THE LOST WORLD OF AGHARTI
The Mystery of *Vril Power*

CW01044422

THE LOST WORLD OF AGHARTI

OF AGHARTI

The Mystery of *Vril Power*

ALEC MACLELLAN

SOUVENIR PRESS

First published 1982 by Souvenir Press Ltd.
43 Great Russell Street, London WC1B 3PA
and simultaneously in Canada

Paperback edition with new introduction published 1996

Reprinted 2001

ISBN 0 285 63314 7

Printed in Great Britain by
The Guernsey Press Co. Ltd.,
Guernsey, Channel Islands

'I can affirm that I have brought it from an utter darkness to a thin mist, and have gone further than any man before me.'

John Aubrey
Miscellanies

CONTENTS

	Acknowledgements	x
	Prologue	xi
	Introduction to the Paperback Edition	xiii
1	A weird experience underground	13
2	The Legend of Agharti	29
3	Seekers after a lost world	41
4	The strange quest of Ferdinand Ossendowski	60
5	The search for Shamballah	72
6	The enigma of Lord Lytton's subterranean world	84
7	Adolf Hitler and the 'super-race'	100
8	The secret passages of South America	116
9	Brazil – and the Atlantis connection	134
10	The 'Underground' of New York	151
11	The mystery of *Vril Power*	170
12	The discovery of Shangri-la!	184
13	The realm of 'The King of the World'	204
	Bibliography	229

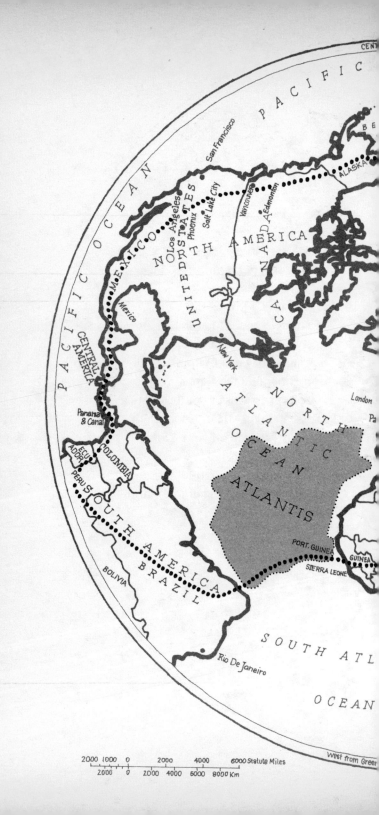

The Agharti Tunnel System.

ACKNOWLEDGEMENTS

This book would not have been possible without the dedicated work of earlier researchers into the legend of Agharti and its associated topics, and I am therefore most glad to offer my thanks to Dr Raymond Bernard, Robert Ernst Dickhoff, Eric Norman, Charles A. Marcoux, Carl Huni, Professor Henrique Jose de Souza, Robert Charroux and Erich von Däniken. In particular I am indebted to the exhaustive investigations of the late Harold T. Wilkins and would like to thank his publishers, Messrs Rider & Co. Ltd, for permission to quote from his books, as well as Messrs Jarrolds Ltd. for those of Nicholas Roerich and Edward Arnold Ltd. for Ferdinand Ossendowski. Other quotations are acknowledged in the text. I should also like to thank the staffs at the British Museum, London, the Bibliotheque Nationale, Paris and the New York Public Library for so conscientiously and painstakingly helping me with my enquiries, as well as my many friends and correspondents in Britain, Europe and America who assisted in so many and varied ways in the compiling of this work. I should perhaps just add that all the opinions and conclusions which are drawn in this book, except where otherwise stated, are my own.

A.M.
1981

PROLOGUE

'Tunnels and labyrinths have played a mysterious part in ancient civilisations in regions of what may wrongly be called the older worlds of Asia and Europe and Africa. Who can say what the ancient priest-emperors of old Peru knew of, or had inherited, from these vanished civilisations which are not even a name, or more than a faint and ghostly shadow? An ancient tradition of Brahmanic Hindustan speaks of a large island of 'unparalleled beauty' which, in very ancient times, lay in the middle of a vast sea in Central Asia, north of what is now the Himalayas. A race of nephilim, or men of a golden age, lived in the island, but there was no communication between them and the mainland, except through tunnels, radiating in all directions, and many hundreds of miles long. These tunnels were said to have hidden entrances in old ruined cities in India – such as the ancient remains of Ellora, Elephanta, and the Ajanta caverns in the Chandore range.

'Among the Mongolian tribes of Inner Mongolia, even today, there are traditions about tunnels and subterranean worlds which sound as fantastic as anything in modern novels. One legend – if it be that! – says that the tunnels lead to a subterranean world of Antediluvian descent somewhere in a recess of Afghanistan, or in the region of the Hindu Kush. It is Shangri-la where science and the arts, never threatened by world wars, develop peacefully, among a race of vast knowledge. It is even given a name: Agharti. The legends adds that a labyrinth of tunnels and underground passages extended in a series of links connecting Agharti with all other such subterranean worlds! Tibetan lamas even assert that in America – it is not stated whether North, South, or Central – there live in vast caves of an underworld, reached by secret tunnels, peoples of an ancient world who thus escaped a tremendous cataclysm of thousands of years ago. Both in Asia and America, these fantastic and ancient races are alleged to be governed by benevolent rulers, or King-archons. The subterranean world, it is said, is lit by a strange green luminescence which favours

the growth of crops and conduces to length of days and health.'
– Extract from a statement made in London in 1945 by Harold T.
Wilkins (1891–1959), explorer and historian, and one of the world's
leading authorities on underground tunnels and subterranean
passages.

INTRODUCTION TO THE PAPERBACK EDITION

Public interest in the legendary subterranean world of Agharti has grown considerably since this book was first published in 1982. In the intervening years further investigations have been carried out in a number of countries into the world-wide system of tunnels said to be linked to this fabled kingdom, and I have received numerous letters and communications from people fascinated by the story, living in Europe, America, Australia, New Zealand and Japan. Several newspapers have also launched their own inquiries into Agharti, and in 1994 Tyne-Tees Television produced an entire programme about one of the alleged entrances to the underworld in the north-east of England.

One of the early champions of the findings disclosed in this book was Erich von Däniken, the trail-blazing author of *Chariots of the Gods?* (1968) and many other equally important works about unsolved mysteries of the past. But I have been equally pleased by the reaction of the general public and their letters to me. Typical of these was one from Joan Boardman who wrote to me from Truro in Cornwall in 1992: 'My husband, Frank, is a gifted clairvoyant and we have received teachings from power sources for some years now. Whilst we were in Italy in 1984 we first came into direct contact with the Agharti force when my husband was taken consciously through space and time forward 15 years to the Continent of South America. We have since received visitations from this power source and been given teachings on what is going to happen in the coming decade as far as world conditions are concerned. A work pattern and spiritual pathway is being set out for us and Agharti seems to be the protecting force, amongst other things.'

Mrs Boardman is one of several readers who have written to tell me about contact with 'beings' from the lost world. Rarely in these communications have the emissaries given themselves a name, but

'Aga' and 'Aghar' have been reported from quite different sources.

Another correspondent, who lives in the town of Henderson near Auckland, New Zealand, and who signed himself Petrus Augustus, also offered some interesting information from his part of the globe. He has apparently been fascinated by the unexplained ever since 1978 when he had a personal encounter with a UFO – an event which was widely publicised in the *Auckland Star* and a number of other newspapers around the world and has never been disproved.

'There has been a lot of interest in New Zealand in your book,' he wrote to me in October 1991, 'and a number of people like myself have been investigating the facts about Agharti. A seaman here has been exploring some tunnels running from the naval base in Auckland and they are like the ones you have described. They run under the harbour and all under the city.'

Perhaps even more dramatic was the news from South Korea in March 1995. This occurred during the celebrations for the fiftieth anniversary of the country's liberation from Japanese occupation during World War Two. I quote from a report in the *Tokyo Shimbun* of 25 March, sent to me by an editor working for my Japanese publishers.

'In a week-long operation near Andong in central South Korea, soldiers with mine detectors searched for metal stakes buried more than 50 years ago by the Japanese army in a war of intercultural magic intended to "disrupt Korean *Feng Shui* earth energies", according to the Yonhap News Agency. During the Japanese rule from 1910 to 1945, the governors ordered thousands of stakes to be driven into the ground at spots that were thought to be springs of the nation's life energy – particularly sacred sites dedicated to local shamanic traditions.'

The report added that during their operations at Andong, two Korean soldiers had made an unexpected discovery: 'While searching in a cave for these stakes, two soldiers had come across a passageway which appeared to have no end. Aided only by torchlight, the men proceeded for some distance before the intense darkness and coldness forced them to turn back with the mystery unsolved.'

Although this may well be another piece of evidence corroborating the existence of the Agharti tunnels, what fascinated me rather more was the reference to *Feng Shui*: another of my correspondents had already postulated the theory that the mysterious Vril power, which is so inextricably linked to the Agharti legend, might actually be a form of this ancient life force, known and studied by the Chinese for more than 3,000 years.

In essence, *Feng Shui* – which literally means 'wind and water' – is a force of nature called the *Chi* or 'breath or life', which circulates in the air in and around all landscapes and buildings. According to tradition, these invisible energy lines, which have been described as the 'electricity of nature', must be allowed to flow smoothly or they will have a detrimental effect on all those who live in their path. By positioning buildings in such a way that the *Chi* has an easy access and exit, the generation of bad *Feng Shui* – or *Sha* as the element is called – is prevented.

Thanks to the development of a system of rules to encourage the *Chi* and bar the entry of the *Sha* through the use of furniture, colour schemes and everyday artefacts, it is now possible to adapt any building, house or even a flat in such a way as to attract the life-enhancing force and improve the lives of occupants. In recent years several books have been published in the West about *Feng Shui* and how it can be utilised to remarkable effect in both urban and rural areas; to one of these, *The Way of Feng Shui* by Philippa Waring (Souvenir Press, 1993), I owe grateful acknowledgement for the above summary.

By comparing what we know of Vril power, as outlined in the pages of this book, with the powers of *Feng Shui*, certain similarities are immediately apparent. Both aim to improve human life, to create better health and to generate more happiness in the world. It is an area of study to which I point the reader and which I intend to follow myself.

As with the previous edition of *The Lost World of Agharti*, I welcome letters from readers with further information to add in the unravelling of this fascinating mystery. I cannot promise to answer them all, as my research frequently takes me abroad for long periods of time. I hope, however, that this paperback edition will reach an even larger audience than its predecessor and will encourage a new generation to go in search of the traces and legacy of what may well have been the oldest civilisation on Earth.

ALEC MACLELLAN,
London, November 1995.

Chapter 1

A WEIRD EXPERIENCE UNDERGROUND

The day which was to provide me with one of the strangest, most unnerving, but ultimately fascinating experiences of my life began ordinarily enough.

I was on holiday in the West Riding of Yorkshire, staying with some relatives in the dour but pleasant town of Keighley, hard by the famous Ilkley Moor. It was a summer's day, and a wide expanse of clear blue sky and strong sunlight threw the ranges and hills to the north in sharp relief. These outcrops scarcely deserve the description mountains, for they are broad and blunt, and the highest, Great Whernside, is only 2,314 feet high.

It was, in fact, in the direction of Great Whernside that I set out that morning. I had risen early and driven to Grassington, from where I planned to walk along the pleasant valley of the River Wharfe. Having something of a love for ancient history, I could hardly have picked a better place to begin my ramble than Grassington, for here, at Lea Green, are the remnants of an Iron Age village occupied from about 200 BC to AD 400. Little circular mounds and grassed-over stoneworks offered mute evidence that this was one of the most thickly populated neighbourhoods in the dales in the Iron Age and also showed why it is considered one of the most interesting prehistoric sites in England. As Lettice Cooper has written in *Yorkshire West Riding* (1950):

> Grassington has always been the metropolis of Wharfedale. There are traces of a prehistoric city there before the Romans discovered the lead mines which gave it occupation and importance. Grassington and Linton in the valley below are particularly rich in wild flowers and fairy tales There are legends of the dreadful 'Barguest', the ghost-dog of the dales, whose appearance foretold disaster, and the Fairy Hole is the name given to a low opening in the limestone rock.

As I began my walk up the valley, all was peace and tran-
quillity. Yet, strangely, some words I had been reading the
previous evening by Daniel Defoe, about his tour of the West
Riding in the early years of the eighteenth century, kept
coming into my mind. Speaking about the mountains of
Upper Wharfedale which lay ahead of me in the warm sunlight, he had written: 'They are more frightful than any in
Monmouthshire or Derbyshire, especially Pingent Hill.' I
looked away to my left and could just make out the flat
summit of 'Pingent Hill', now known as Penyghent, and
wondered why Defoe had been so upset by this scene. I knew
his was an age that did not admire wild beauty, but his
hostility had almost amounted to fear. Unexpectedly, a shiver
ran up my spine. I should have realized then that it was an
omen . . .

I walked on across Grassington Moor and saw the first evidence of the mines which had partly drawn me to this area.
My preliminary reading prior to coming to Yorkshire had told
me that lead mining had gone on along the valley of the River
Wharfe for centuries, the mines being worked by shafts and
levels rather than the more traditional hushes. This has naturally made them easily accessible to the curious as well as to the
miners. Tourists had, in fact, actually been encouraged to visit
the mines by the Reverend Baily Harker in his pioneer guide
book, *Rambles in Upper Wharfedale* published in 1869. 'I
would recommend to visitors a journey underground,' he
wrote, 'though the descent may frighten them a little. The
bottoms of some of the shafts are reached by ladders and
others by ropes.'

The mines have, of course, been closed down for almost a
century now, although the occasional hardy soul can be found
picking over the spoil heaps left by the old miners for bits of
barytes and lead ore. My walk took me past numbers of these
heaps of debris, and I was able to identify from my notes the
quaintly named mines of Moss, Sara, Beaver, Turf Pits and
Peru. It was possible to sense that once this landscape had
been alive with activity as the miners produced lead to the
value of thousands of pounds each year. Now all was still and
silent in the morning sunlight.

To be fair, however, it was not only the mines which had
drawn me to the Wharfe Valley. My interest had also been

fired by the stories of caves and ancient tunnels which were said to abound in the area. A few days earlier I had paid a visit to the Pig Yard Club Museum at nearby Settle, which contains a number of relics, all of which make one appreciate why the caves here have been referred to as 'a *vade mecum* of life in remote times'. Looking at this remarkable collection, I was reminded of G. Bernard Wood's comment in his *Secret Britain* (1968) that it 'could make any person realise his citizenship of an almost illimitable world still bristling with secrets, some of them as yet barely half told'.

Among the items is the skull of a great cave bear, evidence of a straight-tusked elephant and slender-nosed rhinoceros, a fishing harpoon made of deer horn, as well as a variety of ornaments and ancient coins – all unearthed from local caves. My emotions as I gazed at these exhibits were very much those of Mr Wood, who also wrote in his book: 'For me modern problems are soon put in perspective on seeing such evidence of bygone perils, humble household tasks, or perhaps domestic felicity.'

I needed no further spur to explore the Wharfe Valley. However, I also knew that though some of the caves and tunnels had been dated from the Mesolithic, Neolithic, Bronze and Iron Age periods, there were others far more puzzling, far more mysterious, few of which had been completely investigated. And there was the extraordinary statement of one Dr Buckland, who had explored Kirkdale Cave in 1882, and then set out to prove in his book *Reliquiae Diluvianae* that the remains he found 'pertained to men who were swept away by Noah's flood'.

Walking up the valley on that summer's day was no hardship, and in what seemed like no time I was in the shadow of Great Whernside. Already I had seen plenty of evidence of the potholes that form a great natural underground system in the limestone here and attract many potholers each year. But it was caves that I was more interested in.

I was at a point about midway between the little villages of Kettlewell and Starbotton, where steepish, unbroken ridges of hill hem in the valley, when I caught just a fleeting glance of a cave entrance up on the hillside. I was not even sure it was a cave from where I stood, but I was, by now, anxious to explore something, and so I turned my footsteps in that direction.

As I got nearer, I found that I had not been mistaken, although the entrance to the cave was very small and narrow. I took out the torch I was carrying and shone its beam through the tiny opening. Only darkness stretched ahead of me, and the gentle, plopping sound of water dripping from the roof of the cave.

As soon as I stepped inside, a draught of cold air struck me. I hesitated for a moment, and wondered if it was really worthwhile exploring something so unpromising. But was that my real reason, I asked myself, or was I just feeling nervous?

So I made up my mind. I had come this far to look at a cave, and look at one I would. I did up the collar of my shirt and buttoned my jacket. Then I moved off, following in the powerful white beam of the torch. The walls of the cave seemed to slope downwards gradually, and then take on the more regular shape of a tunnel. The floor beneath my feet was hard and rocky, and every now and then I stumbled through small puddles of water.

Only the sound of my own breathing and footsteps broke the silence, while ahead of me the light revealed the tunnel continuing to slope gradually downwards with hardly a bend. I turned once to look behind me, but there was only impenetrable darkness.

I must have walked for about ten minutes before I stopped. The tunnel gave no sign of changing either its height or gradual descent, and I asked myself just how much longer I was going to go on? It seemed I'd found one of the strange underground tunnels of the West Riding and explored it. I was no potholer or spelaeologist, so what could I achieve by going on further? Probably only put myself in danger if anything went wrong, I thought ruefully.

Common sense, and perhaps even a feeling of unease, got the better of me. I swung the torch around and was just about to set off back the way I had come, when something stopped me dead in my tracks. As I had swung the beam of my torch back behind me, I had caught sight out of the corner of my eye of a faint glow away down ahead of me in the tunnel. Evidently, the penetrating light of my torch had obliterated it until that moment.

I peered harder to make sure I had not been mistaken. No, there was clearly a dim glow some distance ahead. For another moment I hesitated. Should I investigate or go back?

Even as I stood there, the light down the tunnel seemed to gain in intensity, although it may only have been an illusion. Cautiously I began to move forward again, the beam of my torch now directed at my feet. I walked carefully, almost holding my breath, for perhaps fifty yards. I could now see that the light was green in colour, and it seemed to be pulsating. Whatever its source was, I had not the faintest idea. I came to a standstill once again.

Then something even more extraordinary occurred. At first I thought the sound was my own breathing, then I discerned a gentle humming noise that gradually grew louder. As it did so, I felt the ground beneath my feet begin to vibrate, at first ever so gently, but steadily increasing in intensity. The humming became a rumble, and as it did so, the green light appeared to pulsate still more strongly. I felt my heart begin to pound and a sudden terror came over me there in the darkness. *Something* almost seemed to be coming towards me.

What on Earth was happening? What was the strange light? And what was causing the rumbling beneath my feet? I believed I was in the tunnel of some long forgotten Yorkshire mine, but my senses seemed to be telling me I had stumbled onto something far more extraordinary.

In the next few moments the pulsating light and shaking of the ground grew stronger still, until I felt the tunnel must surely collapse upon me. That very thought seemed to release me from the feeling of bewilderment which had overcome me, and without a second thought I turned and raced back up the passageway.

I did not stop running until I flung myself, gasping for air, through the entrance of the tunnel and into the sunlight and warmth of that summer day. I sank exhausted onto the ground and tried to recover my breath. Gradually my panic subsided and I wrestled to make some sense of what had happened.

There could be no mistaking the green light I had seen, nor the sensation of the ground trembling beneath my feet. If the mines in this part of the country were still being worked, I might have tried to convince myself I had come a bit too close to some underground blasting. If ever a train had run through an underground tunnel anywhere in this part of Yorkshire, I might have told myself I had somehow got into a ventilation shaft. But no logical explanation I could think of came any-where near satisfying the facts of the experience I had just undergone.*

The eerie green light was unlike any I had ever seen before, and the rumbling sound had almost seemed as if it came from some huge piece of machinery. Could the one have been an underground light and the other some strange subterranean means of transport?

At that moment in time, I was not sure why these thoughts came into my mind. And now, a decade later, I am not sure they are the right solution, although as this book will set out to show, they may not be so far from the truth. I have to admit that I have never returned to try and find that tunnel, and doubt now whether I could.

Back in Keighley later that day, I discussed my experiences with my relatives and other friends. What they told me helped convince me that it had not been a dream or an illusion, and that I had in all probability experienced the selfsame sensa-tions which had given rise to a long held tradition in the West Riding of Yorkshire – a tradition which said that somewhere in the dales was the entrance to an underground world. By common consent this subterranean kingdom was the haunt of fairies and goblins and little people, but there had been one or two other folk who maintained that it was actually the dwell-ing place of people like ourselves who had lived hidden from the sight of man since time immemorial.

Although in my subsequent research to try to solve the mystery of my experience I found plentiful details about a 'Fairy Underworld' (*vide* the Reverend John Hotten, who has written in his *A Tour of the Caves*, 1781, that the caves of Wharfedale were 'alternately the habitations of giants and fairies, as the different mythology prevailed in the country', it was in the work of a man who actually lived in Wharfedale that I found the most striking evidence of all. The man was Charles James Cutcliffe-Hyne (1865–1944) who, though he is a virtually forgotten author today, is still remembered by a few

---

*It has been suggested to me that the green light might have been caused by that strange phenomenon known as *Ignis Fatuus* (Foolish Fire) – sometimes referred to as 'Will-o-the-Wisp' in folklore – which results from the marsh gas in putrefied earth that gives off little flames when trodden upon. And that the rumbling noise was merely the sudden movement of some subterranean rocks. While both explanations are undeniably plausible, they do not entirely convince me.

older readers as the creator of the tough and ruthless adventurer, Captain Kettle.

What interested me first about Cutcliffe-Hyne was that he had lived in Kettlewell, only a few miles from that strange cave which I had entered. Secondly, that he had earned something of a reputation as a daring adventurer who loved exploration, and was obsessed with the legend of Lost Atlantis.* And, thirdly, that he had written a now extremely rare book called *Beneath Your Very Boots* (published in 1889), about an underworld kingdom which gossip in Wharfedale once maintained was based on facts he had actually uncovered.

When I obtained a copy of the book and read it, I found that certain of the facts exactly matched my own experiences. The story recounts the adventures of a certain Anthony Haltoun in an underground world which he enters through a cave 'in the valley of the Wharfe near to its commencement'. The entrance is 'on the northern flank of the dale' and the young man enters despite a stern warning from a local to 'leave the caves alone, or else the folk who dwell in them will catch you'.

Haltoun tells us that the passageway was definitely not that of a lead mine, 'for the Wharfedale mines are nearly all horizontal', while this one progressed downwards in a gradual slope. Walking along it, he is confronted by 'a brilliant light which suddenly flashed through the gloom and displayed a party of men advancing towards me'. At their approach, the ground also begins to shake and tremble, and the startled Haltoun falls into a faint.

When he recovers his senses, the narrator discovers that he has fallen into the hands of an underground race called the *Nradas*, a fair-skinned, blond-haired people who have lived in a state of harmony and peace since prehistoric times. They are opposed to war, and it was 'their hatred of fighting which caused them, in the first instance, to seek shelter beneath the land which was glutting itself with slaughter.' Haltoun inquires of his hosts:

' "Do I understand that there is a regular colony in this cave?" '

---

*Cutcliffe-Hyne wrote an excellent novel on the theme of the last days of Atlantis called *The Lost Continent*, which was published in 1899 and, though rarely read today, is still widely quoted in studies of fantasy fiction.

' "Well, yes, partly; only for colony read nation, and for cave almost interminable labyrinth. Out habitations and the tunnels connecting them, ramify under the whole of the British Isles, and in many places under the seas besides!" '

The *Nradas* explain that they are ruled over by *Radoa*, 'who is supreme both in things temporal and in things spiritual: He is at once Ruler and Deity.' *Radoa* is said to be a majestic figure, dressed in a golden robe, who lives in a beautiful, cavernous city. The number of inhabitants of this subterranean metropolis 'is a trifle over ten thousand . . . though there are twice as many within a ten miles circuit round it.'

The *Nradas* also tell Haltoun how they took advantage of the make-up of the Earth to create their subterranean world. 'Firstly, the crust of the earth is vesicular – i.e. full of holes, formed either by Titanic convulsion or by the water's irresistible erosion; and, secondly, that nearly all these cavities are ventilated by invisible capillary air-shafts.' Of the tunnels, many were naturally formed while 'here and there a more symmetrically carved tunnel pointed to the handiwork of man.' (Later, Haltoun comes to believe that these passageways were bored by rotary tools studded with diamonds which had been mined underground.) To illuminate their world, and also propel the vehicles which transport them through the tunnels, the *Nradas* have tapped 'the earth's internal power, abstracted through deep borings'.

Much in Cutliffe-Hyne's story is pure fantasy – enjoyable fantasy to be sure – but running through the whole work there is also a strong thread of authenticity, a feeling that certain of the facts are true, and others, though unsubstantiated, are based on old traditions in which authentic elements can always be found.*

What Cutcliffe-Hyne denies his readers are any more exact details of the subterranean world than I have quoted here.

But in his autobiography, *My Joyful Life*, published in 1935, he refers to this novel and a legend upon which it is

---

* The belief in there being an entrance to a subterranean world in this part of Yorkshire is also expressed in the grim novel *Land Under England* by Joseph O'Neill (1886–1953), which was published in 1935. O'Neill, who was Permanent Secretary to the Department of Education in the Irish Free State from 1923 to 1944, describes an ancient totalitarian society of people living underground in caves and passageways and using telepathy to control the minds of its inhabitants. The book was widely regarded at the time as an allegorical attack on Nazi Germany.

based – and in so doing adds a whole new dimension to the story, and indeed set me off on the research which has ultimately resulted in this book.

In *My Joyful Life*, which is now a hard-to-find volume, Cutcliffe-Hyne first describes how he became interested in the mines of West Yorkshire when he was a child:

> Somehow I fancy I must be a bit of a throw-back to some cave-dwelling ancestor, because my tastes have always been a trifle troglodytical. My father was Vicar of Bierley, a big, straggling, West Riding village dotted with collieries. One of his churchwardens, with whom I was very matey, was a colliery overseer, and with him I used to descend the local pits whenever he would take me. As I 'got' my first corve of coal when I was ten, one may say I was entered to mining young and early. The Bierley pits were small and (looking back) pretty primitive. The old beam-engines for winding, and the shaft gear, and the furnace ventilation would have sent the present-day Government inspector into a quiet swoon. But they taught me to be impervious to giddiness and claustrophobia, and to keep an instinctive look-out for the safety of my own skin.

This introduction to the world 'beneath our feet' also gave him an interest in the innumerable legends about the caves and mines of the West Riding. Later, when he was at Cambridge University, he learned rock-climbing and was President of the Clare Alpine Club, 'the dignity being granted for jumping across the cañon which divided our chapel from Trinity Hall, depositing on the crow-steps there an empty marmalade jar, and returning home intact!' This escapade stood him in good stead when his later life of adventure took him all over the world to places like Europe, Scandinavia, Africa, Mexico and South America and 'up precipitous rocks as well as down deep mines and caves'.

Cave hunting, indeed, became Cutcliffe-Hyne's main hobby, and in his autobiography he describes exploring subterranean passages in Yorkshire, several places in Europe and Africa, and searching for a lost Inca treasure cave in Mexico. It was while engaged on these expeditions that he first heard stories of a subterranean kingdom said to be linked to all the nations of the world. 'In South America I heard tell that there

were enormous tunnels that traversed the continent, ultimately linking with this forbidden place. More curious still,
there was similar talk in Europe, and even some old people in
the West Riding knew the story and believed there to be
entrances through their own caves. The kingdom was said to
be called Agharti.'

I read Cutcliffe-Hyne's book absolutely fascinated. The idea
of a subterranean kingdom linked to all the continents of the
world by a gigantic network of passageways was an amazing,
mind-boggling idea indeed. If the legend was true, then there
must be a lost world beneath our own which neither time nor
the activities of mankind had disturbed for generations!

And so it was that I began my search for this lost world
called Agharti and its extraordinary and ancient history, as I
shall describe in the pages which follow. . . .

The idea that there is a hidden world beneath the surface of
our planet is a very ancient one indeed. There are innumerable folk tales and oral traditions found throughout many
countries of the world speaking of subterranean people who
have created a kingdom of harmony and contentment un-
troubled by the rest of humanity. Literature, too, can boast
several works on this theme – *Niels Klim's Journey Underground* by the Dane, Ludvig Baron von Holberg (1741), being
perhaps the pre-eminent example – and artists and poets have
also been attracted to the theme over the years.

At first sight many of the accounts appear little more than
fantasies – delightful tales of ethereal beings who hover forever
on the edge of the human consciousness. But when the stories
are brought together and compared, some startling similarities between them all become apparent. No matter what their
origin, there is a curious and compelling thread of truth
underlying them all. Nicholas Roerich, the Russian explorer,
artist and savant, whom we shall be studying in some detail
later in this book, has expressed this fact most convincingly in
his book, *Abode of Light* (1947):

Among the innumerable legends and fairy tales of various
countries may be found the tales of lost tribes or subterranean dwellers. In wide and diverse directions, people
are speaking of identical facts. But in correlating them you

can readily see that these are but chapters from the one story. At first it seems impossible that there should exist any connection between these distorted whispers, but afterwards you begin to grasp a peculiar coincidence in these manifold legends by people who are even ignorant of each other's names.

You recognize the same relationship in the folklore of Tibet, Mongolia, China, Turkestan, Kashmir, Persia, Altai, Siberia, the Urals, Caucasia, the Russian steppes, Lithuania, Poland, Hungary, France, Germany . . . From the highest mountains to the deepest oceans, they tell how a holy tribe was persecuted by a tyrant and how the people, not willing to submit to cruelty, closed themselves into subterranean mountains. They even ask if you want to see the entrance of the cave through which the saintly folk fled . . .

Over the years this kingdom to which the exiles fled has been given various names. If it has been considered a place of evil, then Hell, Hades or Tartarus. If – as is most generally the case – it is seen as a place of goodness and light then Shangrila, Shamballah or, most widely of all, Agharti. (I should perhaps just point out that this word Agharti can be found variously spelled as Asgartha, Agartha or Agarthi, but as it most generally appears in the first form, I have adopted that spelling throughout the book.)

Taking the legend in its most basic form, Agharti is said to be a mysterious underground kingdom situated somewhere beneath Asia and linked to the other continents of the world by a gigantic network of tunnels. These passageways, partly natural formations and partly the handiwork of the race which created the subterranean nation, provide a means of communication between all the points, and have done so since time immemorial. According to the legend, vast lengths of the tunnels still exist today; the rest have been destroyed by cataclysms. The exact location of these passages, and the means of entry, are said to be known only to certain high initiates, and the details are most carefully guarded because the kingdom itself is a vast storehouse of secret knowledge. These manuscripts are claimed to be the works of the lost Atlantean civilization and of an even earlier people who were the first intelligent beings to inhabit the earth.

That there are mysterious passageways beneath the earth's surface, there is no doubt. John Michell and Robert J. M. Rickard have written in their book, *Phenomena* (1977):

> When we look for physical evidence to support these accounts we stumble across the greatest and most suppressed archaeological secret: the existence of vast, inexplicable tunnel systems, part artificial, part natural, beneath the surface of a great part of the earth . . . Baring-Gould's *Cliff Castles and Cave Dwellings of Europe* has amazing records of the extensive cave and tunnel structures beneath France and other countries. In Harold Bayley's *Archaic England* are reports from early travellers of great tunnels stretching under much of Africa, including one beneath a river called Kaoma, 'so lengthy that it took the caravan from sunrise to noon to pass through'. As we write, July 1976, there is news of a military-backed expedition setting off in South America with the double object of investigating the riddle of the 'technologically impossible' stone cities in the high mountains and exploring the vast network of mysterious tunnels, said to run throughout the entire Andes range. If we wanted to prove the existence of a living world beneath our own, we would have no difficulty in pointing to the entrances to the underworld and no lack of historical evidence of contacts between men and subterraneans.

Michell and Rickard also make the interesting point that: 'If we suppose, as many cranks and great men before us have supposed, that there is life in a subterranean world which occasionally interpenetrates with our own, many of our strange phenomena seem more reasonable.'

If we turn to the doctrines of the Buddhists we can also find a number of specific facts about Agharti. According to these teachings the kingdom is located deep within the planet and inhabited by millions of gentle, peaceable people. They are ruled by a wise and incredibly powerful being known as Rigden Jyepo, 'The King of the World', who lives in a magnificent dwelling in the capital of Agharti called Shamballah. From here he has contact with representatives in the 'upper world' and is therefore able to influence the ways of 'surface man'. 'The King of the World' is also said to be in direct communication with the Dalai Lama of Tibet.

The American Buddhist, Robert Ernst Dickhoff, known as Sungma Red Lama, adds to this information in his intriguing booklet *Agharta* (1951):

Agharta began some 60,000 years ago when a tribe led by a holy man disappeared underground. The inhabitants there are said to number many millions and a science superior to any found on the surface of earth directs the activities of these underground citizens in this weird kingdom.

When speaking of Agharta one has to visualise a vast underground terminal city, being a branch of a subterranean, suboceanic network of tunnels . . . Most of these ancient tunnels are now covered at their openings or entrances, due to landslides caused by the deluge of long ago and to the submerging of entire continents. The few remaining ones open to the surface world are in Tibet, Siberia, Africa, South and North America, and on remote islands which were once the mountain peaks of Atlantis.

Dr Dickhoff maintains that the antediluvian civilization which created Agharti flourished on both sides of the Atlantic, and adds:

Tibetan Lamas are of the opinion that in America live in caves of vast proportions the survivors of a catastrophe which befell Atlantis, and that these caverns are connected by means of tunnels running clear to either of the two continents, Asia and America; also that these caverns are illuminated by a green luminescence which aids underground plant life there and lengthens human life.

Another American, Dr Raymond Bernard, who is a leading researcher into the legends of underground kingdoms, has also commented on the Buddhist links with Agharti in his book, *The Subterranean World* (1960):

Throughout the Buddhist world of the Far East, belief in the existence of a Subterranean World, which is given the name Agharti, is universal and is an integral part of the Buddhist faith. Another sacred word among Buddhists is Shamballah, the name of the subterranean world capital.

Buddhist traditions state that Agharti was first colonised

many thousands of years ago when a holy man led a tribe which disappeared underground. This reminds one of Noah, who was really an Atlantean, who saved a worthy group prior to the coming of the flood that submerged Atlantis. The present population of this underground kingdom are believed to possess a science superior to any found on the surface of the earth, through which they wield forces of nature we know nothing about. Their civilisation is believed to represent a continuation of the Atlantean civilisation and is many thousands of years old (Atlantis sank about 11,500 years ago) while ours is very young, only a few centuries old.

Dr Bernard believes that there is a tunnel beneath the Tibetan capital of Lhasa, which leads to Shamballah and is constantly guarded by Lamas. He also claims that Buddhism is actually 'an Aghartan philosophy brought to surface humanity by teachers who came up from the Subterranean World'. Dr Bernard writes:

> The various gigantic statues of Buddha do not represent the human Gautama, but rather these subterranean supermen who came up to teach and help humanity at remote times in the past. These Buddhas all taught the same universal, scientific religion as emissaries of Agharti, the subterranean Paradise, which it is the goal of all true Buddhists to reach.

Perhaps the most remarkable claim advanced by this unusual man – whom we shall be meeting again later in this book – is the theory that the underground people travel through the tunnels in strange vehicles which occasionally emerge and appear in our skies – the phenomena known as UFOs or 'Flying Saucers'! He says they are powered by those mysterious 'forces of nature' possessed by the subterranean people!

From the specific remarks of Dr Bernard and the Buddhist Robert Dickhoff, as well as the more general traditions I have given, the reader will not find it hard to see why there is such a fascination with the legend of Agharti. But it is which details are *fact* and which are *fiction* that I have set out to determine in this book.

It does need to be said right away that this is not another 'Hollow Earth' book. In recent years there have been a number of new books – as well as reprints of the old classic titles like *The Phantom of the Poles* by William Reed (1906), *The Smoky God; or A Voyage to the Inner World* by Willis George Emerson (1908) and *A Journey to the Earth's Interior* by Marshall B. Gardner (1920) – all of which seek to prove that the inside of our world is hollow and that people dwell therein. This is not a theory to which I subscribe, and it is no part of my argument in this book that planet Earth is anything other than an oblate spheroid solid to the core.* What I *do* believe is that it is possible for natural cavities in the ground to have been utilized along with the construction of tunnels to form a secret world just beneath our feet. How much of this still exists, whether it is peopled or not, and what is the truth of its origins is what I have attempted to discover. It is an inquiry that will take the reader back through the pages of history and into some of the darkest recesses on the Earth's surface. The results of this inquiry have led me to a startling conclusion about the extent and route of the tunnel network and the location of Agharti itself – now believed by some authorities to be the fabled Shangri-la for which man has sought since the dawn of time.

Hand-in-glove with the story of Agharti goes a perhaps even more mysterious subject – that of the strange force known as *Vril Power*, which has long been associated with the sub-terranean world. This amazing force is said to give almost un-limited power to anyone who possesses it – and many have wished to do so, including the most sinister and evil figure of the twentieth century, Adolf Hitler. We shall be examining his role in the quest for *Vril Power* as well as studying the force it-self during the pages which follow.

But, first, before attempting to establish *where* Agharti is, *whether* the underground passageways exist, or even *what* the mysterious *Vril Power* might be, we must look into the history of this remarkable subterranean kingdom and the mystery

---

* According to the most widely held belief, the Earth – which has a circumference at the equator of 24,902 miles and a surface area of 197 million square miles – consists of a small inner core of molten iron and nickel (about 800 miles wide), an outer core of molten iron and nickel, a mantle of solid rock (1,800 miles thick), and on top of this a three-to-five miles covering of outer crust. The Hollow Earth believers claim that inside this outer crust is not solid matter but a world of oceans and landmasses which can be entered by holes at either the North or South Poles, or through deep faults in the planet's surface.

which surrounds it. It is a story that takes us back over the centuries and through the records and history books of many and varied nations . . .

Chapter 2

THE LEGEND OF AGHARTI

The Legend of Agharti – the belief in a subterranean kingdom linked to the far corners of the earth by a network of tunnels – can be traced back to Antiquity. Mention of it is found in the oldest traditions, and references to it are recorded in ancient manuscripts belonging to the earliest civilizations. Most of these accounts speak of it being inhabited by people who settled there long before the dawn of history – a peace-loving race concerned with the purity of their lives and exercising as far as possible a moderating influence on the people living above on the Earth's surface.

Just how firmly entrenched the idea is proves not hard to discover, for as Louis Pauwels and Jacques Bergier have stated in their remarkable assessment of 'lost' and 'occult' knowledge, *The Morning of the Magicians* (1960):

> The most ancient religious texts speak of separate worlds situated underneath the Earth's crust which was supposed to be the dwelling place of departed spirits. When Gilgamesh, the legendary hero of the ancient Sumerian and Babylonian epics, went to visit his ancestor Utnapishtim, he descended into the bowels of the Earth; and it was there that Orpheus went to seek the soul of Eurydice. Ulysses, having reached the furthermost boundaries of the Western world, offered a sacrifice so that the spirits of the Ancients would rise up from the depths of the Earth and give him advice. Pluto was said to reign over the underworld and the spirits of the dead. The early Christians used to meet in the catacombs, and believed that the souls of the damned went to live in caverns beneath the Earth.

For further emphasis of the point we need only turn to Sabine Baring-Gould, who has said:

> Wonderful caves, entrances to a mysterious underworld, are

common in many countries. The German stories of the
mountain of Venus, in which the Tannhäuser remains, or
of Frederick Barbarossa, in the Unterberg, or the Welsh
stories of King Arthur in the heart of the mountain, seen
occasionally, or the Danish fables of Holger Dansk in the
vaults under the Kronenburg, all refer to the generally
spread belief in an underworld inhabited by spirits.

If we next refer to the archaeologist Harold Bayley's fascinating book, *Archaic England* (1919), we find he has taken the
subject a stage further and pointed out that a number of the
world's great legendary heroes are supposed to have actually
come from the subterranean world. He writes:

Practically all the 'Mighty Childs' of mythology are represented as having sprung from caves or underground: Jupiter
or Chi was cave-born and worshipped in a cave; Dionysos
was said to have been nurtured in a cave; Hermes was born
at the mouth of a cave, and it is remarkable that, whereas a
cave is still shown as the birthplace of Jesus Christ at Bethle-
hem, St. Jerome complained that in his day the pagans cele-
brated the worship of Thammuz, or Adonis, i.e. Adon, *at
that very cave*.

Mr Bayley goes on to show that it is even possible to find
references in the ancient texts to a persistent belief in primitive
man that he had *originated* from a cave. In a chapter entitled
'Down Under' he says:

Etymology and mythology alike point to the probability, if
not the certainty, that among the ancients a cave, natural
or artificial, was regarded as the symbol of, and to some
extent a facsimile of, the intricate Womb of Creation, or of
Mother Nature. 'Man in his primitive state,' says a recent
writer, 'considers himself to have emerged from some cave;
in fact, from the entrails of the Earth. Nearly all American
creation-myths regard man as thus emanating from the
bowels of the great terrestrial mother.' A sketch of a rotund
female figure, evidently representative of the Great Terrestrial Mother holding in her hand a simple horn, the fore-
runner of the later *cornucopia*, or horn of abundance, is the
outline sketch on a rock carved cliff in the Dordogne. It has

been proved to be of Aurignacian age and is the only yet discovered statue of any size executed by the so-called Reindeer men.

We must not, however, get too embroiled in a discussion about primitive man, but concentrate our efforts on the more specific references to the underworld kingdom we know as Agharti. To this end I should like to quote from another leading authority on the legends of subterranean worlds, Professor Henrique Jose de Souza. In a fascinating article entitled, 'Does Shangri-la Exist?' published in the Brazilian Theosophical Society's *Journal* in 1960 he wrote:

Among all races of mankind, back to the dawn of time, there existed a tradition concerning the existence of a Sacred Land or Terrestrial Paradise, where the highest ideals of humanity were living realities. This concept is found in the most ancient writings and traditions of the peoples of Europe, Asia Minor, China, India, Egypt and the Americas. This Sacred Land, it is said, can be known only to persons who are worthy, pure and innocent, for which reason it constitutes the central theme of the dreams of childhood.

In Ancient Greece, in the Mysteries of Delphos and Eleusis, this Heavenly Land was referred to as Mount Olympus and the Elysian Fields. Also in the earliest Vedic times, it was called by various names, such as Ratnasanu (peak of the precious stone), Hermadri (mountain of gold) and Mount Neru (home of the gods) and Olympus of the Hindus. Symbolically, the peak of this sacred mountain is the sky, its middle portion on the earth and its base in the Subterranean World.

The Scandinavian Eddas also mention this celestial city, which was the subterranean Land of Asar of the peoples of Mesopotamia. It was the Land of Amenti of the sacred Book of the Dead of the ancient Egyptians. It was the City of Seven Petals of Vishnu, or the City of the Seven Kings of Edom or Eden of Judaic tradition. In other words, it was the Terrestrial Paradise.

In all Asia Minor, not only in the past but also today, there exists a belief in the existence of a City of Mystery full of marvels, which is known as Shamballah, where is the

Temple of the Gods. It is also the Erdemi of the Tibetans and Mongols.

The Persians call it Alberdi or Aryana, land of their ancestors. The Hebrews called it Canaan and the Mexicans Tula or Tulan, while the Aztecs called it Maya-Pan. The Spanish Conquerors who came to America believed in the existence of such a city and organized many expeditions to find it, calling it El Dorado, or City of Gold. They probably learned about it from the aborigines who called it by the name of Manca or 'City Whose King Wears Clothing of Gold'.

By the Celts, this holy land was known as 'Land of the Mysteries' – Dust or Dananda. A Chinese tradition speaks of the Land of Chivin or the 'City of a Dozen Serpents'. It is the Subterranean World, which lies at the roots of heaven. It is the Land of Calcas, Calcis or Kalki, the famous Colchida for which the Argonauts sought when they set out in search of the Golden Fleece.

In the Middle Ages, it was referred to as the Isle of Avalon, where the Knights of the Round Table, under the leadership of King Arthur and under the guidance of the magician Merlin, went in search of the Holy Grail, symbol of obedience, justice and immortality. When King Arthur was seriously wounded in a battle, he requested his companion Bedivere to depart on a boat to the confines of the earth, with the following words: 'Farewell, my friend and companion Bedivere, I go to the Land where it never rains, where there is no sickness and where nobody dies.' This is the Land of Immortality or Agharti, the Subterranean World. This land is the Valhalla of the Germans, the Monte Salvat of the Knights of the Holy Grail, the Utopia of Thomas More, the City of the Sun of Campanella, the Shangri-la of Tibet and Agharti of the Buddhist world.

Not all the evidence concerning Agharti is so generalized, however, and as we progress down over the years we can find a number of specific reports which further underline the widespread belief in the underground Kingdom.

One of the earliest and most curious of these traditions is to be found in the East, where a report claims that the first man, Adam, actually came from a subterranean world. According to an ancient sage named St Ephrem, his home was 'in the middle of the Earth' and his dying words were that his 'redeemer and that of his posterity' would come from this place. The tradition goes on to say that Adam's body was embalmed and then kept safely until a priest called Melchizedek, a wise man from the subterranean world, eventually arrived some years later through a tunnel to take it back for proper burial. This story is further substantiated in the Koran, which describes Adam as having been a handsome man 'as tall as a palm tree', while Hindu lore says that he was the king of a group of Elders who had first gone underground at the time of a great cataclysm and then returned to supervise the re-establishment of life on the surface world.

There are several references to an underground kingdom in the classical texts, including that of Hanno, the Carthaginian navigator who undertook a voyage along the west coast of Africa about 500 BC. In his work *Periplous* he tells of hearing stories of underground dwellers who were superior in intelligence to other men and 'ran swifter than horses' when any attempts were made to follow them into their tunnels. (As we shall see later, there is a strong tradition that a tunnel to Agharti runs from Africa.)

Plato, the great historian of lost Atlantis, also speaks of mysterious passageways in and around the mighty continent, 'tunnels both broad and narrow, in the interior of the earth'. He further mentions a great ruler 'who sits in the centre, on the navel of the earth; and he is the interpreter of religion to all mankind'. The legend of Atlantis is, in fact, inextricably entwined with that of Agharti, as we shall find when we discuss the early history of South America and the tunnel 'bridge' between the American continent and Africa.

The Roman, Gaius Plinius Secundus (Pliny), makes reference to subterranean dwellers who had originally fled underground after the destruction of Atlantis, in his *Natural History*. However, unlike his predecessors, he credits them with very little intelligence, as since the cataclysm they 'have fallen below the level of human civilization, if we can believe what is said'. Gaius Plinius does believe, though, that these Troglodytes have hidden in their tunnels a 'great, ancient treasure'.

Talk of hidden treasure naturally attracted the attention of many rulers, and the infamous Roman Emperor Nero actually sent out expeditions to try and locate these hidden hoards. Africa was believed, by common consent, to be the place where the treasure lay – and in a network of subterranean passages to be precise. For eight years between AD 60 until his death in AD 68, Nero dispatched several armies of legionaries to find these treasure tunnels. Fearful of the mad Emperor's wrath, the soldiers frantically combed Africa from the coast to the burning deserts, preferring death rather than returning empty-handed. It was not until after they received news that Nero had died that the half-crazed remnants of the armies were able at last to go back home to Rome. Although they had found neither tunnels nor treasure – perhaps due in no small measure to the deliberately misleading directions they were given by the natives – this did not prevent the legend of a subterranean kingdom continuing to flourish.

Arguably the first detailed account of an actual visit to this 'underworld' appears in the remarkable collection of tales and reminiscences, *De Nugis Curialium*, assembled by the twelfth-century Welsh poet and historian, Walter Map, or Mapes. In his book he recounts the story of a visit by King Herla 'one of the most ancient of British kings' to just such a place. Some authorities have suggested it is merely a fantasy about Fairyland, but the description seems far more likely to be referring to an actual underground tunnel inhabited by a race of subterraneans.

In the tale, King Herla is approached one day by a handsome man who tells him: 'I am the King over many kings and princes, and unnumbered and innumerable people.' The stranger invites Herla to accompany him on a trip to his kingdom which, he says, is below ground. Walter Map's narrative then continues:

> They entered a cave in a high cliff, and after an interval of darkness, passed, in a light which seemed to proceed not from the sun or moon, but from a multitude of lamps, to the mansion of the king. This was as comely in every part as the palace of the Sun described by Naso [in Ovid's *Metamorphosis* – Author].

King Herla enjoys his host's hospitality for what seems like a short period of time and is then given leave to return to the surface world – suitably laden with gifts and presents. He is escorted 'to the place in the tunnel where darkness began' and the two monarchs take their farewell of each other. Walter Map then concludes:

> Within a short space Herla arrived once more at the light of the sun and at his kingdom, where he accosted an old shepherd and asked for news of his Queen, naming her. The shepherd gazed at him with astonishment and said: 'Sir, I can hardly understand your speech, for you are a Briton and I am a Saxon: but the name of that Queen I have never heard, save that they say that long ago there was a Queen of that name over the very ancient Britons, who was the wife of King Herla; and he, the old story says, disappeared at this very cliff, and was never seen on earth again, and it is now two hundred years since the Saxons took possession of this kingdom and drove out the old inhabitants!' And at his words, the King who thought he had made a stay of but three days, could scarce conceal his amazement.

It is evident from this curious account, that King Herla had been below ground far longer than he imagined, although how literally we should take the time period suggested – two hundred years – is debatable! The specific mention of the form of lighting in the subterranean kingdom matches almost precisely those from other sources, and it is only to be regretted that the report does not tell us any more about the king and the impressive world in which he lived. For my part, I am satisfied that the tale does represent an encounter with underworld people.

Another legendary king who is associated with Agharti is Prester John, who in the twelfth century was said to 'reign in splendour somewhere in the dim Orient' according to Sabine Baring-Gould in his *Curious Myths of the Middle Ages* (1894). Although some stories claim that Prester John was a mighty Christian Emperor who held sway over much of Central Asia, all attempts to contact him by the Christian kings and priests of Europe proved in vain. Despite this, marvellous tales about his kingdom, his powers and his wealth were current throughout Europe and for a time a letter was circulated which was claimed to have been written by the mighty ruler himself. Although it later proved spurious, it contained one strange sentence which has excited the attention of scholars. In it, Prester John says: 'Near the wilderness, between barren mountains, is a subterranean world, which can only by chance be reached, for only occasionally the earth gapes, and he who would descend must do it with precipitation, ere the earth closes again.'

This statement, plus the claim that Prester John was 'the Lord of Lords, surpassing all under heaven in virtue, in riches and in power', has given rise to the belief that he was actually the fabled 'King of the World' of Agharti. The belief was first expressed by Athanasius Kircher in his work *Mundus Subterraneus* (1665), in which he placed the heart of Prester John's kingdom in Mongolia. Later supporters have cited evidence that the king's empire embraced 'three Indies and lands which extended beyond India' to further the claim. Most recently, André Chaleil has observed in his book, *Les Grands Initiés de Notre Temps* (1978): 'After all, esotericists through the ages have talked of the subterranean kingdom of Agharti, and if one thinks of the Middle Ages, one can see that the enigmatic Prester John was none other than the entity ruling over the vast, unknowable kingdom.'

In a later one of his books, *Cliff-Castles and Cave Dwellings in Europe* (1911), Baring-Gould recounts another story, set a hundred years later, of a descent to a mysterious underworld. It is a puzzling tale, but nonetheless worth repeating:

A story is told of Father Conrad, the Confessor of St Elizabeth of Thuringia, 'a barbarous, brutal man, who was sent into Germany by Gregory IX to burn and butcher heretics. The Pope called him his *'dilectus filius'*. In 1231 he was engaged in controversy with a heretical teacher, who, beaten in argument, according to Conrad's account, offered to show him Christ and the Blessed Virgin, who with their own mouths would ratify the doctrine taught by the heretic. To this Conrad submitted, and was led into a cave in the mountains. After a long descent they entered a hall brilliantly illuminated, in which sat a King on a golden throne. The heretic prostrated himself in adoration, and bade Conrad do the same. But the latter drew forth a consecrated host and adjured the vision, whereupon all vanished.

It is, of course, purely a matter of conjecture as to whether this 'King on a golden throne' might be the fabled 'King of the World' or whether the whole story was just a dream.

If we turn over the pages of history a little further we find that the German legend of the Pied Piper of Hamelin is also linked to the Agharti legend. Indeed, at least two modern authorities, Harold Bayley and Robert Dickhoff, believe he may actually have been a man from the subterranean world! Let me quote Dickhoff to represent the conviction of both writers:

> There is a well known story told and retold which tells of a town in Germany named Hamelin, which was plagued with rats, and of a stranger who with the sound effect of his magic pipes charmed these pests to follow him to a place where all of them were drowned. And how, after refusal to pay the pied piper his agreed reward, he again used the magic of his pipes, playing yet another tune, which charmed all the children of Hamelin to follow him. When he had his victims lured to a certain mountain there appeared a hidden passageway through which the children and piper passed, never to be seen again.

Dickhoff then asks: 'What knowledge had the stranger of a passage or a tunnel, and where did he actually emerge with his human cargo?' He suggests that their destination was Agharti, and adds: 'All similarities can not always remain coincidences!'

In an interesting footnote to the story, Harold Bayley speculates that the piper and the children entered a passageway in the Koppenburg Mountains of Germany, though 'whether the Koppenburg contains any tunnels I am unable to say'.

That great discoverer Christopher Columbus, who is credited with finding the New World, also features in our legend. According to various accounts of his voyage to America, he heard stories of huge, underground passageways in the vicinity of the West Indies. These accounts were apparently given to him by the Caribs in the year 1493.

The natives claimed that in the ancient kingdom of the female warriors, the Amazons – which was said to have been sited on Martinique – there were tunnels which ran 'beyond the knowledge of man'. The Amazons, however, used them as places of refuge when they were attacked by enemies or pestered by over-amorous suitors. There they could hide themselves and, also, if the advances of the men persisted, they could fire their arrows at them with virtual impunity. There is no record that Columbus discovered either the origin or extent of these passageways.

As we shall see, there is also considerable historical evidence of enormous networks of underground tunnels in both North, South and Central America, but it is not my intention to discuss the facts here, for that would preclude some of the conclusions I have reached concerning them, to which I shall come in later chapters. The same is also true across the Atlantic in Africa, Europe and Asia, which will be dealt with in turn. Suffice it to say for the moment, that the evidence concerning them strengthens the claim that the legend of Agharti was known worldwide from an early period of time.

However, there is one other continent to which we must direct our attention here, for it was particularly from its ancient teaching and traditions that a more complete and fulsome picture of Agharti first emerged. The continent was India and, as we shall see, it was as a direct result of the research carried out here that the subterranean world changed from being just a legend – albeit a widely popular one – to the focal point of intensive study and investigation.

As anyone with even a passing knowledge of India will know, the subcontinent is an absolute mine of ancient lore and cosmic legends, and study of its history is endlessly fascinating and colourful. Although this 'history' is authoritatively documented from about the sixth century BC, much that occurred in prehistoric times helped shape the Indian civilization and gave rise to the great moral philosophies which still today influence millions of people throughout the East. The oldest Indian literary 'works' are the hymns of the *Rig-Veda*, which are certainly based on much older oral traditions, and describe the invasion of Aryan tribes whose fusion with the local population between the years 1700 and 1200 BC ultimately shaped the modern nation. It is the ages before this recorded period, however, which are of greatest interest to us, for from them came the first stories of a subterranean kingdom.

These prehistoric ages are known as *pre-Vedic* (that is, prior to the *Rig-Veda* texts) and it is the view of several authorities that in ancient times India extended over a much greater area than today. According to the great Anglo-German Orientalist

Professor Friedrich Max Muller (1823–1900), in his massive study *Sacred Books of the East* (begun in 1875 and running to fifty-one volumes), there was an Upper, Lower and a Western India. 'In those ancient times,' he writes, 'countries which are now known to us by other names were all called India.' He says that Western India was what is today Iran, and among the other countries considered part of this nation were Tibet, Mongolia and the Tartar regions of Russia.

The Professor says that there are good reasons for suspecting that the great civilizations of the early world, those of Egypt, Greece and Rome, actually received their laws, arts and sciences from this pre-Vedic India, where once dwelt several races which preceded our own. He writes: 'It is one of the universal traditions accepted by all the ancient people that there were many races of men anterior to our present races. Each of these was distinct from the one which preceded it; and each disappeared as the following appeared ' Professor Muller cites an ancient Brahmin manuscript, *The Code of Manu*, which speaks of there having been six races prior to our own, and quotes from it: 'And there issued from Swayambhouva, or the Being Existing Through Himself, six other Manus, each of whom gave birth to a race of men. These Manus, all powerful, of whom Swayambhouva is the first, have each, in his period, produced and directed this world composed of movable and immovable beings.'

Professor Muller also tells us that at the heart of this 'cradle of humanity' was an island set in the middle of a great inland sea. This sea occupied what are now the salt lakes and deserts of Middle Asia to the north of the Himalayan mountain range. The island itself was apparently very beautiful, and on it dwelt the last remnants of the race which immediately preceded our own. These people were a truly remarkable species, according to the Professor:

> This race could live with equal ease in water, air, or fire, for it had an unlimited control over the elements. They were the 'Sons of Gods'. It was they who imparted Nature's most weird secrets to men, and revealed to them the ineffable, and now lost 'word'. This word has travelled around the globe, and still lingers as a far-off dying echo in the hearts of some privileged men.

Despite their absolute powers, however, these people could not prevent their eventual extinction nor the disappearance of their island 'Shangri-la'. The suggestion is that it must have been destroyed by a holocaust of some kind.

Perhaps, though, the most interesting piece of information to come from this research was that this lost island was joined to the mainland all around by secret tunnels!

'There was no communication with the fair island by sea,' says Professor Muller, 'but subterranean passages known only to the chiefs communicated with it in all directions. Tradition points to many of the majestic ruins of India, Ellora, Elephanta, and the caverns of Ajunta (Chandor range), with which were connected such subterranean ways.'

The Professor, along with a number of his successors, have wondered if this description of a lost island might be a variation on the Atlantis legend. They have pondered whether the tradition of a landmass which disappeared beneath the waters had somehow been translated by oral tradition from the Atlantic ocean onto the continent of India? As a matter of *fact*, it is not a theory which will bear much scrutiny.

While Professor Muller was writing and publishing his masterwork, a French lawyer living in India had, quite independently, become fascinated with the occult traditions of India and in particular with the lore of worlds before our own. Like the Anglo-German Orientalist, he had come across references to a lost kingdom and talk of a network of subterranean passages to which it was joined. He determined to find out more about the legend – and decide whether or not it was just that, a legend.

His name was Louis Jacolliot and his research was to really begin to draw back the veil on the mystery of Agharti.

Chapter 3

SEEKERS AFTER A LOST WORLD

The man winding his way through the tightly packed market stalls in the Calcutta bazaar scarcely got a second look from the press of humanity all around him. The noise and stench of the place appeared not to trouble the small figure, though it was immediately evident from his rather dishevelled suit and pale features that he was not an Indian. A faded white hat partly concealed his bearded face, and the light-coloured jacket he was wearing was already stained with sweat down the back and marked with dirt on the front where the man had had to push himself through some narrow gap between the stalls or else rubbed up against a filthy, gesticulating native.

Although foreigners were not altogether unexpected figures in the bazaar of this bustling Indian capital in the middle years of the nineteenth century, they usually conducted themselves in a rather more imperious way than this unprepossessing little man. The city was, after all, the seat of the government of British India, and with its position at the natural outlet of the River Ganges had become a great commercial and industrial centre. As one might well expect, the place was a mixture of magnificent palaces built by Indian princes, splendid administrative buildings constructed by the British Raj, and some of the most appalling slums in all of India. Even at this time, many of the fearful conditions which had been epitomized by the events of the 'Black Hole of Calcutta' a hundred years previously still persisted.

But such memories, and the squalid atmosphere in which the stranger found himself, did not seem to disturb him in the least. Indeed, he seemed to be so deep in thought that he was quite unaware of anything going on around him.

The man was Louis Jacolliot, a French consular official serving in the capital, but a man also passionately devoted to the pursuit and collection of arcane information. He was no comfortable library researcher, seeking for facts in the quiet, ordered confines of such seats of learning. He preferred to hunt for uncollected material, for oral traditions that might only be found among the local people. And to secure such items required him to immerse himself in all stratas of city life, from the palatial, glittering mansions of the high-caste Indians to the disease-ridden streets of the slums and bazaars where the poor of Calcutta eked out their miserable lives.

But despite his apparent absorption in thought, Jacolliot missed little as he wandered about the bazaar. He had long ago learned to make himself unobtrusive, and this helped him win the confidence of people in a place such as this. On the reverse side of the coin, he could also conduct himself with courtesy and dignity when such was required of him. All in all, he had carefully trained his alert mind and questioning brain to the service of his burning desire for information about the ancient history of India.

Jacolliot was driven by a simple and compelling conviction. 'To study India,' he maintained, 'is to trace humanity to its sources.' Writing in the first of the twenty-one books which he was to produce during his lifetime, *La Bible dans L'Indie* (1868), he showed that he had already come to the same conclusions about the influence of this mighty subcontinent on other civilizations that Professor Friedrich Muller and his contemporaries were working on. Jacolliot wrote:

> In the same way as modern society jostles antiquity at each step, as our poets have copied Homer and Virgil, Sophocles and Euripides, Plautus and Terence; as our philosophers have drawn inspiration from Socrates, Pythagoras, Plato and Aristotle; as our historians take Titus Livius, Sallust or Tacitus, as models; our orators, Demosthenes or Cicero; our physicians study Hippocrates, and our codes transcribe Justinian – so had Antiquity's self also an Antiquity to study, to imitate, and to copy. What more simple and more logical? Do not peoples precede and succeed each other? Does the knowledge, painfully acquired by one nation, confine itself to its own territory, and die with the generation that produced it? Can there be any absurdity in the suggestion that the India of 6,000 years ago, brilliant, civilized, overflowing with population, impressed upon Egypt,

Persia, Judea, Greece and Rome a stamp as ineffaceable, impressions as profound, as these last have impressed upon us?

It was from the standpoint of this conviction that Jacolliot carried out much of his research, and the facts which he garnered and presented in his subsequent twenty works further underlined his words. What remains puzzling to this day is why he should be so sadly neglected and little quoted. For we need be in no doubt of his importance, as his 'disciples' Pauwels and Bergier have stated in their book, *The Morning of the Magicians* (1960) – although they themselves devote less than a page to him! They state:

Jacolliot wrote some quite important prophetic works, comparable, if not superior to those of Jules Verne. He also left several books dealing with the great secrets of the human race. A great many occult writers, prophets and miracle workers have borrowed from his writings which, completely neglected in France, are well known in Russia.

Madame Helena Blavatsky, the Russian émigrée who, as we shall see later in this chapter, borrowed freely and often without credit from Jacolliot, also appreciated his importance, although she was guarded in her praise of him! Writing in her *Isis Unveiled* (1877) she says:

His [Jacolliot's] twenty or more volumes on Oriental subjects are indeed a curious conglomerate of truth and fiction. They contain a vast deal of fact about Indian traditions, philosophy and chronology, with most just views courageously expressed. But it seems as if the philosopher were constantly being overlaid by the romanticist. It is as though two men were united in their authorship – one careful, serious, erudite, scholarly, the other a sensational and sensual French romancer, who judges of facts not as they are but as *he* imagines them. His translations from *Manu* are admirable; his controversial ability marked; his views of priestly morals unfair, and in the case of the Buddhists, positively slanderous. But in all the series of volumes there is not a line of dull reading; he has the eye of the artist, the pen of the poet of nature.

Louis Jacolliot was born at Charolles in Sâone-et-Loire in 1837, the son of a small-town lawyer. Although he received only a perfunctory education, his overwhelming desire to learn and his capacity for hard work earned him a place in the French Civil Service, and ultimately a career in the consular division. His brief biographical details as given in *Larousse* indicate that he served for a number of years in India during the Second Empire, was then Chief Justice of Chandernagor and afterwards held the same post in Tahiti. He returned to France in 1874 and devoted the rest of his life to writing, dying at the comparatively young age of fifty-three at his home in Saint-Thibaut-les-Vignes in 1890.

Such facts disguise the full-blooded nature of the man during his time in India, particularly because, by his own account, he witnessed numerous occult rituals and ceremonies, made intensive study of the mystical powers of the fakirs, was initiated into several secret societies, and unearthed a whole host of ancient documents and records which threw new light on the prehistory of India. He was never slow to take himself out among the native population, despite the dangers into which this occasionally ran him, and he was rewarded with much of the information which so enlivens his books, including the important *Occult Science in India* (1884), one of the few works to be translated into English. In a later book, *L'Indie Brahmanique* (1887), he even confessed: 'We have seen things such as one does not describe for fear of making readers doubt one's intelligence . . . but still we have seen them.'

Jacolliot's research also took him beyond the confines of Calcutta, and we have records of him in Southern India, at Pondicherry, and more importantly travelling in the nearby Carnatic region, where he had several discussions about the ancient history of India with a number of old Brahmins in their temples at Villenoor and Chelambrum. It was these holy men – whom he called 'revered masters' – who apparently first told him of a subterranean kingdom somewhere to the north of India.

This story tied up with whispered tales he had heard in the bazaars of Calcutta about an underground world which was supposed to be located to the north, beyond the Himalayas. He had heard reports, too, of a network of tunnels which were

said to stretch from the Ganges underneath the great mountain range and on to a secret destination. Here was said to live
the greatest holy man of all with his followers.

It was from this oral information, augmented with further
research which he carried out among ancient Sanskrit records
in Calcutta, that he was able to commit to paper the first
important modern account we possess about the subterranean
world he called Asgartha, but which we now know to be
Agharti.

This research also strengthened Jacolliot's belief in ancient
civilizations flourishing in prehistoric times, as he wrote in his
later book, *Histoire des Vierges* (1879):

> One of the most ancient legends of India, preserved in the
> temples by oral and written tradition, relates that several
> hundred thousand years ago there existed an immense
> continent which was destroyed by geological upheaval.
> According to the Brahmins, this country had attained a
> high civilization, and the peninsula of Hindustan, enlarged
> by the displacement of the waters, at the time of the grand
> cataclysm, has but continued the chain of the primitive
> traditions born in this place. The Indo-Hellenic tradition,
> preserved by the most intelligent population which
> emigrated from the plains of India, equally relates to the
> existence of a continent and a people lost in antiquity.

From this Jacolliot concluded:

> Whatever there may be in these traditions and whatever
> may have been the place where a civilization more ancient
> than that of Rome, of Greece, of Egypt and of India was
> developed, it is certain that this civilization did exist, and it
> is highly important for science to recover its traces, however
> feeble and fugitive they may be.

It was not in this work, however, but in another published a
year later entitled *Le Spiritisme dans le Monde* (1875) that he
revealed, albeit guardedly, details of a vastly old underground
kingdom which, he said, he had learned about from 'translat-
ing every ancient palm-leaf manuscript which I had the
fortune to be allowed by the Brahmins of the pagodas to see'.
The most specific account he found appeared in a work called
the *Agrouchada Parikshai* (Book of Spirits) which spoke of a

subterranean paradise which flourished 'centuries before our era'. It was presided over by the *Brahm-atma*, or supreme chief, the leader of the *Initiates*, a large body of devoted followers who were the descendants of an earlier civilization.

This Supreme Pontiff, the *Brahm-atma*, was the sole possessor of a mystic formula described as 'symbolizing all the initiatory secrets of the occult sciences' and represented by the letters AUM which signified:

A

Creation

U   M

Preservation   Transformation

According to the *Agrouchada Parikshai*: 'The *Brahm-atma* could only expound its meaning in the presence of the initiates of the third and supreme degree.'

Jacolliot comments:

This unknown world, of which no human power, even now when the land above has been crushed under the Mongolian and European invasions, could force a disclosure, is known as the temple of Asgartha . . . Those who dwell there are possessed of great powers and have knowledge of all the world's affairs. They can travel from one place to another by passageways which are as old as the kingdom itself.

The locating of Asgartha under a land 'crushed by invasions' was Jacolliot's typical way of putting into words his conviction – based as all his beliefs were on research and intuition – that the kingdom lay somewhere under the heartland of Asia. This also doubtless disguised his frustration at never having had the opportunity to put this theory to the test by travelling into Asia, for his later appointments in the consular service took him to the East Indies, Tahiti and then back home to France. The story of Asgartha therefore remained an enigma with him for the rest of his days. But there could be no denying the important role he had already played in making the facts public.

One further strange event occurred to Louis Jacolliot before he left India which I think should be noted here. He had, as he said, become convinced that the people of Asgartha were descendants of a pre-Vedic civilization and were masters of secret powers. In company with an old fakir he watched a ritual in which a 'spirit' was raised who he believed *might* have been the soul of one of these people. I stress might because Jacolliot made no such claim, although at least one commentator on his work feels the possibility is strong. The event is recorded in his book *Phénomènes et Manifestations* (1877), in which he describes the fakirs as being 'the only agents between the world and the *Initiates*, who rarely cross the thresholds of their sacred dwelling place'. The two men were seated in an ancient temple at the time, and this is how Jacolliot describes what followed:

The fakir continuing his evocations more earnestly than ever, a cloud, opalescent and opaque, began to hover near the small brazier, which, by request of the Hindu, I had constantly fed with live coals. Little by little it assumed an entire human form, and I distinguished the spectre – for I cannot call it otherwise – of an old Brahmin sacrificator, kneeling near the little brazier.

He bore on his forehead the signs sacred to Vishnu, and around his body the triple cord, sign of the initiates of the priestly caste. He joined his hands above his head, as during the sacrifices, and his lips moved as if they were reciting prayers. At a given moment, he took a pinch of perfumed powder, and threw it upon the coals; it must have been a strong compound, for a thick smoke arose on the instant, and filled the two chambers.

When it was dissipated, I perceived the spectre, which, two steps from me, was extending to me its fleshless hand; I took it in mine, making a salutation, and I was astonished to find it, although bony and hard, warm and living.

'Art thou, indeed,' said I at this moment, in a loud voice, 'an ancient inhabitant of the earth?'

I had not finished the question, when the word AM (yes) appeared and then disappeared in letters of fire, on the breast of the old Brahmin, with an effect much like that which the word would produce if written in the dark with a stick of phosphorus.

'Will you leave me nothing in token of your visit?' I continued.

The spirit broke the triple cord, composed of three strands of cotton, which begirt his loins, gave it to me, and vanished at my feet.

Not surprisingly, Jacolliot was amazed and puzzled by what he saw. Later he wrote:

The only explanation that we have been able to obtain on the subject from a learned Brahmin, with whom we were on terms of the closest intimacy, was this: 'You have studied physical nature, and you have obtained, through the laws of nature, marvellous results – steam, electricity, etc.; for twenty thousand years or more, we have studied the intellectual forces, we have discovered their laws, and we obtain, by making them act alone or in concert with matter, phenomena still more astonishing than your own.'

If we accept the validity of what Jacolliot saw and reported – and there is no evidence to suggest that we should not – then he may well have experienced the strange force known as *Vril Power* – which the people of Agharti are said to possess – actually in operation! Whether or not this was the case, we shall be returning to discuss this mysterious power in detail later on.

Brief though Louis Jacolliot's references to Asgartha actually were – taken in the context of his wide coverage of ancient Indian history in his twenty-one volumes – they were nonetheless intriguing enough to attract the attention of two other contemporaries: each as different from him and each other as could be imagined. The first was a strange, grandiloquent French occulist named Saint-Yves d'Alveydre, and the other an extraordinary Russian lady who founded the Theosophical Society, Madame Helena Blavatsky. Both, in their particular ways, were seekers after Agharti, and made their specific contributions to the development of interest in the subject.

Joseph Alexandre Saint-Yves d'Alveydre was an extraordinary figure who would probably have remained unknown to posterity and certainly been unable to satisfy his obsessive interest in ancient history and pseudo-science developed in his youth, but for the good fortune of marrying a wealthy lady. Born in Paris in 1842 in humble circumstances, he appears to have spent his early years in exile on the island of Jersey for some undisclosed reason, and then returned to France and settled once again in the capital city. Here he contracted a marriage to the Countess Keller – 'a providential one,' says a contemporary report, 'but one which prompted a considerable amount of slander' – and this gave him both the title Marquis and considerable wealth.

Cushioned from the normal preoccupations of life, d'Alveydre threw himself wholeheartedly into the study of ancient texts, languages and occult sciences. To further his studies he learned Sanskrit, Hebrew and Arabic, and amassed an enormous library of books, both ancient and modern. He evidently became particularly attracted to the legend of Atlantis and conceived a theory that the white race – as distinct from the other races of whatever colour – had originated from the lost continent and that they represented the highest type of humanity. Aside from developing this racist fantasy, d'Alveydre was also an inventor and proposed a plan to feed mankind on algae from the sea, as well as constructing a machine called an Archeometer, which he said provided a key to all the sciences and religions of antiquity. According to André Chaleil in his *Les Grands Initiés de Notre Temps* (1978) this was:

> an instrument formed of signs of the Zodiac, planetary signs, notes of music, colours, letters from Arabic, Hebrew and Sanskrit, and numbers, which gave measurement to the system of universal intercommunication. Thus, it allowed the individual to elaborate forms according to an idea, i.e. the poet to write poetry of the connection between letters and colours, the musician to compose a piece based on numbers.

The Marquis also proposed a new socio-political system called Synarchy, which advocated that society should be regarded as a living organism like that of the human body. Defining this, he said: 'The first function corresponds to nutrition and that is economics. The second can be defined as the will, and that is legislation and politics. Finally, the third corresponds to the spirit and that includes science and religion.' Commenting on this, André Chaleil says:

Synarchy, as Saint-Yves understands it, is the old dream of the meeting of left and right, of workers and capitalists, of scholars and priests, under the same banner and in the same spirit. It is already, in some way, the myth of the defence of the West against itself in face of the threat of Anarchy, or government without principles.

Many of d'Alveydre's theories certainly bewildered ordinary readers, and some even thought him mad – including his own father, who asserted: 'Of all the lunatics I have known, my son is the most dangerous!' For his part, the Marquis seemed to deliberately cultivate the opinion that he was an eccentric – claiming to receive many of his ideas while in a state of trance, and to dictate them to his secretary at one and the same time!

At first glance, it is easy enough to condemn Saint-Yves d'Alveydre as a grandiloquent and megalomaniac author – as many did during his lifetime – but as others have pointed out he was a conscientious and dedicated researcher, always prepared to explore the unknown, and never afraid of expressing his opinions. It was just that his bizarre lifestyle overshadowed everything else. As Jean Saunier has remarked in his *La Synarchie* (1971): 'Saint-Yves d'Alveydre was not such a strange author as one might believe. On the contrary, might he not appear to have been one of the last of the utopians of the nineteenth century?'

This, then, was the man who came across Louis Jacolliot's references to Asgartha, as he waded through his books in a never-ending quest for information – in particular information which referred to 'utopian' societies of any kind. And what more fitting description could there be for the secret kingdom which Jacolliot described? He immediately saw it as another element to be used in developing his theory of Synarchy.

Saint-Yves had apparently been interested in the idea of secret caves where ancient mysteries were said to be hidden ever since his day-dreaming youth, but it was the discovery of the references to an entire subterranean world which really fired his imagination. It was the starting point from which eventually came the book he titled with a typical flourish, *The Mission of India in Europe and The Mahatma Question and Its Solution*. It was published in 1886.

The *Mission* is an extraordinary work by any standard, made all the more so because d'Alveydre claimed that much of the information in it was imparted to him by an emissary from Agartha! (The Marquis, incidentally, has the distinction of being the first writer to refer to the subterranean world by another of the names now most generally used.) According to a contemporary report, d'Alveydre said he had received a visit from a 'mysterious envoy', an Afghan prince named Hadji Scharif, who had been sent by the ruler of the kingdom, 'The King of the World'. This supreme being was evidently aware of the Marquis's interest in Agartha and was prepared to allow him to reveal some of its secrets. The rest of his information, he said, had come by way of telepathic messages from the Dalai Lama in Tibet, who also knew of the subterranean world.

The truth of the matter is that Saint-Yves had come into contact with a Hindu Brahmin priest who had fled from his native country after a revolt and settled in France. The man had already helped him to learn Sanskrit and then offered further information when the subject of Agartha was raised. Unfortunately, the Frenchman could not resist sensationalizing both his source of information and, to a degree, his book.

The Brahmin told d'Alveydre that Agartha was the great initiatory centre of Asia and had a population that ran into millions. It was ruled by twelve members of the 'Supreme Initiation' and 'The King of the World', who 'directs the entire life of the planet in a discreet and unseen way'.

The old Hindu also revealed that there were supposed to be several entrances to the kingdom, all carefully hidden from view, and only those surface dwellers who were specially chosen were ever allowed to find one and enter. The subterranean people had their own language, *Vattan*, a form of speech unknown to linguists and scholars. They had also created a 'secret archive of humanity' into which they placed 'the most perfect machines and specimens of beings and animals which have disappeared; all this forming the potential safeguard of humanity, spiritually and politically'. Finally, there were vast underground libraries with volumes dating back for thousands of years. (What a thought *that* must have been to a bookworm like d'Alveydre!)

In discussing the information he had gleaned, the Marquis

reached the not altogether surprising conclusion, for him, that Agartha was actually governed by a Synarchic society, and he described its constitution thus:

> Thousands of *dwija* and *yogi* united in God from the great circle. Moving towards the centre of the circle we find five thousand *pundits*, their number corresponding to the hermetic roots of the Vedic language. Then come the twelve members of the 'Supreme Initiation' and the *Brahm-ata*, the 'support of the soul in the spirit of God'. The whole of Agartha is a faithful image of the Eternal World throughout Creation.

(As a footnote to this argument, d'Alveydre also makes the remarkable claim that India discovered the ancient art of yoga through its contact with the subterranean kingdom!)

Prayer also played an important part in the life of the underground dwellers, according to the Marquis:

> At the hours of prayer, during the ceremony of the Cosmic Mysteries, although the sacred hierograms are only whispered in the vast underground cupola, strange phenomena take place on the surface of the Earth and the Heavens. Travellers and convoys even a long way off stop, with both men and beasts anxiously listening.

(This is an intriguing as well as important comment, and one that the reader will find significant when we come to the chapter dealing with the experiences of the Russian explorer, Ferdinand Ossendowski, as well as the final section which discusses the association of Agharti with the aerial phenomena known as 'Flying Saucers'.)

Saint-Yves says that it is from Agartha that such 'divine envoys' as Orpheus, Moses, Jesus and many others have come 'when humanity requires them'. And he concludes: 'Supported by the history of the world, I have demonstrated that Synarchy, government by trinitarian arbitration, drawn from the depths of the initiation of Moses and Jesus, is the promise of the Israelites as it is ours.'

Such are the relevant facts which the Marquis recounts in his *Mission of India in Europe*. But according to André Chaleil, no sooner was the book published, 'than Saint-Yves d'Alveydre had it destroyed'. Although some copies escaped, the question as to why the rest were subjected to this fate after all the effort that had gone into them remains a mystery. Chaleil admits that no one knows the real answer, but wonders: 'Had he seen, with the second sight that he claimed to possess, places which ought to remain unknown? Had he misused the secret information he had been given, which he was then obliged to efface completely?'

What we do know for a fact is that just as the book was to be published another Indian came to Paris looking for the Marquis. This mysterious figure, about whom very little is known, according to the occult authority Paul Chacornac is said to have been angry with Saint-Yves because he had used the information passed on to him 'not as traditional information to be received and assimilated, but as elements destined to be integrated into his personal system'. The man said that 'The King of the World' looked with displeasure on any denigrating of Agartha by association with Synarchy.

Whether this visit played any part in the Marquis's decision to destroy his work we shall never know. He never spoke about the matter again in the years up to his death in 1910. Indeed, he never wrote another word about Agartha, and retreated into virtual obscurity. Today his name rarely appears as anything other than a footnote in occult history – and then usually in derisory terms.

The third writer to put news of the subterranean kingdom before the general public in the last quarter of the nineteenth century was Madame Helena Petrovna Blavatsky (1831–1891), and it is a fact that although she is claimed in some quarters to have been the person who actually revealed Agarthi to the world, she initially did little more than embroider on the information that had already been made available by Louis Jacolliot. She was, though, a remarkable woman and arguably the founder of modern occultism.

Born the daughter of a Russian colonel, she was married at seventeen to the Vice-Governor of the Province of Erivan in the Ukraine, Nikifor Blavatsky, but after a few weeks of marriage she ran away, noting in her diary: 'Love is a nightmare a vile dream. Woman finds her true happiness in acquiring supernatural powers.' She was evidently also driven by a belief that she had formulated as a teenager and which she expressed thus:

There have always existed wise men who have all the knowledge of the world. They have total command over the
forces of nature and make themselves known only to those
persons who are deemed worthy of knowing and seeing
them. A person must also believe in them before they see
them.'

For the rest of her life, Madame Blavatsky pursued these
'Masters of Wisdom', as she called them, across the face of the
Earth.

Her first destination after running away was Europe, where
for some years she lived a precarious, Bohemian existence,
dressing in outlandish clothes, smoking hashish and interesting herself in all aspects of the occult. This interest grew into
an obsession and she set off on a number of journeys about
which the details are scant and often confusing. According to
those who became her followers, Madame Blavatsky travelled
in almost every country of the world. She was said to have gone
to Egypt, where she conducted a midnight ritual in the Great
Pyramid of Cheops to raise the spirit of a long dead Egyptian
priest. Then in India she immersed herself in the magical
practices of the Hindu priests, and followed this with a trip to
Tibet where, disguised in men's clothing, she secured entry to
a number of the isolated monasteries of the lamas. A two-year
stint in South America also brought her into contact with
many of the ancient mysteries of that continent.

In 1873 she finally arrived in New York. Here she quickly
became caught up in the public's growing fascination with
Spiritualism, and met one Colonel Henry Steel Olcott, a
renowned investigator of psychic phenomena. The ageing
Colonel found himself spellbound by the liberated and often
outrageous young woman as well as deeply impressed by her
obviously profound knowledge of the occult. Within a few
months they were living together – although the Colonel
insisted that there was no sexual love between them.

The couple began holding gatherings at which all aspects of
the supernatural would be discussed, and as a result of these
meetings they had the idea of creating an organization to
further such work. The result was the Theosophical Society,
based on the word Theosophy, meaning knowledge of divine
wisdom. Madame Blavatsky set herself the task of collating

and setting down all the knowledge she had collected, whether at first hand or through research, for a book which would become the cornerstone of the society. The result was published in 1877 under the title of *Isis Unveiled*. It proved an immediate success, although it was derided in some quarters as 'a gallimaufry of fact and fable on many subjects'.

Among the topics which Madame Blavatsky touched upon was the secret world of Agartha. Mentioning Louis Jacolliot only in passing, she repeated the details about the subterranean kingdom and the *Brahm-atma*, the supreme chief of the initiates, who alone knew the secret of the mystic formula contained in the word AUM. The selfsame details, in fact, that I have already described. But because Jacolliot's books were little known outside France – and had only been published in limited editions, as against the large print-run for the two volumes which comprised *Isis Unveiled* – Madame Blavatsky has subsequently often enjoyed the credit for opening Western eyes to the wonders of this strange mystery.*

There was, however, one new piece of information that she added to the developing file of material on Agartha. In discussing the legend that the underground kingdom was supposed to be linked to the rest of the world by passageways, she reported that she had personal knowledge of one such enormously long tunnel that ran over 1,000 miles through Peru and Bolivia. She had, she said, actually acquired a plan of the tunnel while travelling in South America in 1850. Although the passageway had evidently been used by the ancient Incas as a repository for their treasure to keep it out of the avaricious hands of the Spanish Conquistadors, it appeared to her to be of a much earlier origin – perhaps even with Atlantean connections. Writing in *Isis Unveiled* she said:

> We had in our possession an accurate plan of the tunnel, the sepulchre, the great treasure chamber and the hidden,

---

*In an analysis of *Isis Unveiled*, the American Orientalist William Emmette Coleman found that over 2,000 passages had been copied from other books 'without proper credit', and that Madame Blavatsky had cited 1,300 books of which she had only read 100. He concluded: 'By this means many readers of *Isis* have been misled into thinking Madame Blavatsky an enormous reader, possessed of vast erudition; while the fact is her reading was very limited, and her ignorance was profound in all branches of knowledge.' In his list of books which she plagiarized, he mentions extensive quotations from Ennemoser's *History of Magic* and *The Gnostics and their Remains* by C. W. King, as well as 'seventeen passages from Jacolliot's *Bible in India*'.

pivoted rock-doors. It was given to us by an old Peruvian;
but if we had ever thought of profiting by the secret it would
have required the cooperation of the Peruvian and Bolivian
governments on an extensive scale. To say nothing of
physical obstacles, no one individual or small party could
undertake such an exploration without encountering the
army of brigands and smugglers with which the coast is
infested; and which, in fact, includes nearly the entire
population. The mere task of purifying the mephitic air of
the tunnel not entered for centuries would also be a serious
one. There the treasure lies, and tradition says it will lie till
the last vestige of Spanish rule disappears from the whole of
North and South America.

The old Peruvian who gave Madame Blavatsky the map said
he had actually visited the underground labyrinth. 'It defies
the imagination,' he told her. 'It is like stepping into the land
of Aladdin. The old magicians and the Incan priests say the
tunnels were there when their people first came to America.'
   We shall be returning to this tunnel network as well as some
further confirmatory evidence by Madame Blavatsky from her
travels in South America later in the book.
   Despite the initial success of *Isis Unveiled*, and the
Theosophical Society, in a short while interest in both
declined, and by 1879 Madame Blavatsky and the Colonel had
decided to leave America and go to India, the great fountain-
head of occult wisdom. Here both they, and theosophy, were
warmly welcomed, and soon Madame Blavatsky was once
again gaining converts and performing various supernatural
wonders to demonstrate her 'powers'. In 1882 they purchased
a large mansion on the banks of the Adyar River, near
Madras, and established the headquarters of the Theosophical
Society. It still flourishes there today, and among its memen-
toes is a copy of that ancient tunnel map the old Peruvian gave
to Madame Blavatsky.
   The last years of the remarkable lady's life were darkened
with scandal and accusations that she had 'rigged' her
miracles. Indeed so persistent were the attacks alleging that
she was a charlatan and a fraud, that she fled from India and
went to England, where she lived out her last days producing a
companion work to *Isis Unveiled*, again based on a mixture of

personal experience and intensive research. She called this work *The Secret Doctrine*, and described it as a compendium of all the basic truths from which religion, philosophy and science had sprung. It was published in 1888 and also contained some more of her views about Agartha, in particular the great *Brahm-atma*. Referring the reader to what she had already said in *Isis Unveiled* concerning the secret underground kingdom of Asia and its ruler, she declared:

> He is the mysterious (to the profane – the ever invisible) yet ever present Personage about whom legends are rife in the East, especially among the Occultists and the students of the Sacred Science. It is he who holds spiritual sway over the *initiated* Adepts throughout the whole world. He is the Initiator. For sitting at the threshold of light, he looks into it from within the circle of darkness which he will not cross; nor will he quit his post till the last day of his life-cycle. It is under the direct, silent guidance of this Maha (Great) Guru that all the other less divine teachers and instructors of mankind became, from the first awakening of human consciousness, the guides of early Humanity. It is through these 'Sons of Gods' that infant humanity got its first notions of all arts and sciences, as well as of spiritual knowledge; and it is they who have laid the first foundation stone of those ancient civilisations that puzzle so sorely our modern generation of students and Scholars.
>
> Let those who doubt this statement explain the mystery of the extraordinary knowledge possessed by the ancients – alleged to have developed from lower and animal-like savages, the cave men of the Palaeolithic age – on any other equally reasonable grounds. Let them turn to such works as those of Vitruvius Pollio of the Augustan age, on architecture, for instance, in which all the rules of proportion are those *taught anciently at initiations*, if he would acquaint himself with the truly divine art, and understand the *deep esoteric significance hidden in every rule and law of proportion*. No man descended from a Palaeolithic cavedweller could ever evolve such a science unaided, even in millenniums of thought and intellectual evolution. It is the pupils of those 'Sons of Gods' who handed their knowledge from one generation to another, to Egypt and Greece with

its now lost *canon of proportion*. It is owing to the divine
perfection of those architectural proportions that the
Ancients could build those wonders of all the subsequent
ages, their Pyramids, Cave-Temples, Tunnels, Cromlechs,
Cairns, Altars, proving they had the powers of machinery
and a knowledge of mechanics to which modern skill is like
a child's play, and which [*sic*] that *skill* refers to itself as the
'works of hundred-handed giants'.

In a later section, Madame Blavatsky also confirms her
earlier belief about a network of tunnels joined to Asgartha. 'It
is a fact,' she says, 'known to the initiated Brahmins of India,
and especially to Yogis, that there is not a cave-temple in the
country but has its subterranean passages running in every
direction, and that those underground caves and endless
corridors have in their turn *their* caves and corridors.'

But perhaps most importantly of all as far as our study is
concerned, Madame Blavatsky provided a hint as to almost
precisely *where* Agharti is located. In a footnote to her discussion of the *Brahm-atma's* Initiates, she says that following a
catastrophe in ages gone by: 'The elect of this race took shelter
in the "sacred island", the fabled Shamballah, in the Gobi
desert.'

At first glance, it may seem that in this rather enigmatic
sentence Madame Blavatsky has merely provided the subterranean kingdom with yet another name. But in fact, as I
mentioned in passing in the first chapter and will substantiate
later, Shamballah is the name generally given to the *capital
city* of Agharti, where 'The King of the World' is enthroned.
But this error should not be allowed to obscure the fact that
this extraordinary lady was the first of the historians to give us
anything approaching a possible site for the mysterious underworld.

What remains a mystery is why no one immediately followed
up the hint to try and establish its truth or otherwise. No
doubt the infamy which surrounded the lady's last years, and
her death in 1891 shortly after the publication of *The Secret
Doctrine*, played an important part in this state of affairs. But
it is a fact that almost a quarter of a century was to pass before
the subject of Agharti again came to public attention through
the experiences of another Russian exile. And when it did, the

clue to its location was to prove not so far off the mark as Madame Blavatsky's detractors had claimed all her other ideas and conclusions had been . . .

Chapter 4

THE STRANGE QUEST OF
FERDINAND OSSENDOWSKI

Until the start of the twentieth century, the legend of Agharti remained very much . . . a legend. The old stories of a secret underground kingdom persisted in certain corners of the world, but evidence to support the claims remained as elusive as ever. Indeed, it might well have been expected that in the rational and materialistic new century, such a story would finally be confined to the realms of fantasy: a colourful tradition to be ranked alongside other ancient mysteries such as the lost continents of Atlantis and Mu.

But such a supposition did not allow for the remarkable discoveries of two intrepid explorers who in the 1920s went into the vastness of Asia and there unearthed evidence about Agharti which far exceeded that of any previous reports. Their accounts, indeed, became the cornerstone of our present knowledge of the secret kingdom.

Strangely, neither man knew the other; certainly they never met, nor did they ever read each other's books. Yet, both were of Russian extraction, both were men of courage and wisdom, and neither was easily convinced of falsehoods or taken in by wild stories. One made his discoveries about Agharti while fleeing for his life from the terror of the Bolshevik Revolution in Russia; the other came shortly after from self-imposed exile in America, seeking to penetrate the mysteries of Tibet – that remote and mysterious kingdom deep in the Himalayas into which few Westerners have ever penetrated. Their names were Ferdinand Ossendowski and Nicholas Roerich, and it is their major contributions to our story which we shall consider next.

Ferdinand Ossendowski was a remarkable man by any standards, and it is somewhat difficult to explain why he is so sadly neglected today, his name recorded in so few reference works, and his books forgotten and of the utmost rarity. As we shall see, this is in stark contrast to his fellow explorer of the

Agharti legend, Nicholas Roerich.

Ossendowski was born in Vitebsk in 1876. From his child-hood he demonstrated a passionate love for his native Siberia, in particular its history and wildlife. During schooldays he proved to be an intelligent and alert scholar, showing a great aptitude for both geography and geology. Naturally enough this led to his entering on a career in mining, and by the beginning of the new century he was widely regarded as one of the leading experts on gold mining in Siberia. He was also something of a rebel and an idealist. By 1905 he had become noticeably disillusioned by the Tsar's central government in Moscow, which seemed to him to be paying scant regard to the needs of his beloved Siberia. He therefore became involved in an attempt to obtain partition for Siberia from the rest of Russia, serving as a leading member of a group who called themselves the Far Eastern Revolutionary Government, with their headquarters in the town of Harbin.

It was a passionate, but ill-conceived attempt at defying the Tsar's might and was quickly squashed. Ossendowski, along with thirty-seven others, was arrested and put on trial. Although friends offered to help Ossendowski himself to escape, he preferred to stand trial with his friends and was summarily sentenced to death for treason. However, following powerful appeals on his behalf, plus his undoubted use to the government because of his mining knowledge, this sentence was commuted to two years imprisonment. He returned to normal life in September 1907, a harder but wiser man from his gruelling experience in a Siberian prison.

In the years which followed, Ossendowski devoted himself to his mining studies, serving as Professor of Geology at universities in Petrograd and Omsk, as well as writing extensively on gold and platinum mining for Russian and Polish journals. During the period of the First World War, he was sent as a member of a 'special investigating mission' to Mongolia which, it has been suggested, was a front for certain spying activities on the government's behalf!

In 1920, with the outbreak of the Bolshevik Revolution, Ossendowski's life took its most dramatic turn. As a well-known figure in Russian life, a member of the bourgeoisie, and a suspected government collaborator, he was a natural target for the Reds, and he was high on the list of wanted men when the revolutionaries overran Siberia. But he did not wait a second time for imprisonment and the possibility of death, fleeing instead into the wilds of Siberia and heading for Mongolia. Although he had no clear plan as to where he might go, he sensed that China would probably have to be his ultimate destination once he had crossed the great wilderness of Mongolia.

Lewis Stanton Palen, who later collaborated with Ossendowski on a book called *Man and Mystery in Asia* (1924), explains that the Red soldiers at first pursued their quarry with relentless fervour, but suddenly abandoned the chase when they believed Ossendowski to be dead. A mangled skeleton which had been savaged by wolves was found in the forest of Yenisey and had on it the passport of a Dr Ferdinand Ossendowski. Says Palen: 'As he was so well known and so badly wanted by the Bolshevik rulers, great rejoicing followed the discovery of his documents and the news of the death of so well known an enemy of Bolshevism was spread through all the Red Organs in Siberia and Russia.'

But, in truth, Ossendowski was not dead; he had cleverly outwitted his pursuers. Palen explains:

> In a struggle with a party of Bolsheviks in the forest, Dr Ossendowski in defence of his own life made a Commissioner pay the price the latter would have exacted from this fugitive man of education: and, being in need of documents more useful and less compromising than those in his own name, he simply removed the Commissioner's papers from his pocket and left his own undesirable ones in their place.

Although Ossendowski was now free from pursuit, he knew there was no going back to Siberia. With great determination and skill he made his way into Mongolia – narrowly escaping death at the hands of a band of marauding *hunghutze* or bandits – until he fell into the company of a remarkable fellow-Russian, a priest named Tushegoun Lama, who had also fled from the Red Revolution. He was a fascinating figure who went everywhere with a big Colt pistol stuck in his blue sash and could claim personal friendship with the Dalai Lama, then the supreme ruler of Tibet.

In the months that followed, a great bond of friendship grew up between these two exiles, and each came to admire the other. In was from Tushegoun Lama that Ossendowski was to hear the first hints about Agarthi and be inspired to investigate the stories and ultimately produce the first detailed modern report on the subterranean kingdom, thereby helping to substantiate the truths in the ancient legend. He called this report, *Beasts, Men and Gods* (1923), and it is now a rare and much sought-after volume.

In telling us about his host, Ossendowski wrote in his book:

Tushegoun Lama! How many extraordinary tales I had heard about him. He is a Russian Kalmuck, who because of his propaganda work for the independence of the Kalmuck people made the acquaintance of many Russian prisons under the Czar and, for the same cause, added to the list under the Bolsheviki. He escaped to Mongolia and at once attained to great influence among the Mongols. It was no wonder, for he was a close friend and pupil of the Dalai Lama in Lhasa, amongst the most learned of the Lama, a famous thaumaturgist and doctor. His influence was irresistible, based as it was on his great control of mysterious science. Everyone who disobeyed his orders perished. Such a one never knew the day or hour when, in his *yurta* or beside his galloping horse on the plains, the strange and powerful friend of the Lama would appear. The stroke of a knife, a bullet or strong fingers strangling the neck like a vice accomplished the justice of the plans of this miracle worker.

During their journeying, Tushegoun Lama told Ossendowski something of the almost miraculous powers of the Tibetan priests, and the Dalai Lama in particular – powers, he said, the foreigners could scarcely begin to appreciate. Then, he went on: 'But there also exists a still more powerful and more holy man . . . The King of the World in Agharti.'

For a moment Ossendowski is puzzled as to what his companion means. He presses him to explain.

'Only one man knows his holy name,' the Lama replies slowly and enigmatically. 'Only one man now living was ever in Agharti. That is I. This is the reason why the Most Holy Dalai Lama has honoured me and why the Living Buddha in Urga fears me. But in vain, for I shall never sit on the Holy Throne of the highest priest in Lhasa nor reach that which has come down from Jenghis Khan to the Head of our Yellow

Faith. I am no monk. I am a warrior and avenger!'

Ossendowski, his alert mind fascinated by this speech, is just about to pour out a whole stream of questions, when Tushe-goun Lama jumps smartly into the saddle of his horse and whirls off into the distance calling behind him the Mongolian phrase of parting: 'Sayn! Sayn-bayna!'

The poor Russian is left standing in the settling dust with his still whirling thoughts. King of the World? Agharti? What did the Lama mean? And where could this mysterious place be?

In fact, Ossendowski had to wait several months before he began to get any answers to the questions which haunted his thoughts by both day and night as he continued his journey across Mongolia.

It happened while he was crossing the great plain of Tzagan Luck with a small party of Mongol guides that the Tushegoun Lama had left behind to see him safely along his way. Sud-denly, one of the guides called for the party to halt. The man jumped from his camel, which immediately lay down without being told. The other Mongols immediately did exactly the same, and all raised their hands in prayer, chanting, *'Om! Mani padme Hung!'*

Bewildered by the sudden events, and seeing no immediate cause for the men's actions, Ossendowski waited until they had finished praying, and then demanded of his guide what was happening.

'Did you not see how our camels moved their ears in fear?' the man replied after a moment's hesitation. 'How the herd of horses on the plain stood fixed in attention and how the herds of sheep and cattle lay crouched close to the ground? Did you notice that the birds did not fly, the marmots did not run and the dogs did not bark? The air trembled softly and bore from afar the music of a song which penetrated to the hearts of men, animals and birds alike. Earth and sky ceased breathing. The wind did not blow and the sun did not move. At such a moment the wolf that is stealing up on the sheep arrests his stealthy crawl; the frightened herd of antelopes suddenly checks its wild course; the knife of the shepherd cutting the sheep's throat falls from his hand; the rapacious ermine ceases to stalk the unsuspecting *salga*. All living beings in fear are involuntarily thrown into prayer and waiting for their fate. So it was just now. Thus it has always been whenever the "King of the World" in his sub-terranean palace prays and searches out the destiny of all peoples on the earth.'

Ossendowski felt a puzzled frown creasing his face. He had seen nothing of what the old Mongol had described. But his interest had been aroused once again by the mention of the mysterious 'King of the World'. And, as he records in *Beasts, Men and Gods*, he thereafter began to earnestly search for more information on the 'Mystery of Mysteries' as the legend of Agharti had become known in Central Asia. He analysed and annotated many sporadic, hazy and often controversial bits of evidence in an attempt to form a cohesive picture.

For example, on the shore of the River Amyl some old people told him of an ancient legend which described how a Mongolian tribe had actually fled from the demands of the warlord Genghis Khan by hiding themselves in a subterranean country. And at the Lake of Nogan Kul he was told of a man who had actually found the gate to Agharti, gone below, but on his return had had his tongue cut out by the lamas so that he would be unable to pass on the information to anyone else.

However, Ossendowski's first really substantial account of the subterranean kingdom was given to him by an old Tibetan, Prince Chultun Beyli, who was living in exile in Mongolia accompanied by his favourite priest, Gelong Lama. The two men spoke freely on the matter once they realized Ossendowski's interest was genuine and sincere. The lama spoke first.

'Everything in the world,' said the Gelong, 'is constantly in a state of change and transition – peoples, science, religions, laws and customs. How many great empires and brilliant cultures have perished! And that alone which remains un-changed is Evil, the tool of Bad Spirits. More than sixty thousand years ago a Holyman disappeared with a whole tribe of people under the ground and never appeared again on the surface of the earth. Many people, however, have since visited this kingdom, Sakkia Mouni, Undur Gheghen, Paspa, Khan Baber and others. No one knows where this place is. One says Afghanistan, others India. All the people there are protected against Evil and crimes do not exist within its bournes. Science has there developed calmly and nothing is threatened with destruction. The subterranean people have reached the highest knowledge. Now it is a large kingdom, millions of men, with the "King of the World" as their ruler. He knows all the forces of the world and reads all the souls of humankind and the great book of their destiny. Invisibly he rules eight hundred million men on the surface of the earth and they will accomplish his every order.'

To this astonishing report by his lama, the old Prince added further details:

'The kingdom,' he said, 'is called Agharti. It extends throughout all the subterranean passages of the whole world. I heard a learned Lama of China relating to Bogdo Khan that all the subterranean caves of America are inhabited by the ancient people who have disappeared underground. Traces of them are still found on the surface of the land. These subterranean peoples and spaces are governed by rulers owing allegiance to the "King of the World". In it there is not [sic] much of the wonderful. You know that in the two greatest oceans of the east and the west there were formerly two continents. They disappeared under the water but their people went into the subterranean kingdom. In underground caves there exists a peculiar light which affords growth to the grains and vegetables and long life without disease to the people. There are many different peoples and many different tribes. An old Buddhist Brahmin in Nepal was carrying out the will of the Gods in making a visit to the ancient kingdom of Jenghiz (Siam), where he met a fisherman who ordered him to take a place in his boat and sail with him upon the sea. On the third day they reached an island where he met a people having two tongues which could speak separately in different languages. They showed to him peculiar, unfamiliar animals, tortoises with sixteen feet and one eye, huge snakes with a very tasty flesh and birds with teeth which caught fish for their masters in the sea. These people told him that they had come up out of the subterranean kingdom and described to him certain parts of the underground country.'

Ossendowski, understandably, found much that was puzzling as well as confusing in these two accounts. Nonetheless he was convinced that he had come across something more than just a legend – or even an example of hypnosis or mass vision – but more likely a powerful 'force' of some kind, evidently capable of influencing the course of life in this part of the world. Maybe even far beyond it, if he could accept all that Prince Chultun Beyli had said.

By now, as the fugitive's path across Mongolia neared the Chinese border, he began to make plans for crossing the frontier and then travelling by train to Peking. From there he hoped it might be possible to reach the West, where he could make a new life if, as he sadly suspected, the Bolshevik revolution succeeded.

But before setting out on the final leg of his flight to freedom, Ossendowski had perhaps his biggest surprise. For in the town of Urga he encountered an old lama who almost unwittingly completed his file on the mystery of Agharti. It was not, however, a meeting that began very auspiciously, as Ossendowski relates in *Beasts, Men and Gods*:

> During my stay in Urga I tried to find an explanation of this legend about the 'King of the World'. Of course, the Living Buddha could tell me most of all and so I endeavoured to get the story from him. In a conversation with him I mentioned the name of the 'King of the World'. The old Pontiff sharply turned his head toward me and fixed upon me his immobile, blind eyes. Unwillingly I became silent. Our silence was a long one and after it the Pontiff continued the conversation in such a way that I understood he did not wish to accept the suggestion of my reference. On the faces of the others present I noticed expressions of astonishment and fear produced by my words, and especially was this true of the custodian of the library of the Bogdo Khan. One can readily understand that all this only made me the more anxious to press the pursuit.

Ossendowski was feeling rather crestfallen as he left the room in which he had been received by the Chief Lama. At his side was the librarian who had looked so fearfully at him when the name of the 'King of the World' was mentioned. Ossendowski decided to have one more try at getting further information about Agharti and its ruler. He turned to the old librarian and asked if he might be allowed to see the lamasery's book collection. He also employed what he called 'a very simple, sly trick' on the man.

'Do you know, my dear Lama,' Ossendowski said. 'Once I rode in the plain at the hour when the "King of the World" spoke with God and I felt the impressive majesty of this moment.'

Much to his astonishment, the old lama responded instantly:

'It is not right that the Buddhist and our Yellow Faith should conceal it,' he said, almost in a whisper. 'The acknowledgement of the existence of the most holy and powerful man, of the blissful kingdom, of the great temple of sacred science is such a consolation to our sinful hearts and our corrupt lives that to conceal it from humankind is a sin.'

Seizing his opportunity, Ossendowski quickly asked the librarian about the powers of the 'King of the World'.

'He is in contact with the thoughts of all the men who influence the lot and life of all humankind,' he replied. 'With Kings, Czars, Khans, warlike leaders, High Priests, scientists and other strong men. He realizes all their thoughts and plans. If these be pleasing before God, the "King of the World" will invisibly help them; if they are unpleasant in the sight of God, the King will bring them to destruction. This power is given to Agharti by the mysterious science of "Om", with which we begin all our prayers. "*Om*" is the name of an ancient Holyman, the first Goro, who lived three hundred and thirty thousand years ago. He was the first man to know God and who taught humankind to believe, hope and struggle with Evil. Then God gave him power over all forces ruling the visible world.'

Ossendowski pressed on quickly with his interrogation of the old lama as the two men walked into the book-lined room which housed the library.

'Has anybody seen the "King of the World"?' he asked.

'Oh, yes!' answered the Lama. 'During the solemn holidays

of the ancient Buddhism in Siam and India the "King of the World" appeared five times. He rode in a splendid car drawn by white elephants and ornamented with gold, precious stones and finest fabrics; he was robed in a white mantle and red tiara with strings of diamonds masking his face. He blessed the people with a golden apple with the figure of a Lamb above it. The blind received their sight, the dumb spoke, the deaf heard, the crippled freely moved and the dead arose, wherever the eyes of the "King of the World" rested. He also appeared five hundred and forty years ago in Erdeni Dzu, he was in the ancient Sakkai Monastery and in the Narabanchi Kure.

'One of our Living Buddhas and one of the Tashi Lamas received a message from him, written with unknown signs on golden tablets. No one could read these signs. The Tashi Lama entered the temple, placed the golden tablet on his head and began to pray. With this the thoughts of the "King of the World" penetrated his brain and, without having read the enigmatical signs, he understood and accomplished the message of the King.'

Ossendowski could feel his heart pounding with excitement as he asked his next question.

'How many persons have ever been to Agharti?'

'Very many,' answered the Lama, 'but all these people have kept secret that which they saw there. When the Olets destroyed Lhasa, one of their detachments in the south-western mountains penetrated to the outskirts of Agharti. Here they learned some of the lesser mysterious sciences and brought them to the surface of our earth. This is why the Olets and Kalmucks are artful sorcerers and prophets. Also from the eastern country some tribes of black people penetrated to Agharti and lived there many centuries. Afterwards they were thrust out from the kingdom and returned to the earth, bringing with them the mystery of predictions according to cards, grasses and the lines of the palm. They are the Gypsies . . . Somewhere in the north of Asia a tribe exists which is now dying and which came from the cave of Agharti, skilled in calling back the spirits of the dead as they float through the air.'

For several moments Ossendowski said nothing. A profound silence settled over the high-ceilinged room. The old man had told him much already, and if he was to say any more, Ossendowski sensed it would be of his own volition. His instinct proved correct.

'Several times the Pontiffs of Lhasa and Urga have sent envoys to the "King of the World",' said the Lama librarian after another moment. 'But they could not find him. Only a certain Tibetan leader after a battle with the Olets found the cave with the inscription: "This is the gate to Agharti." From the cave a man of fine appearance came forth, presented him with a gold tablet bearing the mysterious signs, and said: "The King of the World will appear before all people when the time shall have arrived for him to lead all the good people of the world against all the bad; but this time has not yet come. The most evil among mankind have not yet been born." '

Barely had the old man finished speaking than two other lamas came into the library. Before Ossendowski could ask another question, or even thank the librarian, the man had moved silently and swiftly away. The traveller never again saw or spoke to that lama who had shed so much light for him on the mystery of Agharti.

There are only two more points relevant to our story which need to be mentioned in connection with Ferdinand Ossendowski and his book, *Beasts, Men and Gods*, which he completed and saw published a year later from his exile haven in Paris. The first was that the book appeared at the same time as another work which was to have a crucial importance in quite a different area – though both books were later found to be linked by a strange, intangible thread. This was *Mein Kampf*, by a young German named Adolf Hitler, who had dreams of being a 'King' of the world himself. We shall be returning to study this strange association in a later chapter.

The second point concerns another statement by Ossendowski about the enormous powers the people of Agharti were believed to control. Powers which he said they could use to destroy whole areas of our planet, but which could equally be harnessed as the means of propulsion of the most amazing vehicles of transport. It has been suggested that this could be a prediction of nuclear energy and Flying Saucers! (*Beasts, Men and Gods* was, of course, published in 1923, long before such topics were even being discussed.) The other possibility is that it might be a reference to the mysterious force known as *Vril Power*. Similarly we shall be taking up this fascinating and intriguing possibility later.

But what concerns us most immediately is the discoveries of the second man who went in search of Agharti. He was the world-renowned traveller and artist, Nicholas Roerich, who also tramped the wild and desolate regions of Asia like his fellow-countryman, Ossendowski – and by so doing penetrated still closer to the heart of the mystery . . .

Chapter 5

THE SEARCH FOR SHAMBALLAH

Constantine Nicholas Roerich was an extraordinary character whose name features notably in the history of mysticism. Yet equally, as a result of the profoundness of his philosophy, his remarkable abilities as a seer and prophet, and his undeniable skill as an artist, he also has an important place in the biographies of world figures of the twentieth century. Although he died over thirty years ago, many of his works remain in print, his paintings are displayed in galleries around the world, and his philosophy has inspired several generations of thinkers. In New York, an entire museum named after him pays tribute to his undoubted genius.

The influences of this remarkable man who was born in St Petersburg, Russia, in 1874 are many and varied, but here we must simply concentrate on those that relate to the legend of Agharti: a subject, as we shall see, that absorbed and fascinated him.

Roerich came from a distinguished Russian family who could trace their ancestry back to the Nordic Vikings of the tenth century. They were a brave and adventurous clan, men of intelligence and action, and the desire for exploration clearly ran in the blood of young Nicholas from an early age. Perhaps because of this background, he became fascinated with archaeology, in particular that of the Vikings. According to a monograph *Nicholas Roerich* (1935) by K. P. Tampy: 'When he was but ten, Roerich excavated some ancient mounds dating from the Vikings. The discovered objects were presented by him to the Archaeological Society in a blaze of self-achieved glory.' Tampy also tells us that he was 'possessed of a burning desire to get at the beautiful and make use of it for his brethren'. This led to the development of what proved to be a remarkable artistic talent, and by the age of fifteen his work was already being publicly exhibited, as well as being reproduced in a number of art magazines.

Despite his artistic tendencies, Roerich was first sent to study law at the University of St Petersburg, but when it became evident that his natural skills lay elsewhere his parents allowed him to transfer to the Academy of Fine Art. After graduation, he furthered his training in Paris, returning to Russia to become a lecturer and writer on the arts. In 1906 he won a much coveted prize offered by the Tsar for the design of a new church, and was also appointed Director of the Academy for the Encouragement of Fine Arts in Russia. Indeed his life continued to be one of achievement and acclaim until the dark clouds of the Russian Revolution spread themselves across the land. Roerich, who at the time was on an invited visit to America, felt the doors of his country being irrevocably closed to him. In fact, he never set foot in the land of his birth again.

In America, Roerich further developed his interest in Buddhism and the mystical world of Asia which he had begun to study while he was still in Russia. So profoundly in fact did the subject seize his imagination, that in 1923 he proposed an expedition to explore India, Mongolia and Tibet. It was the Himalayas that perhaps excited him most, and certainly their influence on him was to colour the rest of his life and work. (Roerich actually settled in India in the late 1920s and died there in 1947.)

The expedition, consisting of Roerich and eight Europeans plus local guides, set out in 1924 from Sikkim, striking through the Punjab and then on across Kashmir, Khotan, Urumchi, the Altai Mountains, the Oyrot region, Mongolia, the Central Gobi and Tsaidam, finally ending up in Tibet. The small group wandered through the 'remote, dangerous and seldom visited parts of Asia for five years' to quote one contemporary report, encountering 'frustration and hostility' in numerous places. Leading the party took all Roerich's skill, courage and intelligence, and as well as sketching the scenery and people, he kept a diary of their progress written literally 'in the saddle'.

As far as the outside world was concerned, little was heard of the Roerich party until a lengthy cable reached India from Tibet in May 1928. Extracts from this graphically show the kind of experience they underwent:

On Tibetan territory have been attacked by armed robbers
. . . Forcibly stopped by Tibetan authorities on October 6,
two days north of Nagchu. With inhuman cruelty Expedition had been detained for five months at altitude of 15,000
feet in summer tents amidst severe cold about 40 degrees
below Centigrade . . . Expedition suffered from want of
fuel and fodder. During stay in Tibet five men, Mongols,
Buriats and Tibetans died and ninety caravan animals
perished . . . By order of authorities all letters and wires
addressed to Lhasa Government and Calcutta British
authorities seized. Forbidden to speak to passing caravans.
Forbidden to buy foodstuffs from population. Money and
medicines came to an end . . .

Roerich was later to explain that stories were rife about the
party as they journeyed along:

During these years, rumour made me a 'French and
American King', 'Commander of a Russian Corps' and
'King of all Buddhists'. I succeeded in dying twice. I
succeeded in being simultaneously in Siberia, America and
Tibet. According to the words of Mongols of Tsaidam I
carried on a war with the Amban of Sining. And according
to the words of the Taotai of Khotan I brought a small can-
non which would, in ten minutes, destroy entire Khotan
and its 100,000 inhabitants. We became accustomed to all
this and now are no longer astonished by 'authentic'
rumours. The Mongols firmly remember the 'Ameri Khan':
Thus the American has been visualized as a kind of warrior.
Fairy tales about ourselves from Lhasa were related to us, in
which we could only identify ourselves with difficulty.

Despite all the hardships and tribulations, Roerich found
friends and information along the way to enrich his knowledge
of the people and their traditions. And the expedition was only
a few weeks old before the legend of Agharti first engaged his
attention and thereafter became an absorbing study with him.
He jotted down his first thoughts on the underground kingdom as he rode along, and these notes were later published in
a remarkable record of the expedition entitled *Altai
Himalaya: A Travel Diary* (1930). This is what he wrote:

A legend of Central Asia tells of the mysterious nation,

underground dwellers – the Agharti. Approaching gates
into this blessed kingdom, all living beings become silent,
reverently pausing in their course. Recall, now, the Russian
legend about the mysterious 'Tchud' which went underground to escape the persecution of evil forces. To this
secreted place also leads the sacred legend of the subterranean Kitege.

The whole world tells its tales of underground cities,
treasure troves, temples merging under water! The Russian
and Norman peasant relates about this with equal surety.
So, too, does the inhabitant of the desert know of the
treasures which sometimes glimmer from under the sand
waves and then – until the ordained time – recede again
under the earth.

Around one beacon-fire are gathering those who remember the predestined dates. We do not speak of superstitions
but of knowledge – knowledge revealed in beautiful
symbols. Why invent, when truth is so manifold? In La
Manche even now is seen the city which has been 'submerged' under water.

Many sources tell of the subterranean dwellings in the
district of Lhasa and Koko-Nor. A lama from Mongolia re-
calls the following legend: When the foundations of the
monastery Genden were built during the time of the
Teacher Tsong-kha-pa, in the fourteenth century, it was
noticed that through the gaps of the rocks there arose the
smoke of incense. A passage was broken through and there
was found a cave in which, motionless, was seated an old
man. Tsong-kha-pa aroused him from his ecstasy and the
old man asked for a cup of milk. Then he asked what teaching now existed upon earth. After which he disappeared. It
is also pointed out that the Potala, the palace of the Dalai-
Lama, has hidden recesses of greatest antiquity. By the
facial expressions of the lamas one will not discover anything. One must seek through other paths.

If so much lies underground – how much more lies under
the veil of silence. It is naive to insist, after the first cautious
response. An authoritative astrologer assures us that he
knows nothing – has only heard rumours. Another who is
versed in the ways of antiquity just now insists he has not
even heard of such things. And why should they answer

otherwise? They must not betray. Most heinous is treason –
and there are many traitors. We discern the true devotion
and behind it the structure of the future.

Like Ossendowski before him, Roerich was soon on the lookout for any more titbits of information, any more clues, about
this mysterious underground world. In Lamayuru-Hemis, he
encountered a Buriat lama who, though rather reticent about
the subject, revealed that at the heart of Agharti was a great
city called Shamballah where the 'King of the World' dwelt.
'There are several ways into this forbidden place,' the lama
told Roerich, enigmatically. 'And those that are taken are led
by an underground passage. This passage sometimes becomes
so narrow that one can hardly push through. All the entrances
are safeguarded by the lamas.'
If this man told Roerich any more, he makes no mention of
it in his diary, and there is evidence that the explorer found
the conversation rather frustrating except for the important
new information about the city called Shamballah. Another
incident recorded in his diary a few days later must have been
equally tantalizing:

Someone comes in the evening and whispers about a manuscript of Shamballah. We ask him to bring it.
    One must be in these places to understand what occurs!
One must look into the eyes of these coming ones, in order
to realize how vitally important for them is the meaning of
Shamballah. And the dates of events are not a curious
oddity for them but are connected with the structure of the
future. Though these structures are sometimes dust-ridden
and perverted, their substance is vital and stirs the thought.
Following the development of thought you realize the
dreams and hopes. And out of these fragments has been
pieced together the new web of the world!

Despite any feeling of frustration, Roerich was clearly
becoming captivated by the mysticism of the subject, and
perhaps became deliberately enigmatic himself in his notes.
When his party reaches Tourfan, however, and he is shown a
number of caves which, it is claimed, lead ultimately to
Agharti, he is a little more specific in his diary:

In the cliffs towering over Kurlyk, the entrances of the caves loom dark. These caves penetrate deeply: their depth has not been ascertained. There are also secret passages – from Tibet, through Kuen lun, through Altyntag, through Tourfan; the Long Ear knows of secret passages. How many people have saved themselves in these passages and caves! Reality has become a fairy tale. Just as the black aconite of the Himalaya has become the Fire-Blossom.

The exiled Russian explorer indicates that he is now becoming convinced that there is a centre to which the nations of the world are linked by tunnels, with at its heart a golden capital city called Shamballah. While the party rests for a few days in Mongolia, Roerich takes up his brushes and paints 'The Ruler of Shamballah', a colourful interpretation of the 'King of the World' in his domain. (Roerich later presented this canvas to the Mongolian government.)

The remainder of Roerich's diary is dotted with similar references to Shamballah, indicating that he took every opportunity to discuss the legend. He suspects that 'the Mongolian lamas know a great deal' and that 'many other neighbouring nationalities also understand all the reality of the meaning of Shamballah'. But, he adds: 'it is not easy to win their confidence in spiritual matters.'

As if in confirmation, more talk reaches his ears as the party nears the border with Tibet. He tells us about this in a most curious entry in the diary:

We hear legends. That which was told us about the visitation by the 'Ruler of Shamballah' to monasteries in Narabanchi and Erdeni Dzo is confirmed in various palaces. Yum-Beise is an unpleasant, windy place. The monastery itself is not an inviting one and the lamas are not gracious. Beyond and above the monastery, on the mountain, a tremendous phallus is erected . . .

As the party enter Tibet, Roerich confides to his diary that he believes only a High Lama can answer all his questions – *if* he could find one so disposed. He notes down: 'The Tibetans relate that during the time of the flight of the Dalai Lama in 1904, at the Chang-thang crossing, the men and horses felt a severe tremor. The Dalai Lama explained to them that they were at the hallowed border of Shamballah. Does the Dalai Lama know much of Shamballah?' he wonders.

Roerich's fascinating account of his trans-Asia journey closes with his arrival at the holy city of Lhasa, leaving the reader intrigued with his references to Agharti and Shamballah and as frustrated about them as the author himself must have felt. But Roerich had not faced all the hardships and privations, nor searched so diligently for information all in vain, for in Lhasa in the summer of 1928 he encountered a High Lama named Tsa-Rinpoche who at last answered his most pressing questions. Roerich recorded their unique conversation in a second volume which he called simply *Shamballah*, published in 1930.

First, Roerich had to convince the High Lama that he had a serious interest in the subject, and was not merely curious. Evidently the explorer's answers did not immediately convince the holy man, for he described Shamballah as being 'far beyond the ocean'. And to this Tsa-Rinpoche added: 'It is a mighty heavenly domain. It has nothing to do with our earth. So why do you earthly people take an interest in it?'

For a moment there was complete silence in the room as the two men looked at each other. Roerich was aware that he was being sidetracked, but was equally anxious not to offend the High Lama and have him bring their conversation to a premature end. When he started to speak again, he picked his words very carefully:

'Lama, we know the greatness of Shamballah. We know the reality of this indescribable realm. But we also know the reality of the earthly Shamballah. We know how some High Lamas went to Shamballah, how along their way they saw the customary physical things. We know the stories of the Buryat lama, of how he was accompanied through a very narrow secret passage. We know how another visitor saw a caravan of hill-people with salt from the lakes, on the very borders of Shamballah. Moreover, we ourselves have seen a white frontier post of one of the three outposts of Shamballah. So, do not speak to me about the heavenly Shamballah only, but also about the one on earth: because you know as well as I, that on earth Shamballah is connected with the heavenly one. And in this link, the two worlds are unified.'

The lama became silent. With eyes half concealed by the lids, he examined Roerich's face. And then, in the evening dusk, he began to explain:

'Verily, the time is coming when the Teaching of the Blessed One will once again come from the North to the South,' he said. 'The word of Truth, which started its great path from Bodhgaya, again shall return to the same sites. We must accept it simply, as it is: the fact that the true teaching shall leave Tibet, and shall again appear in the South. Really, great things are coming. You come from the West, yet you are bringing news of Shamballah. We must take it verily so. Probably the ray from the tower of *Rigden-Jyepo*, "The King of the World", has reached all countries.

'Like a diamond glows the light on the Tower of Shamballah. He is there – *Rigden-Jyepo*, indefatigable, ever vigilant in the cause of mankind. His eyes never close. And in His magic mirror He sees all events of earth. And the might of His thought penetrates into far off lands. Distance does not exist for Him; He can instantaneously bring assistance to worthy ones. His powerful light can destroy all darkness. His immeasurable riches are ready to aid all needy ones who offer to serve the cause of righteousness. He may even change the karma of human beings . . .'

Sensing that he had broken through his host's reticence, Roerich went on to ask if it was true that many people lived in the underground kingdom and if they possessed great powers.

'Uncountable are the inhabitants of Shamballah,' the old man in his richly ornate robes replied. 'Numerous are the splendid new forces and achievements which are being prepared there for humanity.'

'But how are the secrets of Shamballah guarded?' Roerich asked. 'It is said that many co-workers of Shamballah, many messengers, are speeding through the world. How can they preserve the secrets entrusted to them?'

Once again Tsa-Rinpoche's piercing eyes gazed into those of his guest.

'The great keepers of mysteries are watching closely all those to whom they have entrusted their work and given high missions. If an unexpected evil confronts them they are helped immediately. And the entrusted treasure shall be guarded. About forty years ago, a great secret was entrusted to a man living in the Great Mongolian Gobi. It was told to him that he could use this secret for a special purpose, but that when he felt his departure from this world approaching, he should find someone worthy to whom to entrust this treasure. Many years passed. Finally this man became ill and during his illness, an evil force approached him and he became unconscious. In such a state he could not, of course, find anyone worthy to whom to entrust his treasure. But the Great Keepers are ever vigilant and alert. One of them from the high Ashram hurriedly started through the Gobi, remaining more than sixty hours without rest in the saddle. He reached the sick man in time to revive him and though only for a short time, it permitted him to find someone to whom he might transmit the message.'

Eagerly, Roerich asked another question that had never been far from his thoughts.

'Lama, in Tourfan and in Turkestan they showed us caves with long, unexplored passages. Can one reach Shamballah through these routes? They told us that on some occasions, strangers came out of these caves and went to the cities. They wished to pay for things with strange, ancient coins, which are now no longer used.'

The slightest suggestion of a smile played around the eyes and mouth of the old lama. It was a moment or two before he answered.

'Truly I say to you that the people of Shamballah at times emerge into the world. They meet the earthly co-workers of Shamballah. For the sake of humanity, they send out precious gifts, remarkable relics. I can tell you many stories of how wonderful gifts were received. Even *Rigden-Jyepo* himself appears at times in human body. Suddenly he shows himself in holy places, in monasteries and at times predestined, pronounces his prophecies.'

Not altogether satisfied with the reply, Roerich persisted on the same line of questioning.

'Lama,' he said, 'how does it happen that Shamballah on earth is still undiscovered by travellers? On maps you see so many routes of expeditions. It appears that all heights are already marked and all valleys and rivers explored.'

The lama's lined old face broke into a wide smile at this – the kind of smile that Roerich felt a wiser person might bestow on someone of lesser ability unable to comprehend a simple truth.

'Verily, there is much gold in the earth, and many diamonds and rubies in the mountains, and everyone is so eager to possess them! And so many people try to find them! But as yet these people have not found all things – so, let a man try to reach Shamballah without a call! You have heard about the poisonous streams which encircle the uplands. Perhaps you have even seen people dying from these gases when they come near them. Perhaps you have seen how animals and people begin to tremble when they approach certain localities. Many people try to reach Shamballah uncalled. Some of them have disappeared for ever. Only a few of them reach the holy place, and if their karma is ready . . .

'It is dangerous to toy with fire – yet fire can be of the greatest use for humanity. You have probably heard how certain travellers attempted to penetrate into the forbidden territory and how guides refused to follow them. They said, "Better to kill us." Even these simple folk understood that such exalted matters may be touched only with utmost reverence.'

Despite a feeling of slight embarrassment, Roerich dwelt on the subject of the location of Agharti and Shamballah. 'Lama, can you tell me something of the three great monasteries near Lhasa – Sera, Ganden and Depung? Are there some hidden passages under them? And is there a subterranean lake under the chief temple?'

Again Tsa-Rinpoche grinned. 'You know so many things that it seems to me you have been to Lhasa. I do not know when you have been there. But if you have seen this subterranean lake, you must have been either a very great lama, or a servant bearing a torch. But as a servant you could not know the many things which you have told me.'

Sensing that the old lama was not prepared to be drawn on the question of the tunnels beneath the monasteries, Roerich asked if he knew anything of the Azaras and the Kuthumpas, holy men who were traditionally supposed to know the secrets of Shamballah.

Once more, Tsa-Rinpoche started his reply evasively:

'If you are familiar with so many incidents, you must be successful in your work,' he said. 'To know so much of Shamballah is in itself a stream of purification. Many of our people during their lives have encountered the Azaras and Kuthumpas and the snow people who serve them. Only recently have the Azaras ceased to be seen in cities. They are all gathered in the mountains. Very tall, with long hair and beards, they appear outwardly like Hindus. Once, walking along the Brahmaputra, I saw an Azara. I strove to reach him, but swiftly he turned beyond the rocks and disappeared. Yet I found no cave or cavern there – all I saw was a small crevice. Probably the man did not care to be disturbed.

'The Kuthumpas are no longer seen now. Previously they appeared quite openly in the Tsang district and at Manasarowar, when the pilgrims went to holy Kailasa. Even the snow people are rarely seen now. The ordinary person, in his ignorance, mistakes them for apparitions . . .'

The old lama's voice faded away and with what seemed like a weary movement he drew the folds of his red garment closer around him. Darkness had now fallen outside the monastery, and only a few small candles relieved the gloom. Roerich could see his host was tiring, and wondered how much longer he would be prepared to talk. There was, though, still one strange episode that had occurred during his journey across Asia which puzzled him and which he knew he must ask the holy man about before he departed.

'Lama,' he said softly, 'not far from Ulan-Davan we saw a huge black vulture which flew low, close to our camp. He crossed the direction of something shining and beautiful, which was flying south over our camp, and which glistened in the rays of the sun.'

Even in the half-light, Roerich saw the lama's eyes suddenly sparkle. Then the old man asked him in a voice that was almost breathless: 'Did you sense a perfume like temple-incenses in the desert?'

Now it was Roerich's turn to look surprised. 'Ah – yes,' he said slowly. 'We did. In that stony desert, several days from any habitation, many of us became simultaneously aware of an exquisite breath of perfume. This happened several times. We never smelt such lovely perfume. It reminded me of a certain incense which a friend of mine once gave me in India – from where he obtained it, I do not know.'

When Tsa-Rinpoche spoke again he provided Nicholas Roerich with the biggest surprise of all in that evening of surprises. Indeed, afterwards the great explorer was not sure that the man's words were not the most amazing thing he had heard during all those extraordinary years in Asia.

'So!' the old man went on, his voice rising. 'You are being guarded by Shamballah! The huge black vulture is your enemy, who is eager to destroy your work, but the protecting force from Shamballah follows you in this Radiant form of Matter! This force is always near you, but you cannot always perceive it. Sometimes only, it is manifested for strengthening and directing you. It is, in truth, the greatest mystery of all about Shamballah!'

Today, as I mentioned, the late Nicholas Roerich enjoys a worldwide reputation as a philosopher and artist. Yet while so much of what he wrote and painted is easily accessible, his contribution to our knowledge of the legend of Agharti – and Shamballah in particular – is generally overlooked. Nor has it been appreciated that what Roerich actually experienced in the desert of Ulan-Davan was in all probability the mysterious force we now know as *Vril Power – in operation!*

Extending our gratitude to him and his fellow-explorer, Ferdinand Ossendowski, for widening our knowledge of the secret underworld kingdom, it is now surely time to examine this *Vril Power* in more details – and first the English writer who featured it in a unique and fascinating work of great rarity. The man was Edward George Bulwer Lytton, and his book was called *The Coming Race*.

Chapter 6

THE ENIGMA OF LORD LYTTON'S SUBTERRANEAN WORLD

One of the hardest to find of all books of mysticism is a curious little volume called *The Coming Race*, which was published in 1871. On the title page the author's name is given simply as 'The Right Hon. Lord Lytton' – a man who was, in fact, a widely popular Victorian novelist and short story writer. Indeed his historical novel *The Last Days of Pompeii* (1834) is still remembered today (even if it is not often read), while his much anthologized novella *The Haunted and the Haunters* (1859) has been described by no less an authority than H. P. Lovecraft as 'one of the best haunted-house tales ever written'.

But *The Coming Race* suffers an obscurity and rarity quite out of keeping with the rest of Lord Lytton's works. Few except the world's major libraries possess copies of the book, and my own search for a personal edition took me several years before I finally located a curiously bound volume in a second-hand bookseller's shop in a backstreet of London. I say curious because the binding is of a strangely-textured leather and there is no title or author embossed on the spine. I suspect I should have passed it by and left it among the other mouldering, dusty volumes except for the one word which had been scratched in ink in capital letters at the top of the spine: VRIL.

The word meant little to me at that time, but intrigued me enough to pull the book from the shelf. Imagine my delight when I opened it to the title page to find it was the much sought-after, *The Coming Race*. Like the two books by Ferdinand Ossendowski and Nicholas Roerich which I have discussed in the previous chapters, it was to prove a work of crucial importance in my study of the legend of Agharti.

I remember, too, that as I casually turned the pages of the book, it fell open to a page which appeared to have been much studied by the previous owner. The page also seemed to explain to me why that one word had been written on the spine. As I stood reading the book in that gloomy little shop – the page in question actually formed the concluding paragraphs of Chapter VII – the thought flashed into my mind that perhaps I had found the reason *why* this work, ostensibly a novel about a subterranean race blessed with supernormal powers, had become such a rarity. Did it contain secrets that should be suppressed? Had the author some special knowledge that even dressed up in the guise of fiction should not be made public?

These were thoughts that were never to be far from my mind in the years that followed when I began my investigation first into the life of Lord Lytton, and later into the legend of Agharti. They were to take me on a bizarre trail that would range from the dawn of time to the rise and fall of Adolf Hitler. How this link was forged I shall now explain, beginning first by quoting that fascinating page in the volume which caught my attention in the bookshop:

Then, turning to his daughter, my subterranean host said, 'And you, Zee, will not repeat to any one what the stranger has said, or may say, to me or to you, of a world other than our own.' Zee rose and kissed her father on the temples, saying with a smile, 'A Gy's tongue is wanton, but love can fetter it fast. And if, my father, you fear lest a chance word from me or yourself could expose our community to danger, by a desire to explore a world beyond us, will not a wave of the *Vril*, properly impelled, wash even the memory of what we have heard the stranger say out of the tablets of the brain?'

'What is *Vril*?' I asked.

Therewith Zee began to enter into an explanation of which I understood very little, for there is no word in any language I know which is an exact synonym for *Vril*. I should call it electricity, except that it comprehends in its manifold branches other forces of nature, to which, in our scientific nomenclature, differing names are assigned, such as magnetism, galvanism, etc. These people consider that in *Vril* they have arrived at the unity in natural energic agencies, which has been conjectured by many philosophers above ground, and which Faraday thus intimates under the more cautious term of correlation:

'I have long held an opinion,' says that illustrious experimentalist, 'almost amounting to a conviction, in common, I believe, with many other lovers of natural knowledge, that the various forms under which the forces of matter are made manifest have one common origin; or, in other words, are so directly related, and mutually dependent, that they are convertible, as it were into one another, and possess equivalents of power in their action.'

These subterranean philosophers assert that, by one operation of *Vril*, which Faraday would perhaps call 'atmospheric magnetism', they can influence the variations of temperature – in plain words, the weather; that by other operations, akin to those ascribed to mesmerism, electrobiology, odic force, etc., but applied scientifically through *Vril* conductors, they can exercise influence over minds, and bodies animal and vegetable, to an extent not surpassed in the romances of our mystics. To all such agencies they give the common name of *Vril*.

Zee asked me if, in my world, it was not known that all the faculties of the mind could be quickened to a degree unknown in the waking state, by trance or vision, in which the thoughts of one brain could be transmitted to another, and knowledge be thus rapidly interchanged. I replied, that there were among us stories told of such trance or vision, and that I had heard much and seen something of the mode in which they were artificially affected, as in mesmeric clairvoyance; but that these practices had fallen much into disuse or contempt, partly because of the gross impostures to which they had been made subservient, and partly because, even where the effects upon certain abnormal constitutions were genuinely produced, the effects, when fairly examined and analysed, were very unsatisfactory – not to be relied upon for any systematic truthfulness or any practical purpose, and rendered very mischievous to credulous persons by the superstitions they tended to produce.

Zee received my answers with much benignant attention, and said that similar instances of abuse and credulity had been familiar to their own scientific experience in the infancy of their knowledge, and while the properties of

Vril were misapprehended, but that she reserved further discussion on this subject till I was more fitted to enter into it. She contented herself with adding, that it was through the agency of *Vril*, while I had been placed in the state of trance, that I had been made acquainted with the rudiments of their language; and that she and her father, who, alone of the family, took the pains to watch the experiment, had acquired a greater proportionate knowledge of my language than I of their own; partly because my language was much simpler than theirs, comprising far less of complex ideas; and partly because their organisation was, by hereditary culture, much more ductile and more readily capable of acquiring knowledge than mine.

At this I secretly demurred; and having had, in the course of a practical life, to sharpen my wits, whether at home or in travel, I could not allow that my cerebral organisation could possibly be duller than that of people who had lived all their lives by lamplight. However, while I was thus thinking, Zee quietly pointed her forefinger at my forehead and sent me to sleep.

Before trying to assess the importance of this strange work – and the likelihood of it containing fact presented as fiction, not to mention its far-reaching influence – it is important to know something of the man who wrote it. And the plain truth is that Edward George Earle Bulwer Lytton (1803–1873) was a man of two quite distinct personalities: prolific novelist and secret, practised occultist.

Bulwer Lytton was born into a wealthy, privileged family who took pride in their breeding and position in society. As a youngster he was, naturally enough, privately educated at home until he was old enough to go up to Cambridge. His friends were carefully chosen, his reading supervised and his responsibilities as a Lytton rigorously enforced.

Yet, despite this supervision by his parents, there is strong evidence that he was already an introverted child, drawn towards mysticism, long before his teens. In a biography, *The Life of Edward Bulwer, First Lord Lytton*, by his son the Earl of Lytton (1913) we are told that when he was only eight he announced one day to his bemused mother: 'Mamma, are you not sometimes overcome by the sense of your own identity?' He also persistently asked questions about the portrait of one of his ancestors that hung in the family home at Knebworth. The man was Dr John Bulwer who, his parents told him, had devoted himself to finding a way of communicating with the deaf and the dumb, and had published a treatise on his theories entitled *Chirologia; Or, The Natural Language of the Hand*, in 1644.

What the Lyttons were reticent about telling their son was that Dr Bulwer had spent even more of his time investigating mysticism, and was said to have made a special study of alchemy. There was even a family legend that he had found a means of prolonging life, and actually lived well into his nineties, an exceptional age for the seventeenth century. The youngster's interest in this ancestor remained with him throughout his life, and indeed Dr John Bulwer features in the guise of Glyndon the occultist in Bulwer Lytton's novel about a secret French occult society, *Zanoni*, which he wrote in 1842.

In hindsight, then, it is easy to see how the young man became fascinated with the supernatural, and why he would have become interested in mesmerism while he was at college, and pursued his interest in the occult when he made a 'Grand Tour' of Europe in 1825.

Two years later, however, Bulwer Lytton contracted an ill-advised marriage and was promptly cut off from any form of financial support by his mother. Forced to face the practicalities of life, he turned to writing to support himself and his wife, and began producing the string of historical novels which made him popular with Victorian readers. But the pressures of this work, plus his wife's extravagance, doomed the marriage, and in 1836 the couple separated.

It was not until two years later, on his mother's death, and his accession to the baronetcy, that Bulwer Lytton could return to his secret passion for mysticism. He buried himself in research into all aspects of magic and divination and also joined the Rosicrucians, a mystical order who claimed to possess important and arcane wisdom that had been transmitted down through their members. The organization was believed to have been founded by a seventeenth-century German mystic, Christian Rosenkreuz (literally translated as 'Rosy Cross'), who had allegedly penetrated a 'secret chamber' beneath the ground and there found a library of books full of secret knowledge. In his definitive study *Histoire de la Rose-Croix* (1923), Serge Hutin tells us:

> The Rosicrucian Brethren were credited with possession of the following secrets: the transmutation of metals, the prolongation of life, knowledge of what is happening in distant places and the application of occult sciences to the discovery of even the most deeply hidden objects . . . They represented a group of human beings who had reached a higher state than the mass of humanity.

While in their book *The Morning of the Magicians* (1960), Louis Pauwels and Jacques Bergier suggest that 'the Rosicrucians were the heirs of civilisations that have disappeared.'

Although there is much that is disputed about the Rosicrucians, Bulwer Lytton was evidently passionately interested in the order's history and its store of ancient wisdom. Just how much of this he assimilated will probably never be known, or to what extent he attempted to carry out their secret magical rituals – though we do know he tried to evoke some elemental spirits on the roof of a London building one summer night in 1853. (His power as an adept of arcane sciences has, to my mind, been more than substantiated in C. N. Stewart's *Bulwer Lytton as Occultist*, published in 1927.)

Bulwer Lytton's skill at astrology and his powers of telekinesis, however, are not in dispute. He used this hard-won knowledge to compile the most accurate predictions for people and gave remarkable demonstrations of being able to move objects from a distance – displays that startled all those who witnessed them. These achievements were not without their cost, however, for he became increasingly eccentric towards the end of his life, morbidly afraid of being left on his own and terrified of being buried alive. Years before his death he had written specific instructions about certain tests that were to be carried out on his corpse to ensure he was neither in a state of trance or in a coma.

It was in all probability this eccentricity which weighed in the mind of obituary writers when they recorded his death in 1873. To strait-laced Victorians such behaviour was undoubtedly the direct result of dabbling in the occult and writing strange books about the supernatural. His death notices expressed the conviction that it would be for his historical novels and romances that he would be remembered. In fact, they could not have been more wrong.

But, these facts established, how do his odd life and its debatable achievements help us get at the truth about whether *The Coming Race* is fact or fiction?

Aside from the evidence in the book itself, there are also two important statements Bulwer Lytton himself made. As I mentioned, the secret knowledge possessed by the Rosicrucians was believed to have been obtained from somewhere 'below ground'. Our author clearly accepted this to be true, for he confided to his friend and fellow member Hargrave Jennings in 1854: 'So Rosenkreuz found his wisdom in a secret chamber. So will we all. There is much to be learned from the substrata of our planet.'

Bulwer Lytton also believed in the power of the pentacle as a means of communication. Writing in his book *A Strange Story* (1861), he is clearly expressing a personal conviction when he says: 'The pentacle itself has an intelligible meaning, it belongs to the only universal language of symbol, in which all races that think – around, and above *and below* us – can establish communion of thought' (my italics). If Bulwer Lytton did not actually find a way to the underground world he describes in *The Coming Race* – and there is no evidence that he did – might he not have learned something of it through access to ancient knowledge, his mystical powers and the use of his favoured pentacle?

There can be no denying the enigma which surrounds his work and its author. But is it unreasonable to suggest that there *are* elements in the book that are true – or at the very least *close* to the truth and merely embellished in a way that one might expect the member of a secret organization to do in order to protect those truths? Others before me have thought so, and some do today – vide Nadine Smyth, who asked in her article, 'UFOs and the Mystery of Agharti' published in the magazine *Prediction* in January 1979: 'Is the story of Agharti merely based upon Bulwer Lytton's imaginative novel? Or is the reverse the case, that Lytton presented under the guise of fiction a version of certain occult facts?' Dr Raymond Bernard goes further in his book *The Hollow Earth* (1969) when he says: 'Lytton was a Rosicrucian and probably based his novel

on occult information concerning existing subterranean
cities.'

But we must come to these believers and their opinions all in
good time. First, I think we should look more closely at the details contained in Bulwer Lytton's unique 'novel'.

In essence, *The Coming Race* is about a society of advanced
beings who live in tunnels and caverns beneath the surface of
the earth, possessing an intelligence and powers far in advance
of humanity. It is their ultimate objective to emerge from this
underworld and take control of the rest of the planet.

The storyteller is an unnamed man who, though described
as being a 'native of the United States of America', has an
appearance and background that make it hard to imagine him
being anyone but the youthful Bulwer Lytton himself. In an
unspecified year early in the 1800s, the young man comes to
England and is taken on a conducted tour of some mines, and
there learns of a legend that one of the tunnels leads to a
mysterious subterranean world. (It is my belief, incidentally,
that although these mines are not named, they are in fact in
the West Riding of Yorkshire, a district where Bulwer Lytton
lived for a period of time. And, as I mentioned earlier in this
book, a tunnel ultimately linked to Agharti is believed by some
to run from below the old mines in Wharfedale, Yorkshire;
this may be regarded as another factor in the argument for the
factual background of the book. Bulwer Lytton himself
excuses the anonymity with which he cloaks the locality thus:
'The reader will understand, ere he close this narrative, my
reason for concealing all clue to the district of which I write,
and will perhaps thank me for refraining from any description
that may tend to its discovery.')

The narrator becomes so intrigued with this legend that he
spends several weeks exploring the mines until, quite suddenly
and unexpectedly, he discovers a tunnel which leads to the
underworld. His progress is made possible by a 'diffused,
atmospheric light, not like that from fire, but soft and silvery,
as from a northern star'. In a huge cavern he discovers a settlement built on a mixture of Oriental and Egyptian lines, and
encounters a man dressed in a tunic with a dazzling tiara on
his head and carrying in his hand a little rod of bright metal
like polished steel. But it is the man's face that fascinates our
narrator:

It was the face of a man, but yet of a type of man distinct from our known extant races. The nearest approach to it in outline and expression is the face of the sculptured sphinx – so regular in its calm, intellectual beauty . . . I felt that this manlike image was endowed with forces inimical to man.

It transpires that this impressive yet benevolent figure is Aph-Lin, a leading member of the subterranean people, who are known as the *Vril-ya*. It is he and his beautiful daughter, Zee, who conduct the storyteller through the mysteries of their world, having first subconsciously given him the ability to understand their language. Once, though, he has told them of his life on the surface world, they pledge him to secrecy, as the reader has already learned in the extract from the book quoted earlier. During this conversation, he becomes acquainted with the extraordinary power which gives the race their name. An understanding of it becomes a driving obsession with him throughout the rest of the book.

The narrator of *The Coming Race* learns from his hosts that their remote ancestors had 'once tenanted a world above the surface of that in which they dwelt'. They had been forced to seek refuge below ground as a result of 'many violent revolutions of nature' which had caused great landmasses to be destroyed or submerged. The story goes on:

A band of the ill-fated race, thus invaded by the Flood, had, during the march of the waters, taken refuge in caverns and, wandering through these hollows, they lost sight of the upper world for ever . . . In the bowels of the earth even now, I was informed as a positive fact, might be discovered the remnants of human habitation – habitation not in huts and caverns, but in vast cities whose ruins attest the civilisation of races which flourished before the age of Noah.

For some time the *Vril-ya* had struggled desperately to re-establish their civilization and culture, finally achieving this by 'the gradual discovery of the latent powers stored in the all-permeating fluid which they denominate *Vril*'. Our narrator continues:

According to the account I received from Zee, who, as an erudite professor in the College of Sages, had studied such matters more diligently than any other member of my host's family, this fluid is capable of being raised and disciplined into the mightiest agency over all forms of matter, animate or inanimate. It can destroy like the flash of lightning; yet, differently applied, it can replenish or invigorate life, heal, and preserve, and on it they chiefly rely for the cure of disease, or rather for enabling the physical organisation to re-establish the due equilibrium of its natural powers, and thereby to cure itself. By this agency they rend their way through the most solid substances, and open valleys for culture through the rocks of their subterranean wilderness. From it they extract the light which supplies their lamps, finding it steadier, softer, and healthier than the other inflammable materials they had formerly used.

But the effects of the alleged discovery of the means to direct the more terrible force of *Vril* were chiefly remarkable in their influence upon social polity. As these effects became familiarly known and skilfully administered, war between the *Vril* discoverers ceased, for they brought the art of destruction to such perfection as to annul all superiority in numbers, discipline, or military skill. The fire lodged in the hollow of a rod directed by the hand of a child could shatter the strongest fortress, or cleave its burning way from the van to the rear of an embattled host. If army met army, and both had command of this agency, it could be but to the annihilation of each. The age of war was therefore gone, but with the cessation of war other effects bearing upon the social state soon became apparent. Man was so completely at the mercy of man, each whom he encountered being able, if so willing, to slay him on the instant, that all notions of government by force gradually vanished from political systems and forms of law.

From Zee, the narrator learns that the subterranean people are governed by a single supreme magistrate called the *Tur*: 'he held his office nominally for life, but he could seldom be induced to retain it after the first approach of old age.' Any disputes arising amongst the male and female members of the *Vril-ya* – the males being known as *Ana* and the females *Gyei* – would be referred to the Council of Sages, to which Zee herself belonged. Both sexes were considered equal and shared in all

arts and vocations, although – said Zee – 'the *Gyei* are usually
superior to the *Ana* in physical strength (an important element
in the consideration and maintenance of female rights). They
attain to loftier stature, and amid their rounder proportion
are embedded sinews and muscles as hardy as those of the
other sex.' Marriages apparently only lasted three years, at the
end of which the couples were free to choose new partners!

When our storyteller asks his guide how it is possible for life
to be sustained below ground without the energy of the sun:

> She did but conjecture that sufficient allowance had not
> been made by our philosophers for the extreme porousness
> of the interior earth – the vastness of its cavities and
> irregularities, which served to create free currents of air and
> frequent winds – and for the various modes in which heat is
> evaporated and thrown off. She did allow, however, that
> there was a depth at which the heat was deemed to be
> intolerable to such organised life as was known to the
> experience of the *Vril-ya*. She said also, that since the *Vril*
> light had superseded all other light-giving bodies, the
> colours of flower and foliage had become more brilliant,
> and vegetation had acquired larger growth.

The *Vril-ya* themselves, said Zee, reinvigorated their bodies
by taking regular baths charged with *Vril*. 'They consider that
this fluid, sparingly used, is a great sustainer of life,' she says.
'But used in excess, when in the normal state of health, rather
tends to reaction and exhausted vitality. For nearly all their
disease, however, they resort to it as the chief assistant to
nature in throwing off the complaint.' (In an interesting footnote to this paragraph, the 'author' – and it could be Bulwer
Lytton himself speaking – says: 'I once tried the effect of a *Vril*
bath. It was very similar in its invigorating powers to that of
the baths at Gastein, the virtue of which are ascribed by many
physicians to electricity; but though similar, the effect of the
Vril bath was more lasting.')

The lives of the subterranean people are constantly peaceful, and they need use little physical effort, Zee explains. 'In
all service,' she says, 'we make great use of automaton figures,
which are so ingenious, and so pliant to the operations of *Vril*,
that they actually seem gifted with reason.' And on seeing one
of these robots, the young narrator is forced to admit that: 'It

was scarcely possible to distinguish the figures I beheld, apparently guiding or superintending the rapid movements of vast engines, from human forms endowed with thought.'

The young woman also tells her attentive listener that there are communities of the *Vril-ya* spread at great distances apart below ground, all linked by tunnels and caverns through which they can travel. 'I heard my father say that, according to the last report, there were a million and a half communities,' she says. 'All the tribes of *Vril-ya* are in constant communication with each other. Our hardy life as children also makes us take cheerfully to travel and adventure.'

A little later in the narrative, after the storyteller has become settled with the underground people, he is given two startling demonstrations of *Vril Power* – firstly in the shape of the *Vril Staff* carried by the inhabitants, and secondly as the means of motivating 'Flying Wings' which enable the *Vril-ya* to travel easily about their domain.

The narrator tell us that although he often saw people carrying the small, shining rods, he himself was never allowed to handle one 'for fear of some terrible accident occasioned by my ignorance of its use'. He then goes on to describe the *Vril Staff* in detail:

It is hollow, and has in the handle several stops, keys, or springs, by which its force can be altered, modified, or directed – so that by one process it destroys, by another it heals – by one it can rend the rock, by another disperse the vapour – by one it affects bodies, by another it can exercise a certain influence over minds. It is usually carried in the convenient size of a walking staff, but it has slides by which it can be lengthened or shortened at will. When used for special purposes, the upper part rests in the hollow of the palm with the fore and middle fingers protruded.

I was assured, however, that its power was not equal in all, but proportioned to the amount of certain *Vril* properties in the wearer, in affinity, or *rapport*, with the purposes to be effected. Some were more potent to destroy, others to heal; much also depended on the calm and steadiness of volition in the manipulator. They assert that the full exercise of *Vril Power* can only be acquired by constitutional temperament – i.e. by hereditarily transmitted organisation

– and that a female infant of four years old belonging to the *Vril-ya* races can accomplish feats with the wand placed for the first time in her hand, which a life spent in its practice would not enable the strongest and most skilled mechanician, born out of the pale of the *Vril-ya* to achieve.

All these wands are not equally complicated; those entrusted to the children are much simpler than those borne by sages of either sex, and constructed with a view to the special object in which the children are employed; which as I have before said, is among the youngest children the most destructive. In the wands of wives and mothers the correlative destroying force is usually abstracted, the healing power fully charged. I wish I could say more in detail of this singular conductor of the *Vril* fluid, but its machinery is as exquisite as its effects are marvellous.

The young man watches in amazement when Zee demonstrates the power of her metal rod. 'I saw her,' he says, 'merely by a certain play of her *Vril Staff* – she herself standing at a distance – put into movement large and weighty substances. She seemed to endow them with intelligence, and to make them comprehend and obey her command.'

Again, here, it is possible to draw an immediate parallel between fiction and fact. For that description of Zee's powers of being able to move objects at a distance apparently by the power of her mind, exactly describes Bulwer Lytton's own acknowledged powers of telekinesis!

Our narrator's second surprise comes when he sees some of the *Vril-ya* flying through the air on wings. These, he observes, can be taken on and off at will and are very large, reaching down to the wearer's knees. He goes on:

They are fastened round the shoulders with light but strong springs of steel; and, when expanded, the arms slide through loops for that purpose, forming, as it were, a stout, central membrane. As the arms are raised, a tubular lining beneath the vest or tunic becomes, by mechanical contrivance, inflated with air, increased or diminished at will by the movement of the arms, and serving to buoy the whole form as on bladders. The wings and the balloon-like apparatus are highly charged with *Vril*; and when the body is thus wafted upward, it seems to become singularly lightened of its weight.

I found it easy enough to soar from the ground; indeed when the wings were spread it was scarcely possible not to soar, but then came the difficulty and the danger. I utterly failed in the power to use and direct the pinions, though I am considered among my own race unusually alert and ready in bodily exercises, and am a very practised swimmer. I could only make the most confused and blundering efforts at flight. I was the servant of the wings; the wings were not my servants – they were beyond my control; and when by a violent strain of muscle, and, I must fairly own, in that abnormal strength which is given by excessive fright, I curbed their gyrations and brought them near to the body, it seemed as if I lost the sustaining power stored in them and the connecting bladders, as when air is let out of a balloon, and found myself precipitated again to earth; saved, indeed, by some spasmodic flutterings, from being dashed to pieces, but not saved from the bruises and the stun of a heavy fall.

I would, however, have persevered in my attempts, but for the advice or the commands of the scientific Zee, who had benevolently accompanied my flutterings, and indeed, on the last occasion, flying just under me, received my form as it fell on her own expanded wings, and preserved me from breaking my head on the roof of the pyramid from which we had ascended.

Once more, in a description of the *Vril-ya* themselves flying, there is a remarkable similarity between their appearance and that strange aerial phenomenon which Nicholas Roerich reported in the desert of Ulan-Davan. Could it have been a member of the subterranean race flying rather than a vulture – a bird unknown in those parts?

Although our narrator is deeply saddened by his failure to fly, the episode has awakened another emotion in him. A desire to return home. As he tells us: 'I now pined to escape to the upper world, but I racked my brains in vain for any means to effect it. I was never permitted to wander forth alone, so that I could not even visit the spot on which I had alighted to see if it were possible to re-ascend the mine.'

As he tries to find some practical solution to this dilemma, he also formalizes his opinions on the true nature of the *Vril-ya*:

I arrived at the conclusion that this people – though originally not only of our human race, but, as it seems to me clear by the roots of their language, descended from the same ancestors as the great Aryan family, from which in varied streams has flowed the dominant civilisation of the world; and having, according to their myths and their history passed through phases of society familiar to ourselves – had yet now developed into a distinct species with which it was impossible that any community in the upper world could amalgamate. And that if they ever emerged from these nether recesses into the light of day, they would, according to their own traditional persuasions of their ultimate destiny, destroy and replace our existent varieties of man.

Having arrived at this chilling verdict on the intentions of the *Vril-ya*, it comes as something of a surprise when our narrator is offered a chance of escape by a most unexpected person – none other than his host's daughter and Council member, Zee. She has apparently grown fond of the young man, but aware that any union between them is impossible, and sensing his desire to return home, she offers her assistance. A few days later during the rest hours she leads him back to the tunnel shaft, and he successfully climbs to the surface – only to find that he ultimately emerges from a quite different tunnel to that which he entered! (Here, yet again, Bulwer Lytton runs true to the legend of a worldwide network of tunnels linked with the subterranean world.)

With a grateful prayer for his deliverance, the young narrator concludes his story:

The more I think of a people calmly developing, in regions excluded from our sight and deemed uninhabitable by our sages, powers surpassing our most disciplined modes of force, and virtues to which our life, social and political, becomes antagonistic in proportion as our civilisation advances – the more devoutly I pray that ages may yet elapse before there emerge into the sunlight our inevitable destroyers. Being, however, frankly told by my physician that I am afflicted by a complaint which, though it gives little pain and no perceptible notice of its encroachments, may at any moment be fatal, I have thought it my duty to my fellow-men to place on record these forewarnings of *The Coming Race*.

This last paragraph of a book which I consider an impressive and compelling work – written more in the form of a treatise than a novel and containing a wealth of detail which I have only been able to hint at here – this paragraph has proved to be uncannily prophetic on two counts.

Firstly, Bulwer Lytton, who we know was already under medical supervision, died less than three years after completing the book.

And, secondly, a leader was indeed to emerge who not only believed in the *actual* existence of the *Vril-ya*, but set out to establish a very similar kind of society to that which Bulwer Lytton had described.

That man's name can still cause a shudder of unease when spoken today: Adolf Hitler. And it is his activities which provide the next, and perhaps even more extraordinary chapter, in our search for Agharti.

Chapter 7

ADOLF HITLER AND THE 'SUPER-RACE'

On the morning of 25 April 1945, a group of Russian soldiers cautiously picking their way through the rubble of war-torn Berlin made one of the most astonishing discoveries of the Second World War. The men who had surged into the devastated capital of Nazi Germany on the previous day and were now within days of bringing the terrible and bloody six-year conflict to an end were constantly on the lookout for the pathetic little pockets of resistance still being put up by groups of German soldiers, mostly old men and young boys, vainly trying to save Adolf Hitler's 'Thousand Year Reich'.

The Russians moved carefully from one shattered building to the next, methodically combing the rubble-filled rooms and cellars for any signs of life. They had to trust to their battle-sharpened instincts as they wormed their way through the bomb damage, and such was the destruction that it was impossible to tell where one street ended and another began. They could tell little other than that they were somewhere in the eastern sector of Berlin.

It was amidst the skeleton that had once been a three-story building that the soldiers made their discovery. For in one of the ground floor rooms they found the corpses of six men lying in a small circle. In the centre of the circle was another body, lying on its back, the hands clasped tightly, almost as if in prayer.

At first glance, the corpses looked little different to the many others that the Russians had come across in this ghastly city of death. But on closer examination, they proved to be very different indeed. For although the corpses were in faded and worn German military uniforms, their faces looked like those of Orientals. They were, in fact, Tibetans – as one of the Russian soldiers, a young man who came from the adjoining area of Mongolia, was not slow to point out. And it was he who also noticed that the figure in the centre of the circle of dead men was wearing a pair of bright green gloves on his clenched hands.

But what on earth were such people doing here, thousands of miles from their homeland, and in the midst of a battle in which their country was playing no part?

Although sudden gunfire from a short distance away quickly distracted the searching Russians, not one of the group was in any doubt that they had stumbled across something quite extraordinary. For apart from their appearance, there was every indication that the Tibetans had not been killed in action, but had probably taken part in some kind of ritual suicide, perhaps under the orders of the strange man in green gloves who lay in their midst.

Before the Russians linked up with the Allies striking into Berlin from the west, and the city fell on 2 May, the bodies of several hundred more Tibetans – some sources have suggested as many as a thousand – were found in similar circumstances. Quite a substantial number had also apparently committed suicide, but others had obviously died under the hail of bombs and gunfire which reduced the once magnificent city to smouldering ruins. The corpses provided a mystery that was some time in the solving – but when the facts about the dead men were painstakingly assembled they formed a quite amazing link with the underground kingdom of Agharti, Adolf Hitler, and Bulwer Lytton's extraordinary book, *The Coming Race*. Indeed, it is true to say that the book had been to a degree responsible for both the presence of those men in the city, and to a lesser extent the very carnage that the Fuehrer of the Third Reich had inflicted on Europe and much of the world during the years from 1939 to 1945.

As I indicated in the previous chapter, there have been numbers of people who, over the years since the publication of *The Coming Race* in 1871, have believed it to be literally true – the description of an actual race of people living below the surface of the world. But of these believers, few were more passionate in their conviction than Adolf Hitler, the former house painter and army corporal who scarred half the nations of the globe with his terrible dream of world domination.

It remains an extraordinary fact that outside of the pages of *The Coming Race*, Bulwer Lytton has left us no clues about the exact nature of his enigmatic work. Is it just a novel or more fact than fiction? And if so, where did he get his information from? At the time of its publication the book was scarcely noticed: the few critics who reviewed it found it a minor work, and all of them echoed the anonymous writer in the London *Times* who hoped that 'the author would return to the historical themes to which his talents are best suited'. Perhaps if the work had excited any sort of controversy, Bulwer Lytton might have been pressed for such details, but its reception was indifferent, and whatever emotions he may have felt about this, he disguised them by getting on with his next work. Of course he may even have hoped for such a reaction, for fear that he might have injudiciously revealed too much of his 'secret knowledge'.

But leaving this conjecture aside, we can be in no doubt that Adolf Hitler believed the story to be true. Indeed, he not only based part of his philosophy on it, but actually dispatched expeditions across the length and breadth of Europe and Asia to find the way to the underground world. If we look briefly at the philosophy of the people in Bulwer Lytton's book we can easily identify the influence it had on Hitler and how his plans for a Thousand Year Reich ruled by a master race of pure-blooded Aryans emerged.

For example, he tells us that the *Vril-ya*, the people of the underworld, were 'descended from the same ancestors as the great Aryan family, from which in varied streams has flowed the dominant civilisation of the world'. They considered themselves a superior race looking on other nations 'with more disdain than the citizens of New York regard the negroes'. They were believers in the survival of the fittest, the triumph of the weak over the strong, and the dominance of the Aryan race. The *Vril-ya* considered democracy, free institutions and a Republican type government as 'one of the crude and ignorant experiments which belong to the infancy of political science'. They were led by a supreme ruler, the Tur, in whom all authority was vested, a man who possessed the secret of *Vril Power*, the mysterious force which could control all the forces of man and nature. And to all this could be added the subterranean people's ultimate objective, 'to attain to the purity of our species . . . and supplant all the inferior races now existing.'

To a man like Adolf Hitler, fascinated by mysticism and racial purity and obsessed with power, *The Coming Race* expressed his deepest desires.

It has become increasingly evident in recent years, that while there has been considerable study undertaken into Hitler and his rise to power, there has not been as much attention paid to the part played in it by his interest in mysticism and the occult as perhaps there should be. For Hitler was unquestionably a man fascinated with ancient Germanic lore and attracted to the powers of the supernatural. He was, of course, also gifted with almost hypnotic powers himself, as his biographer, Professor Alan Bullock, has observed in *Hitler: A Study in Tyranny* (1953): 'Hitler's power to bewitch an audience has been likened to the occult arts of the African medicine-man or the Asiatic shaman; others have compared it to the sensitivity of a medium and the magnetism of a hypnotist.'

Although there is evidence that Hitler showed a certain interest in hypnotism when he was a young man – reading a number of the standard works on the subject – his fascination with the occult can be traced back to his association with a mysterious but undeniably sinister figure, Professor Karl Haushofer, who has been called the 'Master Magician of the Nazi Party'. And the person who brought these two together was none other than Rudolf Hess, Hitler's deputy, the man who made the abortive flight to England to try and halt the war between England and Germany, and who is, today, the sole surviving high-ranking member of the Nazi party.

Karl Haushofer was born in Bavaria in 1869, and appears fleetingly in most works about the life of Hitler – yet when their association is examined in detail it is plain to see that he was an important, if not major, influence on the demagogue-to-be. He was evidently a man of forceful intellect, deeply knowledgeable about Eastern mysticism, and obsessed with the origins and ultimate destiny of the German people.

Coming from a wealthy, military background, Haushofer, after being educated at Munich University, naturally enough entered upon a career in the German army. His obvious ability quickly earned him promotion, and his interest in the Far East – which he had begun to develop while still at university – led to a number of appointments in the Orient serving on the Staff

Corps. His tour of duty took him to India, where he devoted all his spare time to the study of Indian mysticism and in particular the ancient traditions, while later he went to Japan. Of these years, Louis Pauwels and Jacques Bergier have written in *The Morning of the Magicians*:

> He paid several visits to India and the Far East, and was sent to Japan, where he learned the language. He believed that the German people originated in Central Asia, and that it was the Indo-Germanic race that guaranteed the perman-ence, nobility and greatness of the world. While in Japan, Haushofer is said to have been initiated into one of the most important secret Buddhist societies and to have sworn, if he failed in his 'mission', to commit suicide in accordance with the time-honoured ceremonial.

At this time, Haushofer also began to demonstrate another remarkable talent – the ability of prophecy. And when, during the First World War, he put this skill to practical use by pre-dicting the precise moment the enemy would attack and the actual locations where bombs and shells would fire – his pre-dictions later being proved correct – his stature among his men and his superiors grew enormously. He became one of the youngest generals in the German army, and only the eventual defeat of his country prevented him reaching the most senior posts.

In the aftermath of war, Haushofer had no difficulty in finding another occupation for his varied talents. He returned to his earlier fascination with political geography and earned a doctorate at Munich University. Armed with this qualification he threw himself wholeheartedly into teaching the young people of his defeated nation that the war had merely been a setback in the ultimate ambitions of the German people. It was their destiny to one day rule Europe and Asia – the home-land of the Aryan people – and thereby exercise the world control which only they were fitted to administer.

Haushofer also took his campaign into print, writing several books and founding the *Geo-Political Review*, in which he endlessly expounded his beliefs about Aryan supremacy. He also made a number of interesting revelations about what he had learned during his time in India in the early years of the century. While travelling in Central Asia in 1905, he said, he had heard of a vast underground encampment under the Himalayas where dwelt a race of Supermen. The name of this place was Agharti, and its capital was called Shamballah.

According to Haushofer, Agharti was a 'place of meditation, a hidden city of Goodness, a temple of non-participation in the things of the world'. Shamballah, though, was 'a city of violence and power whose forces command the elements and the masses of humanity, and hasten the arrival of the human race at the "turning-point of time" '. (It is interesting to note that Haushofer is the only writer on Shamballah to refer to it as a place of violence as well as power. It has been suggested. with some justification I think, that this was Haushofer's own idea to substantiate his belief that world domination could only be achieved by force: he saw the support of the mighty inhabitants of the underground city as a way of ensuring this, and attributed to them powers that made an association with them all the more desirable.)

Haushofer believed Agharti to be at the centre of the 'heartland' from which the Aryan race had come, and that whoever controlled this 'heartland' – in conjunction with the all-powerful underground race, of course – would rule the world. As Trevor Ravenscroft has so splendidly summarized this philosophy in his *The Spear of Destiny* (1972):

> He clothed geography in a veil of racial mysticism, providing a reason for the Germans to return to those areas in the hinterland of Asia from which it was generally believed the Aryan Race originated. In this subtle way he incited the German nation towards the conquest of the whole of Eastern Europe and beyond to the vast inner area of Asia which extends 2,500 miles from west to east between the Volga and the Yangtze rivers and includes in its most southerly aspect the mountains of Tibet. It was Haushofer's opinion that whoever gained complete control of this heartland, developed its economic resources and organised its military defence, would achieve unassailable world supremacy.

Among the young men who eagerly accepted Professor Haushofer's ideas, and devoured the philosophy extolled in the pages of his *Review*, was one Rudolf Hess, who for a time served as his assistant at the University of Munich. He was to prove the link between Haushofer and Adolf Hitler. In fact, we have Rudolf Hess to thank for a lot of what we know about Haushofer, for as Jack Fishman has reported in his *The Seven Men of Spandau* (1954), it was the former deputy Fuehrer who revealed that his one-time Professor had been 'the secret "Master Magician of the Reich" – the power behind Hitler'. (Fishman also informs us that the ill-fated flight to England was undertaken because Haushofer had had a dream in which he saw Hess 'striding through the tapestried halls of English castles, bringing peace between the two great Nordic nations'. And with Haushofer's record as a prophet, it is not surprising that Hess obeyed the premonition exactly.)

The first meeting between the ageing Professor and the fanatical young revolutionary took place in Landsberg Prison in 1924 when Hitler was in prison there following the failure of the Munich *Putsch*. Hess arranged it from his own cell, where he was sharing imprisonment for his part in the conspiracy to overthrow the Bavarian government. He was convinced that the two men had much in common in their stated beliefs about the future of the German people. As Pauwels and Bergier tell us:

> Introduced by Hess, General Karl Haushofer visited Hitler every day and spent hours with him expounding his theories and deducing from them every possible argument in favour of political conquest. Left alone with Hess, Hitler amalgamated, for the purposes of propaganda, the theories of Haushofer, as the basis of *Mein Kampf*.

The influence of the Munich professor on Hitler's book has been further underlined by Edmund A. Walsh in his *Total Power* (1953), where he writes:

> One can almost feel the presence of Haushofer, although the lines were written by Hess at the dictation of Hitler. What Haushofer did was to hand a sheathed sword of conquest from his arsenal of scholarly research. Hitler unsheathed the blade, sharpened the edge, and threw away the scabbard.

Among the books which Haushofer lent to his enthusiastic listener was Bulwer Lytton's *The Coming Race*. The Professor explained that, like the author, he himself had been a member of a German lodge of the Rosicrucians, and that the book harboured many secrets from that order disguised as fiction. Haushofer said the work was specific in its descriptions of the underground super-race and corroborated much of the evidence he himself had gathered at first-hand in Asia about the world of Agharti.

To Haushofer, *The Coming Race* was merely one brick in his argument. To Hitler, when he came to read it, the book proved much more influential on his vision of the future. There seems little doubt that as he read through the pages of Bulwer Lytton's strange story in the seclusion of his prison cell, he began to yearn for the day when he might establish for himself the actuality of the secret civilization beneath the snows of Tibet . . .

Although by this time Haushofer had sown the seeds of what became Hitler's most driving obsession – the need for the emergence of the 'superman' to rule the world – his importance in our story is not quite at an end. For in the following year, 1925, three more important events occurred, all of which provide further threads in the rich tapestry.

Firstly, Adolf Hitler's *Mein Kampf* was published. Secondly, Ferdinand Ossendowski's *Beasts, Men and Gods* appeared and made the public in general aware of the legends of Agharti and Shamballah. And, thirdly, a secret organization with the unlikely title of 'The Luminous Lodge of the Vril Society' was formed.

Haushofer, as we know, was influential on Hitler's book, and naturally enough was fascinated by Ossendowski's work, which again confirmed many facts he had himself gathered about the underground world in Asia. And as to the secret society, he was one of the people instrumental in setting it up.

Facts about this Society have remained elusive to this day, and the best information has come to us from Dr Willy Ley, the brilliant rocket scientist who was in Berlin at the time and later fled from Germany in 1933. In an essay published in 1947 called 'Pseudo-Sciences Under the Nazi Regime', he describes the carefully shrouded formation of the Society whose philosophy was based almost totally on Bulwer Lytton's book, *The Coming Race*. Ley says the group invited specially selected members from all over the world to help further the research into, and creation of, an Aryan super-race. Among

these members were a large contingent of Tibetan lamas sum-
moned because of their association with Agharti.

Ley also reported that the members of the Lodge believed
they had secret knowledge of the force Bulwer Lytton had
called *Vril* (hence their name), and this they hoped would enable them to ultimately become the equals of the race hidden
in the bowels of the earth. They had developed methods of
concentration and a 'whole system of internal gymnastics by
which they could be transformed', he said. Although Ley only
expressed a general opinion as to what he thought this *Vril
Power* might be, he was not far short of the truth (as we shall
see later) when he described it as the inherent energy in our
bodies of which we use only a minute proportion in our daily
lives – leaving untouched and unexploited the greater proportion which has virtually unlimited powers if only we can find
the key to its exploitation.

Investigation has been carried out into this weird society by
Pauwels and Bergier, as well as by Trevor Ravenscroft, who
writes in his *The Spear of Destiny*:

> The sole aim of this lodge was to make further researches
> into the origins of the Aryan Race and the manner in which
> magical capacities slumbering in the Aryan blood could be
> reactivated to become the vehicle of superhuman powers.
> Surprisingly enough, one of the works which proved an end-
> less source of inspiration to the leading members of this
> Lodge had been written by an Englishman, Bulwer Lytton
> . . . In one of [his] little-known books called *The Coming
> Race* he veiled many of the truths he had learned through
> personal initiation in the Secret Doctrine. He had no idea
> that this book, in which he described the emergence of a
> new race with lofty spiritual faculties and superhuman
> powers, would become the evil inspiration of a small group
> of Nazis intent on breeding a Master Race in order to en-
> slave the world.

Another opinion expressed by Gunther Rosenberg of the
European Occult Research Society and quoted in *Fate*
magazine (July 1972) puts the group's intentions somewhat
more simply: 'They believed that the Lords of the Universe
lived in the centre of the earth. Men on the surface must become God-like and make an alliance with the inner race.

THE KING OF THE WORLD?

Is there an underground cave city called Agharti ruled by a Venusian who holds our future hopes?

ALL through the world today are thousands of people who claim to have knowledge of an underground city, not specifically located although generally assumed to be in Tibet, called Agharti, or Shambala. In this city, they say, is a highly developed civilization ruled by an "Elder" or a "Great One" whose title is among others "The King of the World." Some claim to have seen him, and it is also claimed that he made at least one visit to the surface. It is also claimed that when Mankind is ready for the benefits he can bring, he will emerge and establish a new civilization of peace and plenty.

To quote the words of a "witness": "He came here ages ago from the planet Venus to be the instructor and guide of our then just dawning h u m a n i t y. Though he is thousands of years old, his appearance is that of an exceptionally well-developed and handsome youth about sixteen. But there is nothing juvenile about the light of infinite love, wisdom and power that shines from his eyes. He is slightly larger than the average man, but there are no radical differences in race."

Apparently the ruler of Agharti is a man; apparently he possesses great power and science, including atomic energy machines. Apparently also he is dedicated to bring to us great benefits. Apparently he has power to end warfare on the surface at will. We, the people of Earth, ask: What man can judge another? Wars must end now! Judge not, Great One, lest you be judged. For we ARE ready for peace!

The Legend of Agharti – as presented by Ray Palmer in *Amazing Stories*, May, 1946.

C. J. Cutcliffe Hyne (left) the Yorkshire cave hunter and author whose work inspi
this book.

tration from *Niels Klims' Journey Underground* (1741), the most famous novel of
terranean world.

Louis Jacolliot, the French writer who first revealed the existence of Agharti.

Right: The Russian mystic, Madame Helena Blavatsky, who popularised the lost w‹
legend.

Ferdinand Ossendowski who brought back information on Agharti from the wild Asia.

...cholas Roerich, the ...ist and mystic, who ...nt in search of ...amballah.

N. Roerich.

...istian Rosenkruez, ...nder of the ...icrucians, who ...gedly discovered ...et knowledge ...erground.

1604

Above: The enigmatic Lord Lytton who described a subterranean world in his str
book, *The Coming Race* (1871).

Right: The Cave of Borodla at Aggtelek, Hungary, which Adolf Hitler had explor
his search for a tunnel to Agharti.

A stone relief carving from Palanque in Mexico. Does it depict the 'King of the Worl in one of the passageways to his kingdom?

The ancient site of Atlantis according to a seventeenth-century engraving.

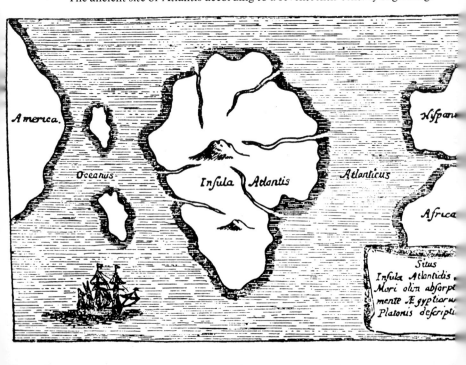

A stone statue of an Atlantean, according to historian Lewis Spence.

A very early impression of Quetzalcoatl showing him in the tunnel he used to journey backwards and forwards between Atlantis and South America.

A mysterious tunnel system discovered in the Chandore Mountain Range of India. Do these lead to the secret kingdom of Agharti?

The mysterious 'Caves of a Thousand Buddhas' in China – beyond which some experts believe may lie a passageway to Agharti.

The striking Tibetan township of Shigatze, underneath which lies the hidden city of Shamballah.

A rare painting of Lake Manasarowar, held sacred by all Tibetans, and believed to
close to the heart of Agharti.

A vision of Shamballah as seen by the mystical painter, Nicholas Roerich.

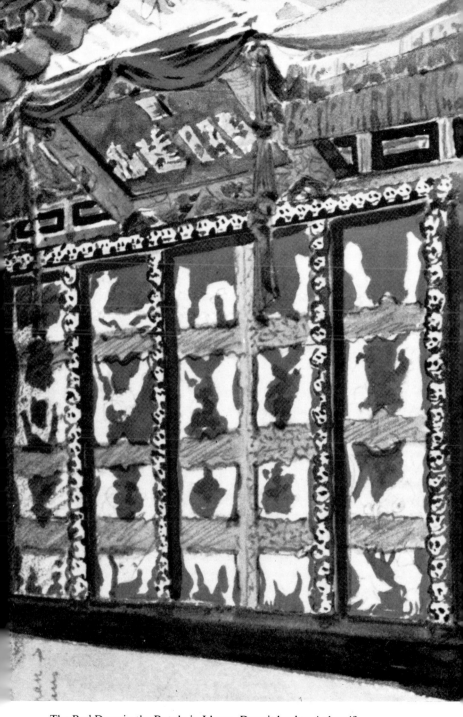

The Red Door in the Potola in Lhasa. Does it lead to Agharti?

Do UFOs like this one originate from the Subterranean World rather than the gala

Otherwise, we will be enslaved to build the New Cities for the Coming Race.'

Because of Haushofer's profound knowledge of mysticism in Asia and the Far East, he was a leading – if not *the* leading – member of the Luminous Lodge. It has been suggested that the Professor had actually mastered the use of *Vril Power*: and there is certainly no doubt that he was on intimate terms with several of the Tibetan high lamas who lived in Berlin, and who might be expected to know its secret. These mysterious figures, led by a supreme lama identified only as 'The Man with the Green Gloves', were to stay in the heart of the Reich through its triumphs and its ultimate downfall. As far as we can tell, all of them died either by their own hand or under fire in the days before the German nation finally surrendered to the Allies.

There is evidence that Haushofer informed Hitler of the Luminous Lodge (although the Fuehrer never joined its ranks) and that he also took the Tibetan in green gloves to meet the Nazi leader on several occasions. Hitler was, of course, much influenced by astrology, and apparently consulted with this lama regularly, according to Eric Norman in his curious book, *This Hollow Earth* (1972). 'This Tibetan also made several public predictions that were printed by Nazi newspapers,' says Norman. 'These included the number of Hitler's deputies who would be elected to the Reichstag. The Nazi propaganda papers also reported that the lama "knew the secret of the entrances to Agharti".'

It seems reasonable to surmise that it was the combined influence of all these factors that further convinced Hitler of the reality of Agharti and redoubled his determination to deploy time and manpower to its discovery. He had learned from the legends that a network of tunnels running across Europe ultimately led to this fabled home of the super-race, and after his rise to power he instituted the search for it which was to continue for the rest of his life. The first expeditions were dispatched purely under the auspices of the Luminous Lodge, beginning in 1926, but later, after coming to power, Hitler took a more direct interest, overseeing the organization of the searches himself.

This involvement was doubtless stimulated by the Fuehrer's conviction that certain representatives of the underground super-race were already abroad in the world – a conviction that has been graphically recorded by Hermann Rauschning, the *Gauleiter* of Danzig, whose intimate conversations with the German leader have caused him to be described as 'the only authentic biographer of Adolf Hitler'.

Rauschning's book, *Hitler Speaks: A Series of Political Conversations with Adolf Hitler on his Real Aims*, was published in 1939, and stimulated widespread interest. However, it was only later that the importance of some of his statements came to be fully appreciated.

In the book, Rauschning describes how he recorded the conversations in a period covering the last year before Hitler's seizure of power and the first two years of the Nazi regime (1932–1934). 'In the course of these discussions,' says Rauschning, 'Hitler speaks openly about his innermost ideas – ideas which have been kept secret from the masses.' Rauschning makes no secret of his fear of Hitler and calls him 'the master enchanter and the high priest of the religious mysteries of Nazidom'.

It seems evident that from early on in their relationship, Hitler regarded Rauschning as a confidant, and would discuss things with him that much more senior members of his hierarchy were not privy to. In particular, his fascination with mysticism. Rauschning records:

> Hitler was fond of mystical talk. One cannot help thinking of him as a medium. For most of the time mediums are ordinary, insignificant people. Suddenly they are endowed with what seem to be supernatural powers which set them apart from the rest of humanity. These powers are something that is outside their true personality – visitors, as it were, from another planet. The medium is possessed. Once the crisis is past, they fall back again into mediocrity. It was in this way, beyond any doubt, that Hitler was possessed by forces outside himself.

From Rauschning's appreciation of Hitler's mystical qualities developed their discussions about the superman that the Fuehrer dreamed would ultimately emerge. Two instances in particular are recorded by Rauschning which, if taken literally, seem to prove that Hitler *actually saw* one of these beings. What, in fact, seems more probable is that they are rather deranged fantasies – to which the Fuehrer was, of course, often prone – although they do underline the depth of his faith in this particular idea.

On the first occasion, after a lengthy conversation about the superman of the future, Hitler suddenly confided to his listener: 'The new man is among us. He is here! Now are you satisfied? I will tell you a secret. I have seen the vision of the new man – fearless and formidable. I shrank from him.'

Then, in a still more dramatic moment in his 'eagle's eyrie', the glass-walled building in the Bavarian mountains, honey-combed with tunnels like some strange facsimile of the place called Shamballah which he so desperately sought, Hitler revealed another encounter with one of these men. Rauschning describes the incident thus:

> My informant described to me in full detail a remarkable scene – I should not have credited the story if it had not come from such a source. Hitler stood swaying in his room, looking wildly about him. 'He! He! He's been here!' he gasped. His lips were blue. Sweat streamed down his face. Suddenly he began to reel off figures, and odd words and broken phrases, entirely devoid of sense. It sounded horrible. He used strangely composed and entirely un-German word-formations. Then he stood quite still, only his lips moving. He was massaged and offered something to drink. Then he suddenly broke out –
> 'There, there! In the corner! Who's that?'
> He stamped and shrieked in the familiar way. He was shown that there was nothing out of the ordinary in the room, and then he gradually grew calm.

It has been suggested that the strange word-formations that Hitler used on this occasion might have been the language of the *Vril-ya* which Bulwer Lytton describes in *The Coming Race*; that Hitler had resorted to them in an attempt to communicate with his visitor. But such, of course, is no more than speculation.

Details of the various expeditions that Hitler ordered to Tibet to search for Agharti and Shamballah are conclusive, if somewhat disappointing. Writing in *This Hollow Earth*, Eric Norman says:

Nazi records seized after the fall of the Third Reich indicate
that Hitler and his henchmen launched several unsuccessful
expeditions . . . Frustrated German geographers and
scientists were ordered to find tunnel entrances that led to
the *Vril-ya*. German, Swiss and Italian mines were charted
for possible shafts leading down to the interior land of
cavern cities. Hitler even ordered an intellectually-inclined
Army Colonel to check out Bulwer Lytton's life, hoping to
find where – and when – the author had visited the caverns
of *Vril-ya* . . . From 1936 onwards the Nazis were regularly
sending teams of elite corpsmen into caves and mines in
Europe. Entire crews of *spelunkers* prowled caves hunting
for the new advanced man.

Despite failure after failure – each of which brought tirades
of rage from Hitler and an insistence that still more effort was
to be put into the project – only one discovery of any real
significance has subsequently come to light. This was made in
Czechoslovakia in 1939. Before the invasion of that country
Hitler's researchers had also combed the Reich's archives for
any European folk tales which spoke of caves, tunnels or mines
associated in any way with the idea of a subterranean world.
From this line of inquiry emerged the fact that there were a
number of places in Czechoslovakia where old legends
mentioned superior beings living beneath the ground.

Two separate parties went to check out these locations, but
no records have survived of their results. Indeed, the entire
operation in Czechoslovakia might have been forgotten altogether but for the accidental discovery of a mysterious tunnel
in October 1944 by a member of the Slovak Uprising. It tied
up with one locality the Germans *were* known to have explored. The man's name was Dr Antonin Horak, the captain
of a group of Resistance fighters, who also happened to be an
expert spelaeologist. His extraordinary discovery was not made
known until 1965, however, when he published a detailed
account in the *National Spelaeological Society News*.

In this report, Dr Horak described how he and two other
men – all that remained of a group of Resistance fighters –
came across the tunnel near the settlements of Plavince and
Lubocna, in a location recorded at 49·2 degrees north, 20·7
degrees east. The three men were on the move after a skirmish

with the Germans. One was badly injured and the other two were on the verge of collapse. Fortunately they were able to find a local peasant who led them to a large underground grotto where they could hide up and rest.

The peasant warned Dr Horak against going any further into the cave. 'It is full of pits, poison gas pockets and it is haunted,' he said. So tired were the captain and his companion named Jurek that they only had time to make their wounded compatriot, Martin, comfortable, before they fell into the sleep of exhaustion.

The following day, however, as Horak waited for the injured man to recover his strength, he decided to ignore what he considered the superstitious advice of the old peasant and explore the tunnel. For some time he worked his way along the passage until suddenly he came face to face with a totally new section which gave every indication of being man-made. 'Lighting some torches,' he said, 'I saw that I was in a spacious, curved, black shaft formed by cliff-like walls. The floor in the incline was a solid lime pavement.'

Dr Horak was amazed as well as puzzled by this mysterious tunnel which continued far beyond the flickering light of his torches. He determined to take some samples, but when his pickaxe failed to make any impression on the solid lime 'pavement', he tried to loosen some material from the walls by firing his pistol.

'The bullet slammed into the substance of the walls with a deafening, fiery impact,' he wrote in his article. 'Sparks flashed, there was a roaring sound, but not so much as a splinter fell from the substance. Only a small welt appeared, about the length of half my finger, which gave off a pungent smell.'

Frustrated in his attempts to obtain a sample, Dr Horak returned to his two companions and discussed what he had found with the man Jurek. After they had both inspected the tunnel – which left neither feeling any closer to solving the mystery – Dr Horak began to ponder over his impressions:

I sat there by the fire speculating. How far did it reach into the rocks, I wondered. Who, or what, put it into the mountain. Was it man-made? And was it at last proof of the truth in legends – like Plato's – of long lost civilisations with magic technologies which our rationale cannot grasp or believe?

Sadly, no one has followed up these questions posed by Dr Horak, and the tunnel has remained unexplored since the Germans were there in 1939 – if, indeed, they were – and certainly since Dr Horak in 1944.

Despite all the fevered energy poured into locating Agharti, Hitler's efforts were to be as doomed as his Thousand Year Reich. Though Karl Haushofer and those associated with him in the Luminous Lodge continued to feed their Fuehrer's interest until the end, he was no nearer a solution in 1945 than when his interest had been first kindled. It was just one more ambition that died frustrated with him, as we believe, in the Berlin bunker. And, as I have already described, his fate was also shared by the Tibetans who had nursed his fascination. Had even one of that extraordinary group survived to tell his story, our knowledge of the Nazi quest for Agharti would surely be without so many unanswered questions.

The man who had played such a central role in this chapter of our story, Karl Haushofer, did briefly survive the war, the extent of his participation evidently unappreciated by his captors. But the failure of all that he had worked towards obviously weighed heavily on him. For on 14 March, 1946, apparently in fulfilment of the promise he had made all those years ago when he was admitted to the secret society in Japan, he killed his wife, Martha, and then committed suicide. He had sworn to take his own life if he failed in his 'mission' – and did so in the time-honoured Japanese way by committing *hara-kiri* – thrusting a knife into his abdomen.

With his passing, the last remnant of Nazi interest in Agharti ended. Soon the story was little more than a footnote in the larger account of the evil that Adolf Hitler had unleashed on the world. There was, though, one persistent rumour emanating from this obsession that persisted – and indeed has persisted in certain quarters to this day. It also leads us very conveniently into our next area of discussion.

The rumour was, and is, that certain members of the Nazi hierarchy – among whom were no lesser persons than Martin Bormann and Hitler himself – actually escaped from the funeral pyre of Berlin *through secret tunnels* and found their way to South America, where some still live to this day.

It is a fact, as we shall see, that there *are* secret tunnels in South America, and that ancient traditions link these with Europe and Asia and ultimately Agharti itself. If there is any truth in these rumours, then we might surmise that the Nazi search for the secret underground kingdom was not all in vain. They may not have found Agharti, but perhaps instead they found an escape route from the hell of their own making, to a Shangri-la where they could live out the remainder of their wretched lives.

This is, of course, at first glance, a hypothesis of the wildest improbability. Yet, as we shall see, there is a great deal of convincing evidence about secret tunnels beneath South and North America, and indeed more than a little documentation on the idea of a linking passageway between the continents of America and Europe by way of the 'Lost Continent' of Atlantis. Our story is one with yet more amazing facts to be brought to light . . .

Chapter 8

THE SECRET PASSAGES OF
SOUTH AMERICA

In March 1942, just three months after the United States had been precipitated into the Second World War by the attack of Japanese planes on the naval base at Pearl Harbor, President Franklin D. Roosevelt made time in his busy schedule to receive a rather unusual young couple at the White House in Washington. Their names were David and Patricia Lamb, and they had just returned to their home in Los Angeles, California, after travelling for almost a year in the Mexican frontier state of Chiapas. Amazing rumours had preceded their return to America that they had discovered a tribe of highly dangerous, almost dwarfish, *white-skinned* Indians who were the guardians of a vast network of subterranean tunnels.

President Roosevelt had expressed as strong an interest in this story as any of his fellow-Americans, perhaps even stronger than most, for his distant cousin, the late President Theodore Roosevelt, had been an inveterate explorer of the American continent in the period prior to, and following, his years in high office, and some of this interest had rubbed off on FDR, through his reading the older man's travel journals and books. Indeed, the President knew that his predecessor had led an expedition through South America in 1914 during the course of which he had picked up stories of a network of tunnels beneath the continent in which vast hordes of gold were said to be hidden.

One old guide had told Theodore Roosevelt that these tunnels were supposed to be guarded by a strange breed of white Indians who drove off with great ferocity anyone who came within the vicinity. It was the possibility that these might be the same 'guardians' that the Lambs had encountered which intrigued FDR, and caused him to invite the husband and wife to the White House.

The hour which the three people spent together proved to

be a fascinating encounter. The Lambs told the President that they had been travelling in the dense jungle country of Chiapas when they had suddenly been surrounded by a group of small, pale-skinned men whose features were similar to those of the native Indians, but of an almost pinkish hue. Although the Lambs' guides were head and shoulders taller than their ambushers, they were clearly quite terrified of them.

David and his wife were quick to admit that they were frightened themselves, but it became apparent that the strange little men were not planning to kill them. They just wanted them to go back the way they had come – and quickly.

The party had been trekking in this particular vicinity in pursuit of what David Lamb had been prepared to admit was probably a fool's quest. There were stories of a lost Mayan city somewhere about, beneath which ran a network of tunnels filled with a priceless treasure. As he stood looking at the fierce little men surrounding them, the thought crossed David Lamb's mind that perhaps there was some truth in the legend after all.

For some moments no one moved as the fierce sun beat down on the two so dissimilar groups confronting each other – the two Americans from one of the most modern cities on earth and the white-skinned Indians whose primitive way of life had probably been unchanged for centuries. At last David Lamb plucked up the courage to whisper a message to his chief guide. He told him to ask the Indians who they were and what they wanted. After a moment's hesitation, the guide nervously mumbled his request.

The words had to be repeated several times, and in different dialects, before any kind of response was forthcoming. And even that proved far from perfect. Yet, from what was then translated to the Lambs, they were able to form a rough idea of who the Indians were.

It seemed the men were members of the Lancandone tribe, a degenerate group of Indians who had lived in the jungles for generations. They said they were the guardians of a 'Great Temple' where dwelt the 'Old Ones' whom they worshipped. No outsider was ever allowed to approach this holy place and they would take the lives of any who tried.

David Lamb, who was something of an expert on the

legends of South America, listened to this halting conversation with increasing interest. He had heard mention of the Lancandones before – they were said to be the survivors of an ancient civilization that had once flourished in Central America. He recalled having read a little about them in notes by the French scholar and geographer, the Abbé Charles-Etienne Brasseur de Bourbourg (1814–1874), who had been the ecclesiastical administrator in Chiapas in the 1850s and had unsuccessfully tried to decipher Mayan sign language. (His most important work in this field, *Voyage sur l'Isthme de Tehauntepec*, 1861, has not yet been translated.) De Bourbourg said that these little white-skinned natives appeared from time to time in the frontier pueblos and townships of Chiapas and Western Guatemala and actually bartered with the natives. However, when any attempts were made to follow them to the 'great stone city' where they were said to live they responded by killing their pursuers.*

Although David Lamb satisfied himself that the men were indeed Lancandones, he could find out nothing else about them. And – he told the President – he and his party then had to make tracks back the way they had come. On their journey back to civilization, the Lambs picked up a few more fragments of information about the little men.

Apparently, in the tunnels beneath the city which the Lancandones guarded, there were supposed to be stored a number of sheets of solid gold on which was written in hieroglyphics a history of the ancient peoples of the world. These sheets also spoke of a Great Deluge and were said to have accurately predicted the Second World War, 'which involved all the mightiest nations of the earth'.

President Roosevelt was evidently as fascinated by the

---

* Harold Wilkins in his *Mysteries of Ancient South America* (1946) tells us a little more about these natives. He says that about every forty years rumours develop about the existence of men of a lost Mayan or Aztec race, and from time to time strange, elusive Indians appear in the market places of lonely villages in this area. 'They contact only with Indians,' he says, 'barter goods, and vanish as suddenly as they come, no Mexican or Guatemalan official being any the wiser. They are emissaries from a lost city of the ancient, civilized race that once governed old Mexico. No white man has ever penetrated the region of this wilderness, where, it is rumoured, these lost-world men live as did their fathers, erect or maintain the same majestic stone buildings, palaces and temples, large courts and lofty towers with high terraces of stone staircases, and are still carving in stone the mysterious hieroglyphics that no modern scholar can decipher in the ruins of old Yucatan.'

encounter as the Lambs themselves had been, but neither the Head of State nor the couple could be sure if the lost city really existed or whether the stories about the subterranean tunnels were true.

In the intervening years we have learned a little more about the lost city and a great deal more about the underground passages.

Harold T. Wilkins, the former schoolmaster turned journalist who became an inveterate investigator of the legends of South America, has come up with further evidence about a lost city in the same vicinity and also assembled much useful information on the old traditions of subterranean passages. His research provides a useful basis on which to begin such an inquiry.

Wilkins briefly mentions the meeting between President Roosevelt and the Lambs in his *Mysteries of Ancient South America* which appeared shortly afterwards in 1946. He also records some intriguing supporting evidence which came to hand at the same time:

An English engineer who spent many years of his life in both Mexico and Argentina, and who died in Gloucester Royal Infirmary, in 1938, told me that, in the state of Jalisco, somewhere in the little-known southern extension of the great range of the Sierra Madre, about 121 kilometres [about 75 miles] east of the Cabo de Corrientes, are prehistoric ruins known to the Indian *peónes*. The region is one that is never visited by Mexicans, unless in times of insurrection when a band of *revolucionarios* has sought to escape the Government troops by fleeing to the recesses of the savage mountains. Jalisco is, of course, a province well known as one of the centres of the Aztec race, just as is the valley of Anahuac in the territory round the capital.

The *Aztecos Indiós* in Jalisco state say that these ancient ruins were once the home of a people who were civilized and benevolent. Whether they were of the Mayan race or some even more ancient people with Atlantean connections derived from the Hy-Brazilian pioneer and civilizer Quetzalcoatl, only exploration by competent field workers can decide. The dead city lies on a *mesa* [plateau] and from it, at certain hours of the day, or at dawn, comes the sound of an eerie, vibrant drumming. The sound is heard from afar, even on the Pacific! The Indians declare that the drumming emanates from *los Espiritós* (ghosts), and comes from stone vaults of a great temple where there was once worshipped 'The ruler of the Universe'. One day, say the Indians, the wheel of life, or cycle of events, will come full circle, and the ancient people will return and re-introduce a golden age.

As soon as we begin our inquiries into underground tunnels in South America we find that there is as rich and long-lasting a tradition as that we have already learned about in Asia in general and Tibet in particular. Indeed, there is perhaps even more physical evidence – in the shape of tunnels that can actually be located – as well as even more remarkable and widespread reports about them, in this continent which has been described as 'the cradle of the dim and ancient world's earliest civilization'. And here, too, there is some remarkable evidence that these tunnels, though seemingly separated by the vast Atlantic from the acknowledged centre of Agharti in Asia, were nonetheless linked to it and once formed part of that great underground kingdom's domains!

In searching for evidence we can go back to the very dawn of recorded history, for there is an ancient South American legend that the mighty Inca empire was founded by a group of people who emerged from a tunnel in Peru. The origins of this story are now lost in the mists of time, and only the barest details have come down to us in the form of folk tales. According to these tales, four brothers and four sisters emerged from a tunnel at Pacari–Tambo, which is east of Cuzco. The eldest brother then climbed a mountain and with mighty throws hurled four rocks to each of the four points of the compass. He then claimed possession of all that land within the range of the stones: a mighty empire, according to the legend.

However, dissent soon grew up amongst the brothers as to who should rule the empire, and the cruel, youngest brother, Ayar Uchu Topa, contrived the death of his three elder brothers. He then proceeded to subjugate all the local peoples and strengthened his hold on the kingdom by marrying all four of his sisters! His final act of conquest was to found a number of cities within the kingdom, including the seat of his empire, Cuzco. According to the legend, this city later became the capital of the Inca empire.

Although this story is frustratingly devoid of any more details about the tunnel from which the four brothers and sisters emerged, there are suggestions that they were all fair-skinned people, of above average height, who claimed to be members of the ruling family of an underground world. Some over-zealous proponents of the Agharti legend have claimed they were children of the 'King of the World' and had been sent by him to found a great empire in his image. This is a claim that is difficult to substantiate, beyond the fact that we know the Incas were a gentle, peace-loving nation to whom crime and war were unknown until the arrival of the Spaniards.* Against this, of course, is the undeniable fact that the Incas indulged in the most bloody human sacrifices, a practice said to be foreign to anything known in Agharti or Shamballah.

More definite information about underground tunnels in South America is to be found in the records of the Spanish invasion of Peru. In 1526, a party of Spanish Conquistadors, under the leadership of Francisco Pizarro (c.1475–1541), landed on the northwest coast of South America and proceeded to explore and plunder the land and harass the people. In the years which followed, Pizarro and his band of 180 followers began the almost literal destruction of the Inca civilization as they sought after the amazing artifacts into which the country's enormous supply of gold had been turned by their craftsmen. Although accurate figures are impossible to come by, it has been suggested that there were more than ten million Incas when the Spaniards arrived, and by 1571, just forty years later, the population had been reduced to a little over one million. (In his book, *This Hollow Earth*, Eric Norman notes a bizarre suggestion that many of these Incas

*Of the character of the Incas, the Spanish Conquistador and historian, Don Mancio Serra de Leguisamo, wrote in his *Comentarios de los Yncas* (1589): 'The Inca Peruvians were so free from crimes and excesses, the men as well as the women, that the Indian who had 100,000 pesos of gold and silver in his house, left it open, merely placing a small stick across the door as a sign that the master was out, and no one could enter or take anything that was inside. When they found we put locks and keys on our doors, they supposed it was for fear of them that they might not kill us, not because they believed that anyone would steal the property of another. So, when they found we had thieves among us and men who sought to make their daughters commit sin, they despised us.'

did not die but simply disappeared underground! He writes: 'Those who believe in the hollow earth theory declare that the Incas took a large number of their people, and most of their treasure, into a gigantic tunnel that led down into the inner-earth.')

The story of the murderous activities of Pizarro and his men need not be repeated here, save for those details which bear on our theme. In hindsight it is possible to see that the rapacious nature of the Spaniards ultimately worked against them, for had they shown the same friendship towards the Incas that the natives offered to them, they might well have been *given* the vast hoards of gold they tried to take by force. For the Incas placed only a relatively small value on a commodity which was so plentiful. Instead, of course, when the Incas realized the Spaniards' true purpose, they hid much of their great treasure – and hidden it has remained to this day.

The culminating act of violence during this invasion was the seizure of the leader of the Incas, Atahualpa, and the ransom demand by Pizarro that his subjects should fill an entire treasure room with gold to secure his release. (According to contemporary Spanish chroniclers who saw the treasure room, such a treasure would have consisted of between 600 to 650 tons of gold, worth 384 million gold *pesos de oro*, and probably beyond calculation today!) Anxious to save her husband's life, the Inca Queen complied with the demand, but the greedy Pizarro was so amazed at the sight of all the gold stacked in the room that he refused to release his prisoner, saying instead that he would 'murder him [Atahualpa] unless you tell me whence all these treasures come'. It appears that Pizarro had in the meantime heard that the Incas possessed a secret and inexhaustible depository which lay in a 'vast sub-terranean tunnel, or road, running many miles underground beneath the kingdom'. The unfortunate Queen begged for a delay in complying with this new demand and went to consult her soothsayer. The grim-faced oracle looked in his magic black mirror and told the lady that whatever she did would be to no avail, for the Spaniards intended to kill Atahualpa in any event.

The horrified Queen then gave orders for the Inca treasure to be distributed in hiding places throughout the empire so that none of it would ever fall into the hands of the treacherous invaders. After this task was secretly and safely accomplished, the heartbroken lady took her own life. According to Harold Wilkins, this treasure still lies buried today beneath jungle clearings and in lonely mountain tarns as well as in:

> sealed caves to which mystic hieroglyphs, whose key is possessed only by one descendant of the Inca, at a time, in each generation, give the open sesame; and in strange 'subterraneans', thousands of years old, which must have been made by a mysterious and highly civilised vanished race of South America in a day when the ancient Peruvians, themselves, were a mere wandering tribe of barbarians, if not savages, roaming the cordilleras and the high passes, or still living, perhaps, in some long-disrupted Pacific continent, from which they came in ships.

Since that day, the hope of discovering the priceless hoards of Inca treasure has attracted fortune hunters from all over the world to the wilds of South America. Yet all have been denied because of Pizarro's simple act of treachery, for as the Spanish soldier-priest Pedro Cieza de Leon wrote a few years after the event:

> If, when the Spaniards entered Cuzco they had not committed other tricks, and had not so soon executed their cruelty in putting Atahualpa to death, I know not how many great ships would have been required to bring such treasures to old Spain, as is now lost in the bowels of the earth and will remain so because those who buried it are now dead.

It was to be over one hundred years before the subject of underground tunnels appeared again in a South American commentary. The location this time was Guatemala, and there was no immediate suggestion that it might be connected in any way – literally or figuratively – with that which had been reported running beneath Cuzco. That was to come later. The chronicler of this new tunnel was another Spaniard, a missionary priest with the impressive-sounding name of Francisco Antonio de Fuentes y Guzman. He served for a number of years in the country and about 1689 wrote a history of Guatemala, which has remained in manuscript to this day.

In the course of his dialogue, Fuentes – as the priest is more familiarly known – describes a number of ruined settlements in Guatemala which he believed to have been inhabited by a race of Indians long since vanished. They might even have been the same degenerate Lancandones mentioned earlier. Beneath these settlements run underground tunnels, and one in particular caught his interest. Fuentes writes:

> The marvellous structure of the *tunnels* (*subterranea*) of the pueblo of Puchuta, being of the most firm and solid cement, runs and continues through the interior of the land for the prolonged distance of nine leagues to the pueblo of Tecpan, Guatemala. It is a proof of the power of these ancient kings and their vassals.

It is a puzzling statement, but still remarkable when you realize that the tunnel's length of 'nine leagues' is the equivalent of thirty miles! Unfortunately, Fuentes tells us little else about the tunnels of Guatemala, as clearly such things did not greatly interest him. Perhaps this indifference accounts for the fact that it is another one hundred and fifty years before anyone again mentions the tunnels of Guatemala, or South America for that matter. However, the next commentator, an American named John Lloyd Stephens, was to furnish a book of reports and illustrations of major importance.

Stephens was a successful lawyer and globetrotter who had already undertaken extensive tours in Europe and the Near East before he was attracted to Central America. He was particularly interested in Mayan cities and relics. To this end he arranged to lead a diplomatic mission to the country, and also took along his close friend, Frederick Catherwood, a skilful English artist who had already produced some remarkable illustrations of Egyptian antiquities while travelling about that country in native dress! From their journey together came a remarkable book, *Incidents of Travel in Central America, Chiapas and Yucatan* (1838–9), to which Stephens contributed eye-witness reports and Catherwood marvellously detailed engravings. As copies of the work are now of considerable rarity it is a pleasure to be including examples of both their talents in this volume.

In the first part of the book, Stephens describes his leisurely progress across Central America, collecting information on the people and compiling dossiers on the ruins. Then in Santa

Cruz del Quiche, a pueblo in Western Guatemala, he was introduced to an old Spanish priest who suddenly fired his enthusiasm with tales of a mysterious lost city. But this was no unsupported legend, the priest said: he had seen the place with his own eyes. Stephens writes in his book:

> The thing that really roused us was the assertion by the padre that, four days on the road to Mexico, on the other side of the great sierra was a living city, large and populous, occupied by Indians, precisely in the same state as before the discovery of America. He had heard of it many years before at the village of Chajul, and was told by the villagers that from the topmost ridge of the sierra this city was distinctly visible. He was then young, and with much labour, climbed to the naked summit of the sierra, from which, at a height of ten or twelve thousand feet, he looked over an immense plain extending to Yucatan and the Gulf of Mexico, and saw at a great distance a large city spread over a great space, and with turrets white and glittering in the sun. The traditional account of the Indians of Chajul is, that no white man has ever reached this city; that the inhabitants speak the Maya language, are aware that a race of strangers has conquered the whole area around, and murder any white man who attempts to enter their territory. They have no coin or other calculating medium; no horses, cattle, mules or other domestic animals except fowls and the cocks they keep underground to prevent their crowing being heard.

Although Stephens was evidently torn by the desire to try and see the mysterious city – 'one look at it would be worth ten years of an everyday life', he wrote – he concluded that it would be too dangerous and difficult for such a mission as his. 'No man,' he says in his book, 'even if willing to peril his life, could undertake the enterprise with any hope of success, without hovering for one or two years on the borders of the country, studying the language and character of the adjoining Indians, and making acquaintance with some of the natives.'

Nonetheless, during the remainder of his time in Central America, Stephens continued to search for information about the mysterious city. This brought to light some further fascinating details which he revealed at a press conference in New York when his book was published.

Stephens was asked how it was possible for the natives of such a place to have remained undiscovered for so many years. 'They moved underground,' he replied. 'They had to, to save themselves from the Spanish invaders.'

But how was this possible, another journalist asked. Surely they would be unable to survive without sunlight?

'Not according to what an Indian guide told me,' Stephens said. 'These people have a great light which shines in their underworld, the secret of which was apparently given to them many ages ago by the gods from beneath the earth.'

The hard-bitten New York journalists may well have felt that such a tale smacked of the fantastic, for the line of questioning was not pursued, beyond a further inquiry as to whether Stephens himself had ever seen one of the underground tunnels he mentioned. He had, he replied, beneath the ruins of Santa Cruz del Quiche. He directed his listeners to a passage in his book which referred to the incident:

> Under one of the buildings was an opening which the Indians called a cave, and by which they said one could reach Mexico in an hour. I crawled under, and found a pointed-arch roof formed by stones lapping over each other, but was prevented exploring it by want of light, and the padre's crying to me that it was the season of earthquakes. How far it reached and what was its ultimate destination I could not then even begin to conject. It was clearly another of the profound mysteries of the Americas.

It perhaps comes as no surprise to learn that the publicity John Lloyd Stephens gave to the mysterious city of Central America, and to the underground tunnels, revived interest once again in the lost treasures of the Incas which Atahualpa's Queen had hidden away centuries before. The Peruvian authorities in particular decided to recommence searching for the entrances to the secret tunnels following a rather curious incident in 1844. The incident, related by Harold Wilkins in his book, *Mysteries of Ancient South America*, concerned the dying words of a Quichua Indian (a direct descendant of the Inca Peruvians) and the secret he confessed to an old Catholic priest:

The story was about a mystery of a labyrinth and a series of amazing tunnels going back far beyond the days of the Inca emperors of the sun. It was told under the inviolable seal of the confessional and could not be divulged by the priest under pain of hell fire; and it would probably have remained a secret had not the old priest, in a trail of the mountains, come into the company of a sinister Italian, who was on his travels to Lima. This Italian, with very dark, piercing eyes, and a hypnotic stare, talked to the old priest, who, unwittingly, let drop a hint about a long-sought hidden and very ancient treasure. The sinister gentleman, said to have come from Naples, somehow managed to hypnotise the old priest into telling him the story the priest had learnt, under confession, from the dying Peruvian peasant. The latter had said that his strange secret was known to many pure-blooded Quichua Indians, descendants of the old Incas, but not to the half-caste Mestizos, who were deemed unreliable.

What the dying Indian was supposed to have revealed was where an entrance to the amazing tunnel-labyrinths could be found, and when the sinister Italian took word of this confession to the authorities – in return for a share of any discoveries, needless to say – the Peruvians instituted a large-scale hunt for the concealed opening. Although details of this search remain scant, it seems the hunters were disguised as scientists and archaeologists to conceal the true nature of their mission from the suspicious Quichua Indians. True or not, the men searched in vain for two years, and then returned to Lima no wiser than they had set out. Atahualpa's treasure remained inviolate.

There is a curious sequel to this story which involves Madame Helena Blavatsky, the remarkable lady we met earlier in this book. It also takes us another major step forward in our search for concrete details about the subterranean tunnels of South America. Apparently Madame Blavatsky met this selfsame mysterious Italian who had hypnotized the old priest. The encounter occurred in Lima, and the Italian told Madame Blavatsky that although the authorities had abandoned their search, he believed *he* had found an entrance to the labyrinths of tunnels. However, he said he had neither the time nor the money to continue the search any further.

As Madame Blavatsky was herself going to the vicinity where the man said the entrance was located – Arica, near the Peruvian border – she decided to investigate for herself. Here is what she discovered, as she relates in her book *Isis Unveiled* (1877):

Going southward from Lima by water we reached a point near Arica at sunset, and were struck by the appearance of an enormous rock, nearly perpendicular, which stood in mournful solitude on the shore, apart from the range of the Andes. It was the tomb of the Incas. As the last rays of the setting sun strike the face of the rock, one can make out, with an ordinary opera-glass, some curious hieroglyphics inscribed on the volcanic surface.

When Cuzco was the capital of Peru, it contained a temple of the sun, famed far and near for its magnificence. It was roofed with thick plates of gold, and the walls were covered with the same precious metal; the eave-troughs were also of solid gold. In the west wall the architects had contrived an aperture in such a way that when the sun-beams reached it, it focused them inside the building. Stretching like a golden chain from one sparkling point to another, they encircled the walls, illuminating the grim idols, and disclosing certain mystic signs at other times invisible. It was only by understanding these hieroglyphics – identical with those which may be seen to this day on the tomb of the Incas – that one could learn the secret of the tunnel and its approaches. Among the latter was one in the neighbourhood of Cuzco, now masked beyond discovery. This leads directly into an immense tunnel which runs from Cuzco to Lima, and then, turning southward, extends into Bolivia. At a certain point it is intersected by a royal tomb. Inside this sepulchral chamber are cunningly arranged two doors; or, rather, two enormous slabs which turn upon pivots, and close so tightly as to be only distinguishable from the other portions of the sculptured walls by the secret signs, whose key is in the possession of the faithful custodians. One of these turning slabs covers the southern mouth of the Liman tunnel – the other, the northern one of the Bolivian corridor. The latter, running southward, passes through Trapaca and Cobijo, for Arica is not far away from

the little river called Payaquina, which is the boundary between Peru and Bolivia.

Disclosing the existence of this tunnel in her matter-of-fact
way, Madame Blavatsky almost conceals from the reader its
true extent. For if we glance at a map, we can see that the
distance from Cutzco to Lima is approximately 380 miles, and
then, having turned southwards, the tunnel goes on into Bolivia, a distance of almost 900 miles! (It has been suggested by
several authorities that after passing beneath Tarapaca and
Cobijo – now in Chile – the tunnel turns eastwards, progres-
sing under the cordillera, and ends, or more likely is lost,
somewhere in the mysterious salt desert of Atacama. In this
context Harold Wilkins has queried whether, if it did end
there, 'Maybe when the mysterious tunnel was made, perhaps
thousands of years ago, the climate was very different from
today, and the landscape one of beauty and fertility?'). This
would seem at last to be confirmation of the ancient tradition
of an underground tunnel running beneath much of the continent of South America. Nor is the lady quite finished with her
revelations:

> Not far from this spot [the border of Peru and Bolivia]
> stand three separate peaks which form a curious triangle;
> they are included in the chain of the Andes. According to
> tradition the only practicable entrance to the corridor lead-
> ing northward is in one of these peaks; but without the
> secret of its landmarks, a regiment of Titans might rend the
> rocks in vain in the attempt to find it. But even were some-
> one to gain an entrance and find his way as far as the turn-
> ing slab in the wall of the sepulchre, and attempt to blast it
> out, the superincumbent rocks are so disposed as to bury the
> tomb, its treasures, and – as the mysterious Peruvian
> expressed it to us – 'a thousand warriors' in one common
> ruin. There is no other access to the Arica chamber but
> through the door in the mountain near Payaquina. Along
> the entire length of the corridor, from Bolivia to Lima and
> Cuzco, are smaller hiding places filled with treasures of gold
> and precious stone, the accumulations of many generations
> of Incas, the aggregate value of which is incalculable.

To any reader who might find himself sceptical of these
remarkable claims, Madame Blavatsky offers what she trusts

will be considered proof of her assertions: the existence of a map of the tunnel. (This is still extant, and is now housed in the Theosophical Society's archives near the Adyar river, Madras, India.) Writing of this map in *Isis Unveiled*, she says:

> We have in our possession an accurate plan of the tunnel, the sepulchre, and the doors, given to us at the time by the old Peruvian. If we had ever thought of profiting by the secret, it would have required the cooperation of the Peruvian and Bolivian governments on an extensive scale. To say nothing of physical obstacles, no one individual or small party could undertake such an exploration without encountering the army of smugglers and brigands with which the coast is infested; and which, in fact, includes nearly the whole population. The mere task of purifying the mephitic air of the tunnel, which had not been entered for centuries, would also be a serious one. There, however, the treasure lies, and there the tradition says it will lie till the last vestige of Spanish rule disappears from the whole of North and South America.

Madame Blavatsky also tells us of meeting an aged Peruvian priest – a Quichua Indian – who had actually travelled in the tunnel. A strange, embittered man, he had spent his life concealing his hatred of Peruvian officials and the Spanish conquerors. He told her:

> 'I keep friends with them, these *bandidos*, and their Catholic missioners, for the sake of my own people. But I am as much a worshipper of the sun as if I had lived in the days of our murdered emperor, the Inca Atahualpha. Now, as a converted native and missionary, I once took a journey to Santa Cruz del Quiche (in Western Guatemala), and, when there, *I went to see some of my people by a subterranean passage leading into a mysterious city behind the cordilleras*. Herein, it is death for any white man to trespass!'

Madame Blavatsky confirms her own belief in the story, and cites the evidence offered by John Lloyd Stephens in his work about the secret tunnel near Santa Cruz del Quiche. And she adds: 'Besides, a man who is about to die will rarely stop to invent idle stories.'

I have myself been able to trace further evidence to support the story of the tunnel – as well as it being the depository of a rich treasure. This evidence takes the form of an old parchment document written by a Spaniard named Felipe de Pomares sometime in the early years of the seventeenth century and now on file in the Cuzco archives. The document tells of a Spanish lady who had married a descendant of the murdered Inca emperor, and believing him to know where some of the great treasure was buried, plagued him to show it to her.

The lady, Dona Maria Esquivel, insisted that her husband, named Carlos Inca, was not keeping her in the style which befitted her rank, and she should be allowed to have some of the rich treasure to which Carlos was heir. Despite the unfortunate man's insistence that the treasure should not be touched, Dona Maria persisted so vehemently that he finally gave in and agreed to take her, blindfolded, into the treasure chamber. This he had to do for fear of the 'guardian' who he said kept watch over the entrance to the tunnel.

And so, one night, under the cover of darkness, and still fearful that he might be caught and punished for his audacity, Carlos took Dona Maria into the secret tunnel. They walked for some distance until the lady was unbandaged to find herself in a treasure chamber of dazzling splendour. The place was full of gold and silver ingots as well as temple ornaments and life-size statues of long-dead Inca kings made of solid gold. Carlos Inca only allowed his grasping wife a handful of precious items before hastening her out, blindfolded as before. Later, when she began importuning him once again for further treasures from the secret chamber, he unceremoniously packed her off back to Spain.

This unedifying story of greed is apparently cited whenever a persistent rumour is mentioned that there still exists a secret band of 'guardians' keeping watch over the tunnel entrance beneath the fortress of Cuzco. As Harold Wilkins has written: 'Carlos was the custodian of the secret, and from him it passed to a successor . . . Even today the secret of that vault may still remain locked in the breast of some descendant of the Inca.' For three hundred years, he adds, nothing has occurred to eradicate the notion of that enormous treasure resting in a subterranean passage beneath the ancient Inca capital.

Recently, that indefatigable writer Erich Von Daniken has come up with some fascinating evidence of a lengthy tunnel in Peru's neighbouring country, Ecuador. In his book, *The Gold of the Gods* (1972), he describes visiting an underground tunnel entered by a secret entrance near the town of Guala-quiza. It was part, he said, of a 'gigantic system of tunnels, thousands of miles in length and built by unknown construc-tors at some unknown date, deep below the South American continent'. Von Daniken believes the tunnels in Ecuador to be linked with those in Peru and described the one in which he walked as having smooth, polished walls, with a flat ceiling looking almost as if it was covered with some kind of glaze. 'Obviously,' he says, 'these passages did not originate from natural causes.'

Von Daniken says that a great deal of golden treasure has been found in this tunnel and that its entrance is guarded by a tribe of wild Indians – facts uncannily similar to those we have already noted in Mexico, Guatemala and Peru. He, appar-ently, only gained access because his guide, the man who discovered the tunnel, Juan Moricz, 'had been accepted as a friend by the chieftain of the cave guardians'. These Indians seemingly entered the tunnels only once a year to offer ritual prayers to the 'spirits of the underworld'.

As a result of his inspection, Von Daniken concluded that the tunnel system had been built thousands of years before the Inca kingdom came into being. 'How,' he asked, 'and with what tools are the Incas supposed to have built hundreds of miles of passages deep under the earth? The Channel Tunnel has been planned by the engineers of our highly technical cen-tury for fifty years and they still have not decided which method should be used to build this comparatively minor tunnel.' Von Daniken also correctly concludes that the system was known to the Inca rulers and was used by them for depositing and hiding their treasure from the rapacious Spanish Conquistadors. I shall be returning to discuss just *how* these amazing tunnels might have been engineered, and by whom, later in the book.

With this evidence from Ecuador, we have now examined all the major information concerning subterranean passages in South America – with one important exception, Brazil. From this evidence I believe it is possible to substantiate that there is, in fact, one gigantic tunnel stretching maybe as far as 2,500 miles from Mexico in the north to Peru and Bolivia in the south. (According to an old South American tradition there is even a name for this tunnel, 'The Roadway of the Incas'.) And, as I shall show in the next chapter, there is a branch of the tunnel running eastwards beneath Brazil towards the Atlantic Ocean. Here, I hope to prove, the tunnel was once linked with the Lost Continent of Atlantis.

Later in the book I shall also be examining the evidence that this selfsame tunnel in South America is also linked to another similar network of passages in the United States with what is claimed to be a terminal point beneath New York City! And with this network in Continental America established, I hope to be able to show that it is just part of an even more gigantic system which links America with Europe and Asia – the ultimate destination of all these fabulous passageways being the subterranean world of Agharti.

Chapter 9

BRAZIL – AND THE ATLANTIS CONNECTION

Brazil is the fourth largest country in the world, occupying nearly half the total area of South America. Its great capital city, Brasilia, and two magnificent ports of Rio de Janeiro and São Paulo are internationally famous and present an air of sophistication and culture that has led some people to suggest that ultimately the nation will become one of the world's leading nations.

Yet beyond the coastal lowlands facing the Atlantic Ocean lie some of the most impenetrable jungles and hostile environments to be found anywhere – as well as perhaps *the* most mysterious area in the world, the Amazon basin. On the northern frontier of Brazil there also stands the cloud-capped plateau of Mount Roraima, 'The Lost World', immortalized in Sir Arthur Conan Doyle's great novel.

It is, in truth, a mysterious country, much of it still awaiting thorough exploration, and harbouring the most amazing and controversial legends. What is already evident is that there are clear signs that an incredibly ancient civilization – at least 30,000 and possibly as much as 60,000 years old – once flourished here, and that there is much evidence that cultivated *white men* of an unknown race once walked the country in company with their dark-skinned brethren. There is also no denying that in the comparatively short time that Brazil has been known to the rest of the world – the first European, the Portuguese Pedro Cabral, did not reach the shore until 1500 – we have barely started to penetrate the outer realms of all this mystery. Here, though, we must try and assemble as much material as we can on the twin mysteries of the ancient white race of Brazil and the network of subterranean tunnels with which they are inextricably associated. In neither case is this a dead or dying tradition.

For example, Harold Wilkins remarks at one point in his *Mysteries of Ancient South America*: 'It is probable that

descendants of this white empire exist, *today*, in more than
one part of unexplored Brazil, and among the Andean out-
liers, in regions rich with gold, on the confines of the Amazon's
headwaters.' And again, later: 'There are many stories of the
existence of strange white people today – handsome bearded
men and beautiful, white nude women with symmetrical
Greek features – in the unknown *sertão* of the central Mato
Grosso and the Brazilian highlands, and northwards and
northwestwards in the mountains beyond the headwaters of
the Amazon and its tributaries.' Equally, in his book, *The
Hollow Earth*, Dr Raymond Bernard, a resident in Brazil,
assures us that 'mysterious tunnels, an enigma to archaeologists, exist in great numbers under Brazil, where they open on
the surface in various places. The most famous is in the Ron-
candor Mountains of northwest Mato Grosso, to where
Colonel Fawcett was heading when last seen.' We shall be
investigating the information on both of these topics – as well
as the mystery of Colonel Fawcett – a little later in this chapter
as we pursue our quest for the secret of Agharti.

Brazil has, of course, a good many legends of ancient cities
now in ruins, all hidden in the vast hinterland. Many expeditions have set out to find them since the country was claimed
by Portugal in 1500 and coastal colonies were established in
1532. From the very beginning, the explorers were fired by
stories the natives told of lost cities where enormous hoards of
gold and silver just lay awaiting discovery. The terrible climate, the hostile jungle natives and the enigmatic nature of so
many of the reports doomed expedition after expedition to
failure. From the earliest attempts of small bands of Portuguese fortune hunters, by way of the Brazilian *bandeiristas* of
the eighteenth century, to the expensively equipped expedition
financed by the Krupp Armament Works of Germany in the
early years of this century* – as ill-fated as most of its predecessors – the ruins and vast wealth left by people long since

*The Krupp expedition in the early 1900s went in search of an ancient city believed to
be located somewhere in the western province of the Mato Grosso. The party was
financed to the tune of £100,000 and with its modern equipment, armed men, Indian
guides and sturdy pack animals was perhaps the finest expedition which ever set off
into the unknown heart of Brazil. However, the guides soon deserted the party, wild
Indians began to attack them at every turn, and the explorers and their animals fell
prey to the terrible jungle heat and appalling conditions. They, like their less well-
prepared predecessors, ultimately had to turn tail and head back to civilization.

gone from memory have proved singularly elusive. But from all this endeavour has come the information which, with the passage of time, we have been able to shape into an explanation of some of the mysteries of Brazil.

Based on the geological evidence that we have, there seems little doubt that tropical South America includes some of the most ancient land on the Earth's surface that was never submerged by the ocean nor ground under the tremendous glaciers of the Ice Age. This has led archaeologists to speculate that this now mysterious heartland may very well have been the cradle of the Earth's civilization from which it later spread outwards to Europe and Africa on one side, and Asia on the other. (By comparison, at this period some 60,000 years ago, our European ancestors were living in caves in the regions of what are now Pyrenean France, Cantabrian Spain and Lacustrine Switzerland.)

Being a region of such antiquity has, inevitably, caused the South American continent to be linked with that ancient and mighty lost landmass of Atlantis. And it is the belief of a number of scholars and archaeologists, myself included, that Atlantis once formed a virtual land link between its neighbour continents of Europe to the east and South America to the west. Such a belief explains the similarities in culture and relics found on either side of what is now the Atlantic ocean, and helps demonstrate how it was possible for the tunnels of South America to be linked with the subterranean passages in Europe and Asia, all ultimately converging on Agharti. Let us look at the evidence.

In the *Popul Vuh*, an ancient Guatemalan manuscript whose title means 'The Collection of Written Leaves', and which has been described as 'the great storehouse of Mayan and Central American legend and mythical history', there is much talk of 'a land in the east on the shores of the sea'. Such a location neatly fits our knowledge of the position of Atlantis. This same work tells us that it was from this land 'that the fathers of the people had come' and that they also endured a 'great catastrophe' after which the land to the east disappeared. And having said this, can these following words from the *Popul Vuh* be anything other than a description of the destruction of Atlantis and its effect on its neighbour?

There came a great flood, followed by a thick rain of bitumen and resin, when men ran, here and there, in despair and madness. They tried, beside themselves with terror, to climb on the roofs of houses, which crumbled and threw them to the ground. Trees they tried to ascend, which threw them far away. They sought to enter caves and grottoes and immediately they were shut in from the exterior. The earth darkened and it rained night and day. Thus was accomplished the ruin of the race of man which was given up to destruction.

Cautiously, and based on the evidence of the *Popul Vuh*, plus his own researches, our archaeologist Harold Wilkins draws the ties between Atlantis and South America still closer together. He writes in *Mysteries of Ancient South America*:

One of the South American colonies of Atlantis may, probably, have been the land called Brazil, and Brazil, indeed, was actually the ancient name of the land and borne thousands of years before the arrival at Rio de Janeiro of old Pedro Cabral, the Portuguese navigator. That occurred in AD 1500 and has given rise to the sheer legend that King Emanuel of Portugal named the land Brazil, because the dye-wood, brazil-wood (*Biancaea sappan*) was found there. As a matter of very curious fact, the name Brazil was known to the old Irish Kelts as *Hy-Brazil*.

There are also a number of traditions well known throughout South America about a group of men in long, black, flowing gowns, with white skins and golden hair, who appeared rather like missionaries just before the deluge in about 11,000 BC. The chief among these was known as Quetzalcoatl, and although later he was usually represented as being a god, he was in fact a holy man. He came, it was said, by way of a tunnel from an island to the east of Brazil.* The Marquis de Nadaillac in his *Pre-Historic America* (1885) is intriguing on the subject:

A singular fact in all the legends collected is the reported

---

*This view is substantiated in Ordonez de Aguiler's *Historia de Cielo*, written late in the sixteenth century, in which the author says that Quetzalcoatl made several visits to and from Brazil from his home in Atlantis and 'he was permitted to reach "the rock of heaven" [Atlantis] by a subterranean passage.'

arrival of white and bearded strangers wearing black
clothes, who have been absurdly identified as Buddhist
missionaries . . . Of these strangers there is no certain
information, all that is definitely alleged being that the
chief was Quetzalcoatl or 'the serpent covered with
feathers'. The first Spanish writers chose to see in Quetzalcoatl, St Thomas, who passed from India to America.
Legends about him are numerous, and their variety justifies
us in supposing that imaginary or real actions of several
Maya and Nahua gods were attributed to him.

Harold Wilkins, however, is in no doubt where Quetzalcoatl
came from or what his purpose was: 'He came from Atlantean
Brazil on a civilising mission to barbarian and savage Central
America . . . warning also of destruction to come.'

Mr Wilkins then goes on to describe 'the great catastrophe
that sank Atlantis, the island-continent, into the depths of the
ocean'. It was, he says, accompanied by simultaneous volcanic
outbursts in America, Africa, and the chain of mountains of
Central Asia, and far out in the Pacific. His description is so
vivid I should like to quote it in full here:

In the land of Hy-brazil and the dead cities into which the
bandeiristas were to blunder, 10,000 years later, no day
could be told from night. The skies were darkened. Up
from the ground swirled dense clouds of thick ash and
vapours, choking and mephitic, poisoning all round.
Terrific electric flashes rent the endless blackness, making it
the more unearthly and darker. The maddened sea, in the
mightier Maranon-Amazon gulf, rising like a thing
demented, surged and roared in over the Amazon basin,
dashing on the walled cities, with their massive breakwaters
of stone.

In the highlands of this great Atlantis colony – the new
Atlantis of old America – it was the fire from heaven and
the earth below that ruined them. When the earth shook,
and day turned to night, in these dead cities of the unexplored Mato Grosso, of today, there came from great and
bottomless crevasses in the ground, in the paved roads, by
the side of their splendid temples and palaces, volumes of
deadly gases. Blinded, asphyxiated, maddened beyond
human endurance, rendered insane by the appalling

suddenness of the cosmic catastrophe, men and women, white-skinned, beautiful, some red-haired like Berenice the Golden, others fair and blonde as the Greek goddess Aphrodite, fled out of the cities, leaving all behind them. Parts of the cities sank into the ground, swallowed up by terrific earthquakes. Maybe great fires swept through some of the buildings; for the old *bandeiristas* were puzzled by the absence of the least vestige of furniture and utensils. The great palaces and temples were shaken to their foundations. Those people of Atlantis Brazil who did not manage to escape into the surrounding mountains, along the splendidly paved roads, now cracked and fissured and overwhelmed by great boulders and rocks which the appalling earthquakes and torrential deluge had toppled from the peaks into the gorges, were either burnt and calcined, or engulfed in the yawning earth What was not incinerated was destroyed by the wild beasts and birds of prey who, for many thousands of years to come, would inhabit alone these cities of old Hy-Brazil, swept by the besom of destruction.

Wilkins, along with that other great expert on the ancient history of South America, Lewis Spence (*vide* his books *The Problem of Atlantis*, 1924, and *The History of Atlantis*, 1926), says that there were survivors of this terrible holocaust and that evidence of them has come to light from time to time over the intervening years. Stories of lost tribes of white people being seen in the jungles of Brazil . . . reports of strange, pale-skinned guardians of secret cities in Peru and Guatemala . . . All of them, apparently, descendants of the Atlanteans who colonized Brazil.

For example, there are a little-known race of white Indians known as *Los Paria* who live in a settlement called, significantly, *Atlan*, in the dense forests between the Rio Apure and the Orinoco. These people have an oral tradition about a cataclysm which destroyed their ancient Fatherland, in Brazil, and also a large island in the eastern ocean where dwelt 'a rich and civilized race' – Atlantis, no doubt!

Lewis Spence also tells us of one of the native Indian races of Brazil, the Tapuya, who he believes are the descendants of a white helot race who served the ancient Hy-Brazilian master-race, and also fled with them from the deluge which engulfed

Atlantis. He writes in *The Problem of Atlantis*: 'These Tapuyas are fair as the English. They have small feet and hands, delicate features of great beauty, and white, golden and auburn hair. They were skilful workers in precious stones and wore diamonds and jade ornaments.'

I have, in the previous chapter, referred to the white Indians who have been reported guarding secret cities from intruders, so I perhaps need cite only one other instance of *physical* evidence of the Atlantis-South America connection before moving on to the more specific question of the underground passageways in Brazil.

This interesting observation again comes from Harold Wilkins and is recorded in his *Mysteries of Ancient South America*:

> There is a tradition current in the mystic east and, perhaps, derived from Atlanteans who quitted their great motherland before the time of the terrible cataclysm, that the central cathedral temple of old Atlantis's capital, the hill city, 'Sardegon', had a dome-shaped ceiling from which flamed a magnificent *central sun of blazing gold*. The late inheritors of the remains of the civilization of the Atlantean imperial colony of Hy-Brazil, of South America, the Incas of Peru – Peru, as one has stated, being derived from a word (*not* found in the *Quichua*, or native Peruvian tongue) *Vira*, meaning the god of the sun – had a glorious sun of purest gold which shone with truly dazzling refulgence from the walls of Cuzco's great temple of the Sun. It was there when the keels of Don Francisco Pizarro's caravels and galleons touched the shallows of the Peruvian coast in AD 1530. The very eye-balls of the beholder were pained by its scintillations.
>
> But when Pizarro's conquistadores laid their bandits' hands on this ancient civilization, as the Carian-Colloans had done before them in relation to what was left of the communities of the old, white, bearded Atlanteans of Hy-Brazil in the islands of Lake Titicaca, Peru, that glorious sun of gold vanished. For four centuries its whereabouts have remained a mystery, the close secret of one, or not more than two, of the Inca's posterity. Be sure, that there is living today, on one of the valleys of the Peruvian cordil-

leras, some Peruvian, little suspected by his fellows, who knows where this sun went to ground.

Any study of the mysteries of Brazil, and in particular its lost race, and ancient, ruined cities, must invariably pay some attention to the famous exploration work of Colonel Percy Harrison Fawcett (1867–1925), who has himself become the centre of an unexplained mystery. For he himself disappeared into the Mato Grosso in 1925 and has not been seen or heard of since.

He is of particular interest to us here, because (a) the intention of his exploration was to find 'the cradle of Brazilian civilization' and (b) the theory has been advanced that he did not die in the jungle but found his way into one of the subterranean passages and has remained there ever since!

The facts of Colonel Fawcett's exploration need only be mentioned in brief, because his younger son, Brian, has, of course, edited a fine account of the events in *Exploration Fawcett* (1953). At the time of his last expedition, Fawcett was already well known in South America for his work delineating frontiers in Peru, Ecuador, Bolivia and Brazil during the rubber boom. During these years he had become obsessed with the legend of a lost city somewhere in the Mato Grosso which was supposed to be inhabited by a highly civilized race of white people. (Indeed, before setting off on his expedition, he said simply: 'I have but one object: to bare the mysteries that the jungle fastnesses of South America have concealed for so many centuries. We are encouraged in our hope of finding the ruins of an ancient, white civilisation and the degenerate offspring of a once cultivated race.')

Fawcett was driven on by two particular facts – the first that there were known to be several incredibly old ruins in the jungles. 'These amazing ruins of ancient cities are incomparably older than those in Egypt,' he said. And, secondly, by the story told in a historical document unearthed in the archives in Rio de Janeiro which described the discovery of a lost civilization in the Mato Grosso in 1734. This document (which can still be seen today in the Biblioteca Nationale in Rio de Janeiro) records how a Portuguese expedition discovered a small passage in one of the mountains and, crawling through it, found the ruins of a city which had obviously been devastated by some huge upheaval. Treasure and gold coins were spilled about everywhere. The explorers were even more amazed to be confronted by two men with white skin and golden hair. As the Portuguese settled down to record their find, they dispatched a native runner back to Rio de Janeiro with news of their discovery. The explorers, however, never returned to civilization and were never heard of again. The only solution that could be offered to solve their disappearance was that they had either been detained – or killed – by the strange white men . . .

Before setting off on this fateful trip with his elder son, Jack, and their companion, Raleigh Rimell, Colonel Fawcett had made an intensive study of the lore and legends of Brazil. He had heard all about cities supposed to date back 60,000 years, all about white Indians with blue eyes, and all about the fabulous hoards of treasure waiting in the ruined cities. That he suspected they might be the remnants of the ancient Atlantean race was revealed in a letter he wrote to Lewis Spence in 1924. This same letter also highlighted a growing conviction that there was a link between the ancient people of South America and those on the other side of the Atlantic – for he had noticed a similarity between inscriptions found on porticoes and pillars on certain Brazilian ruins and those he had seen thirty years before on some ancient stonework in Ceylon (now Sri Lanka)!

Fawcett wrote to Lewis Spence:

I have good reason to know that these original [white Atlantean] people still remain in a degenerate state . . . They use script and also llamas, an animal associated with Andean heights above 10,000 feet, but in origin a low country, hybrid animal. Their still existing remains show the use of different coloured stones in the steps leading to temple buildings and a great deal of sculpture in demi-relief.

So it was in high spirits that the Fawcett party set off for the Mato Grosso. The Colonel left his friends convinced that he knew what he was looking for and where he was going to find it – but he denied them any precise details. Only one final message was forthcoming before the three men stepped into the unknown and created the legend which still surrounds them and their fate to this day. It consisted of just a few lines from Colonel Fawcett - but lines redolent with mystery and the suggestion they were on the verge of some amazing discovery:

> If there is any attempt to send an expedition after us, to discover our fate or fortune - and we expect to be right away from civilisation for two or more years - for God's sake, stop them! England has nothing to do with this quest. It is a matter for Brazil, entirely.

After that, all was silence, and only rumours have since emerged from the strange, dense jungles as to what happened to the three Englishmen - perhaps the most extraordinary being a claim voiced by Moscow Radio that Fawcett had become 'a British secret agent in Brazil, regularly sending radio reports to the Foreign Office in London'!

Mrs Nina Fawcett, the Colonel's wife, grew convinced with the passage of time that her husband had not died at the hands of savage jungle Indians, but was being held a captive - in all probability because he had stumbled across some great secret like the Portuguese explorers in the document of 1734 that had so intrigued him.

This is a point taken up by one of today's greatest experts on subterranean legends, Dr Raymond Bernard, the American philosopher and archaeologist who now lives in Brazil. Writing in his monograph *The Subterranean World* (1960), he says:

> Many Brazilian students of the occult share with the wife of Colonel Fawcett the belief that he is still living with his son Jack as residents of a subterranean city whose entrance is through a tunnel in the Roncador Mountain range of northeast Mato Grosso where he was heading when last seen after leaving Cuiaba. The writer met in Cuiaba a native who claimed that his father was Fawcett's guide and who offered to take him to a certain opening leading to the Subterranean World in the region of Roncador, which would indicate that Fawcett's guide believed in the existence of subterranean cities and brought Fawcett to one, where he was held prisoner lest he reveal the secret of its

whereabouts, which he might be forced to do on his return, whether he wished to or not.

Dr Bernard believes that the lost city Fawcett was seeking was indeed of Atlantean origin, but was actually situated *below ground*. He says: 'It is claimed that the Atlantean city for which he searched was not the ruins of a dead city on the surface, but a subterranean city with still living Atlanteans as its inhabitants.'

The Roncador tunnel opening is said to be guarded by fierce Murcego – or Bat – Indians, according to several authorities, including the American naturalist Carl Huni, who has made a special study of the tribe and their relationship to the tunnel legends based on his years of residence in the Mato Grosso area. I quote from his essay, 'The Mysterious Tunnels and Subterranean Cities of South America' (1960):

The entrance to the caverns is guarded by the Bat Indians, who are a dark-skinned, undersized race of great physical strength. Their sense of smell is more developed than that of the best of bloodhounds. Even if they approve of you and let you enter the caverns, I am afraid you will be lost to the present world, because they guard the secret very carefully and may not let those who enter leave.

The Bat Indians live in caves, too, and go out at night into the surrounding jungles, but they have no contact with the real people down in the caverns below, who form a community by themselves and have a considerable population. People believe the subterranean cities they inhabit descended from the Atlanteans, who originally constructed them, but no one knows for sure. The name of the mountain range where these subterranean Atlantean cities exist is Roncador in northeast Matto Grosso. If you go in quest of these caverns, you take your life in your own hands as you may never be heard of again, like Fawcett.

When I was in Brazil I heard a lot about the underground caverns and cities. It is however a long way from Cuiaba. It is near the river Araguaya, which empties into the Amazon. It is to the northeast of Cuiaba at the foot of a tremendously long mountain range named Roncador. I desisted to investigate further because I heard that they jealously guard the entrance to the tunnels from people.

I know that a good part of the immigrants who helped in the uprising of General Isidoro Lopez back in 1928 disappeared into these mountains and were never seen again. It was under the reign of Dr Benavides who bombarded São Paulo for four weeks. Finally they made a truce for three days and let the 4,000 troops, who were mainly Germans and Hungarians, go out of town. About 3,000 of them went to Acre in the northwestern part of Brazil and about 1,000 disappeared into the caverns. I heard the story consistently. I remember it was at the southern end of Bananal Island (near Roncador Mountains).

There are also caverns in Asia and many Tibetan travellers mention them. But as far as I know, the biggest ones are in Brazil and they exist at three different levels. I am sure I would get permission if I wanted to join them and they would accept me as one of theirs. I know they use no money at all, and their society is organised on a strictly democratic basis. The people do not become aged and live in everlasting harmony.

This description of a subterranean 'Utopia' has caused Dr Raymond Bernard, whom I mentioned just now, to comment that it seems very similar to the society that Bulwer Lytton describes in his work, *The Coming Race*. Dr Bernard shares the opinion that Bulwer Lytton based his 'novel' on occult information that he had learned as a Rosicrucian.

Dr Bernard is quite a remarkable figure himself, having settled some years ago in the city of Joinville in Santa Catarina, Brazil. Here he has established a small community known as the New California Subtropical Settlement which, he believes, is ideally placed for further research into the underground tunnels as well as being clear of any nuclear fallout in the event of a war between America and Russia, a subject which deeply absorbs him.

Joinville, he says, is situated in the world's 'Radioactive Safety Zone', for:

It is a fact of meteorology that winds carrying radioactive dust from the Northern Hemisphere, when they reach the equator, are met and opposed by contrary winds coming up from the south, causing them to rise and circle back in a northerly direction. This protects the Southern Hemisphere against windborn fallout from the north, which will be the part of the world where World War III will be fought.

With this in mind, Dr Bernard has urged readers of his works to instant action:

A new migration should get under way from the Northern Hemisphere to the lower part of the Southern Hemisphere, the best part of which is the New Promised Land of Everlasting Spring and Tropical Fruits which I found in subtropical Santa Catarina in South Brazil after a 26 years search for a Terrestrial Paradise in the countries of Latin America. Here I am establishing a settlement of American vegetarians, organic gardeners and advanced thinkers anxious to live in a part of the world where alone a New Age can arise.

Perhaps not surprisingly, Dr Bernard believes that the disaster which destroyed Atlantis was not merely fire and flood, but a 'radioactive catastrophe, probably caused by a nuclear war, the legendary War of the Titans, which led to the earth shifting on its axis and bringing on a world deluge'.

Dr Bernard's concern with nuclear war has not, however, prevented his continued research into the subterranean passages of his adopted country, and indeed some of the settlers in his community have assisted in the work. Their discoveries have led him to believe that there may be an entrance to this network of tunnels somewhere in the vicinity of Joinville, though its actual location still remains elusive. He says:

I have devoted years to investigating and studying the mysterious tunnels which honeycomb Santa Catarina, obviously built by an ancient race to reach subterranean cities. Research is still in progress. On a mountain near Joinville the choral singing of Atlantean men and women has been repeatedly heard – also the 'canto gallo' (cock crowing), which is the standard indication of the existence of a tunnel opening leading to a subterranean city. The crowing is not produced by a living animal, but probably by some machine.

Dr Bernard also shares Harold Wilkins's belief that Brazil was once a colony of Atlantis. Recently he said:

It is claimed that Brazil was once an Atlantean colony. A later report states that an Atlantean city, with elaborate buildings, streets, etc., was found in the midst of the jungles of the Amazon. Also the Brazilian radio and press reported the discovery of a subterranean city by a group of scientists who entered a tunnel which opened on top of a mountain near the boundary of Parana and Santa Catarina and descended until they came to a subterranean city. A strange fright came over the party and instead of studying it, they fled. What did they see? Probably the inhabitants of this subterranean city. Two ranchers living near the border of Parana and Santa Catarina came to the writer claiming they entered a tunnel there and travelled three days, finally descending and coming to an illuminated city in which they saw men, women and children. A member of their party got frightened and so they all returned.

Although Dr Bernard treats such stories with understandable scepticism, he does believe that the Atlanteans built cities in the Amazon and Mato Grosso, and that they might well have constructed some of the tunnels to 'migrate to the subterranean world of Agharti' when the holocaust overwhelmed their homeland. Others, of course, made for the colonies in South America. He writes:

It is claimed that the earth is honeycombed with a network of tunnels, which are especially abundant in South America; and that these tunnels lead to subterranean cities in immense cavities in the earth. Most famous of these tunnels is the 'Roadway of the Incas' which is said to stretch for several hundreds of miles south of Lima, Peru via Cuzco, Tiahuanaco and the Three Peaks, going on to the Atacama Desert where all traces of it is lost. Another branch runs to Brazil, where it is connected by tunnels to the coast. Here the tunnels go under the bottom of the ocean in the direction of the lost Atlantis. In this way Atlantis once had direct connection with its colonies in Brazil and Peru, through tunnels that run under the

Atlantic Ocean and then under Brazil, passing through Parana and Santa Catarina to Mato Grosso and then on to Peru. They then ran down the Andes to Chile.

In his monograph *The Subterranean World*, which I mentioned earlier, Dr Bernard says that there are persistent rumours among older residents in the Santa Catarina area where he lives about the existence of a subterranean race. There are also rumours about 'subterranean vehicles' that travel through the underground tunnels and are believed to be similar to those mentioned by Ferdinand Ossendowski in Tibet. There are those who believe these vehicles to be the 'Flying Saucers' which have so exercised the public imagination in recent years: we shall be returning to this controversy later in the book.

Dr Bernard says that when he visited a group of Theosophists at São Lourenço he heard the story of one of their members (now, unfortunately, dead) who had apparently found a tunnel entrance and travelled all the way from Peru to Brazil in a subterranean passage. He also heard it said that in the slave days, runaway slaves used to enter a tunnel at Ponte Grosse, Parana, and travel all the way to the Mato Grosso underground, later returning by the same route after slavery was abolished.

In the course of the monograph, Dr Bernard cites a number of colourful and supposedly true accounts by Brazilians about journeys they claim to have made through the underground tunnels. One typical example will suffice for them all, and is included because of the doctor's pertinent observations at the end:

Another Brazilian came to the writer saying he travelled through a smooth-cut, illuminated tunnel for three days, 20 hours a day, accompanied by two subterranean men he met at its entrance, until he came to an immense illuminated space filled with buildings and a fruit orchard and where lived men, women and children, also various animals, including lions and tigers, who were as tame as cats and dogs. The sexes lived apart and the women all looked as if in their teens, even though some were centuries old. Also these people were all an exact copy of each other, with no individual variation. Women produced children by parthenogenesis, and were all virgin mothers.

One of the children ran over to him apparently unafraid and when he tried to pick it up (which is forbidden among these people) an avalanche of rocks fell upon him, but did not harm him, leading him to believe they were really projected images rather than real rocks. He escaped to the outside through an exit tunnel. There he met a man who told him he often visited this city, where he was well received, and rode on a subterranean vehicle from it to other cities. The illuminated central tunnel that led to this city was connected by about fifty or more radiating side tunnels to other subterranean cities in various parts of Brazil.

Regarding this and previous Brazilian reports, the writer cannot guarantee that they are true, since the persons who made them had in most cases been impelled by monetary motives. However, in the main they agree with each other regarding (1) these subterranean cities being all illuminated, (2) inhabited by a super-race, (3) connected with each other by a network of tunnels. Where there is smoke there is fire, and while these reports may be fictitious, there is absolute certainty that subterranean people exist there, due to certain tunnels which positively exist in which the voices of men were heard, and which the writer hopes to investigate.

The research of Harold Wilkins, Lewis Spence, Dr Raymond Bernard and others has, I think, substantiated the connection between Brazil and Atlantis, and similarly left us in no doubt as to the extent and importance of the ancient tunnels which once linked the lost continent and its 'colonies' in South America. Whether or not it was the Atlanteans who built the tunnels is a moot point, and as the passageways appear to be the handiwork of a period prior to that when the Atlantean empire flourished, this seems unlikely. We must therefore return to this absorbing mystery at a later point in the book.

In the meantime, Dr Bernard has opened up an intriguing new field of inquiry with his comments about the tunnels being 'illuminated'. For in a little booklet entitled *Agharti* published in Boston in 1951, we find that the author Robert

Ernst Dickhoff, a Buddhist teacher who describes himself as 'Sungma Red Lama', confirms this statement. He says that Tibetan lamas have told him that: 'these caverns are illuminated by a green luminescence which aids underground plant life there and lengthens human life.'

Perhaps even more importantly for our study, Dr Dickhoff tells us that the subterranean tunnels which we have already discovered in Asia and South America are also to be found in *North* America. More extraordinary still, that the tunnels link up with those in South America and ultimately reach Agharti, thereby creating a gigantic underground network which literally links the United States with the rest of the world!

Dr Dickhoff writes: 'Tibetan Lamas are of the opinion that in America live in caves of vast proportions the survivors of a catastrophe which befell Atlantis . . . and that these caverns are connected by means of tunnels running clear to either of the two continents, Asia and America.'

And, indeed, when we begin to look into the facts, we find that the United States most certainly *has* a tradition of subterranean passageways as ancient and fascinating as those we have already discovered. . . .

Chapter 10

THE 'UNDERWORLD' OF
NEW YORK

Frank White was a gnarled old prospector who had spent many years of his life wandering about the remoter regions of California. The grandson of one of the famous 'Forty-niners' who had struck it rich in the great gold rush of 1848 (and then squandered the fortune on wine, women and bad investments), Frank was a loner who had never quite been able to bring himself to give up the search for the elusive gold mine he *knew* was just waiting for him somewhere in the region.

But in the spring of 1935 Frank at last made a strike – though his discovery was not the precious metal he so desired. Instead it was an underground tunnel which contained some of the most extraordinary artifacts modern eyes have ever looked upon.

Frank's discovery came to public notice when he arrived in the town of Brawley not far from the River Colorado and the Mexican border. He had been wandering through the mountains and deserts of California as far north as Death Valley and south to the Gila mountains, he said. During this time he had accidentally stumbled upon a small cleft in the rocks and, investigating, found that it opened out into an underground passage.

Armed only with a small prospector's lamp he had walked along the tunnel, which was about eight feet high with smooth, carefully crafted walls, for about half an hour. Suddenly, he had noticed a strange light up ahead.

'It was green – a sort of sinister green light,' he said. 'It got brighter as I walked along, and then the tunnel opened into a large cave.'

In the cave, Frank White was greeted by the extraordinary sight of a number of mummified bodies lying either on the floor or propped up against rocks. The fluorescent light which glowed over everything seemed to make the bodies even more gruesome, and their distorted poses gave Frank the distinct impression that death had crept up on them unexpectedly.

The old prospector shivered despite himself and quickly looked around the chamber of death. Along one wall were a number of statues that seemed to sparkle dimly in the green light, as if they might be made of gold. The faces, too, appeared to be strangely similar to those of ancient Inca gods he had once seen. Frank also noticed that the corpses were dressed in strange garments that looked as if they might be leather. Yet he told himself he had never seen anything quite like it before. His only thought was that it might have been a treasure house of some kind. 'I felt as if I had stepped into somewhere very ancient,' he said later. 'That the people had somehow been laying like that quite unchanged from the very earliest times. But how long I just couldn't even begin to guess.'

Despite his driving obsession to find gold, Frank felt too nervous to stay in the green-lit room for long. For one thing he could see no source for the strange light. And for another, several of the bodies were grouped around a hole in the far wall of the cave which looked like a continuation of the tunnel. Although he couldn't be sure, he had the uncomfortable feeling that they might have been its guardians – as well as the keepers of the gold statues – when they were still alive . . .

That, in essence, is the story which Frank White revealed to a few sceptical listeners in Brawley in April 1935, although he was careful not to be too specific about the location of the tunnel. The 'discovery' of the strange underground passage was briefly reported in a few of the Californian newspapers (in particular those of nearby San Diego) and then forgotten. A small group of other prospectors later set out with Frank to see if they could rediscover the secret cave and perhaps make their fortunes from recovering the gold statues, but there is no indication they even succeeded in finding the place again.

True story? Or yet another of the colourful mysteries that have come out of old California? The puzzle remains to this day, and indeed it would probably not be worth recounting in this book but for a number of important and substantive facts. Firstly, the knowledge that there *are* indeed a number of underground tunnels running beneath California and its surrounding states. That there *had* been earlier accounts of such subterranean places reported both in the twentieth century and back over the years to the days when the great Red Indian tribes roamed the continent before the arrival of the white men from across the oceans. And, thirdly, that the description of the tunnel, the gold statues in the 'treasure chamber' and the strange green light, all correspond with the facts we have already been assembling about the underground roadway to Agharti.

For it is my belief that Frank White found another of the entrances to this great network and if he had had the courage to go on beyond the place of death he might just have discovered ancient knowledge more precious than any gold. I am encouraged in this view by the redoubtable Harold Wilkins in his *Mysteries of Ancient South America*, who makes a specific comment on this area of California:

> There are spots along the *canon* of the Rio Colorado, where arrows cut deeply into the face of the sheer walls can be seen in certain lights and incidences of the solar rays. They are, by roamers who go hunting treasure westwards across the Gila Desert and unpeopled, thirststricken and heat-crazed Arizona, believed to be pointers towards ancient caches of unknown and extremely ancient races, and, it may be, are memorials of the unknown race whose buried temples, lofty stone pyramids, seven of them within a mile square, and massive granite rings and dwellings, circular walls round venerable trees, and blocks of hieroglyphics, speak of ruins of some very ancient Egypt, or Phoenicia of the wild region, at the head of the Gulf of California, 'a day's march from San Diego', in 1850, when they were discovered.

Nor do we need to be satisfied with just this remark, for if we examine the old legends and reports of prehistoric America we can find plenty of references to underground caves and tunnels which help us build up our own picture.

One of the very earliest North American legends tells us that mankind actually emerged onto the earth's surface from an 'underworld'. As Sabine Baring-Gould has written in his *Cliff Castle and Cave Dwellings* (1911): 'According to Indian legend, the first men were bred like maggots in the heart of the earth, but laying hold of some depending fibre drew themselves up into the light of day.'

The American Indians are, of course, generally regarded as the earliest inhabitants of what is now the United States of America. According to that great pioneer researcher Henry R. Schoolcraft in his *Historical and Statistical Information Respecting Indian Tribes of the United States* (1851–57):

At the close of the Fifteenth Century, the tribes of the present area of the United States were spread out, chiefly, in seven principal groups, or generic families of tribes – bands, or large totemic circles. Each of these spoke a language differing in some respect from the others. Each circle had some peculiarities, in custom or manners. These groups were the Apalachian, Achalaque, Chicorean, Algonquin, Iroquois, Dacota and Shoshone.

It comes as no surprise to learn that as soon as the 'New World' was discovered by the European sailors, a great interest developed in the 'red men' who lived there. They were referred to, mistakenly of course, as Indians, because Columbus at first believed he had found the Indies. What was not a subject for argument was the fact that they seemed in all respects like a unique race who had dwelt in a mystic continent isolated from the rest of mankind for countless centuries.

Later research showed that the American Indians were, in all probability, an offshoot of tribes from the continent of Asia and had originally reached their 'mystic continent' by crossing the narrow Bering Strait. The Marquis de Nadaillac explains in his classic work, *Pre-Historic America* (1885):

The physical characteristics of the American aborigines are generally admitted to point towards affinities with people belonging to the Northern Asia region. The approximation of Asia and America at Bering Strait lends probability to the hypothesis of migration. It has been shown that the route to America via Bering Strait is feasible, and in glacial times if the shallow waters near the strait were, as there is some reason to suppose, filled with grounded ice, there is no reason why people like the Eskimo of the present day, or even lower in the scale, might not make their way along this temporary bridge and subsist on the marine animals which probably swarmed along its borders.

Such is the scholar's view of the populating of America. But, as I quoted Baring-Gould saying, the Indians themselves speak of originating from either a subterranean world or, alternately, and perhaps even more surprisingly, from a lost continent which it might be argued was Atlantis! Let us look at these legends.

According to Lewis Spence in *Myths of the North American Indians* (1914) the mythologies of the 'Red Man' are infinitely more rich in creation and deluge myths than those of any other race in the world. He says that tales which deal with the origin of man are exceedingly frequent, and many are strikingly similar to European and Asiatic myths of the same kind.

'In some of the creation-myths of the various Indian tribes,' he tells us, 'we find the great gods moulding the universe, in others we find them merely discovering it. Still others lead their people from subterranean depths to the upper earth.' In this context, Mr Spence then cites F. H. Cushing's retelling of a Zuni Indian legend which appears in his *Outlines of Zuni Creation Myths* (1896):

> Then from the nethermost of the four caves of the world the seed of men and the creatures took form and grew; even as with eggs in warm places worms quickly form and appear, and, growing, soon burst their shells and there emerge, as may happen, birds, tadpoles, or serpents: so man and all creatures grew manifoldly and multiplied in many kinds. Thus did the lowermost world-cave become overfilled with living things, full of unfinished creatures, crawling like reptiles over one another in black darkness, thickly crowding together and treading one on another, one spitting on another and doing other indecency, in such manner that the murmurings and lamentations became loud, and many amidst the growing confusion sought to escape, growing wiser and more manlike. Then P-shai-an-K'ia, the foremost and the wisest of men, arising from the nethermost sea, came among men and the living things, and pitying them, obtained egress from that first world cave through such a dark and narrow path that some seeing somewhat, crowding after, could not follow him, so eager mightily did they strive one with another. Alone then did P-Shai-an-K'ia come from one cave to another into this world, then island-like, lying amidst the world-waters, vast, wet and unstable.

He sought and found the Sun-Father, and besought him to deliver the men and the creatures from that nethermost world.

In his own collection of creation-myths, Mr Spence relates the more specific legend of the Mandan Indians (a tribe of the Siouan linguistic stock living in the Missouri region), who believed they originally emerged from a subterranean world. Again it is worth quoting in full because it demonstrates what we are told was a 'widespread belief' among the early inhabitants of North America and because it is obviously the source of Baring-Gould's quotation:

> The Mandan tribes of the Sioux possess a type of creation-myth which is common to several American peoples. They suppose that their nation lived in a subterranean village near a vast lake. Hard by the roots of a great grape-vine penetrated from the earth above, and, clambering up these, several of them got a sight of the upper world, which they found to be rich and well stocked with both animal and vegetable food. Those of them who had seen the new-found world above returned to their home bringing such glowing accounts of its wealth and pleasantness that the others resolved to forsake their dreary underground dwelling for the delights of the sunny sphere above. The entire population set out, and started to climb up the roots of the vine, but no more than half the tribe had ascended when the plant broke owing to the weight of a corpulent woman. The Mandans imagine that after death they will return to the underground world in which they originally dwelt, the worthy reaching the village by way of the lake, the bad having to abandon the passage by reason of the weight of their sins.

By no stretch of the imagination could it be argued that this fantastic myth does anything other than underline a belief in a subterranean world. But from the more general myths of the Sioux nation comes the story of an Indian brave who made a journey to an underground kingdom. The Sioux, of course, dwelt in what are now the states of North and South Dakota. And, as we shall see later, there is an enduring tradition of subterranean passages in this region.

The story – one version of which is related in Spence's *Myths of the North American Indians* – concerns a chief of one of the Sioux tribes who lost a son in an underground passage. The boy had been hunting buffalo with some other braves and had cornered one animal, which then dashed into a cave. Without a second thought the boy plunged in after it.

The cave was regarded in superstitious awe by the tribe, and the other braves were afraid to follow their chief's son. When he did not reappear after some time they returned to their camp and reported what had happened. Angrily, the chief returned with the braves to find out why his son was still missing.

At first none of the braves would enter the cave, but when the chief offered the hand of his daughter in marriage to anyone who would go into the passage to find what had become of his son, one young man stepped forward. He would go, he said, and without another word stepped into the darkened passageway which sloped away steeply under his feet. With pounding heart, the brave walked for some distance until he stumbled upon something lying on the floor. In the gloom, he could just make out that it was the chief's son – and that he was obviously dead.

Somewhat saddened, the Indian hauled the body back to near the entrance of the tunnel. Then he called to the chief and the other braves that he had found the missing son. He did not wait for them to arrive, however, but turned back the way he had come. Something had fascinated him about the tunnel and he decided to explore further.

After walking for some distance the brave suddenly found himself in a brightly illuminated cavern, where a pale-skinned man and woman with golden hair were sitting on the floor. They were evidently very sad.

Cautiously, the brave approached the couple who did not look up until he was almost upon them. As soon as they saw him, both began to cry. When the brave inquired what was wrong, the man and woman said that their only son had just died.

A short conversation ensued, in which the brave explained how he had come to be in the tunnel. The couple listened quietly and then said that they were dwellers of this subterranean world, and though they knew all about the people who lived on the surface, he was the first person they had actually met.

The Indian did his best to cheer up the couple and indeed finally made them smile with stories of his life in the Sioux encampment. Following this, the boy asked if they would help him find his way back to the surface, as the tunnel had had many twists and turns in it.

The couple readily agreed to do this and as a gesture of gratitude gave two presents to the Indian – a white horse and a talisman made of iron which they said had the power to satisfy his every wish. It could even melt rocks and thereby facilitate his return to the surface.

Shortly afterward, goes the legend, the brave once again emerged in his own country and was soon recounting his adventure. The chief, true to his word, allowed the young man to marry his daughter and also made him a head chieftain.

Soon his fame and the story of his journey underground spread throughout the whole Sioux nation, and his reputation became assured when he used his magic piece of iron to charm buffaloes and thereby kill more than any other brave. He looked set to live out the rest of his days in honour and peace. But it was not to be, as Lewis Spence tells us in concluding his version of the legend:

> Now it so happened that the chief's remaining son was very jealous of his brother-in-law. He thought his father should have given him the chieftainship, and the honours accorded by the people to his young relative were exceedingly galling to him. So he made up his mind to kill the youth and destroy his beautiful white horse.
>
> On the occasion of another great buffalo hunt the wicked schemer found his opportunity. By waving his robe he scared the buffaloes and caused them to close in on the young brave, seemingly to trample him to death. But when the herd was scattered and moved away, there was no trace of the brave or his milk-white steed. They had returned to the Underworld.

There are other similar legends to this one about Indians entering the Underworld, but I can see no point in repeating them here. Instead, I should like to move on to what these same myths tell us about the race of people dwelling below the surface.

According to Lewis Spence, their domain is known as the

'Land of Supernatural People'. They have dwelt in their tunnels and caves since time immemorial and are said to be 'a spiritual race some degrees higher than mankind'. These people apparently eat, drink, hunt and amuse themselves in the same manner as those on the surface of the world, and are by no means invulnerable or immortal. Their main difference from the Indians, however, was that they were white-skinned and fair-haired.

That most famous race of Indians, the Apaches, who so fiercely opposed the intrusion of the settlers into their territory of Arizona and North Mexico, have a strong tradition of a race of pale-skinned people who dwelt in tunnels beneath their reservations. Again, this adds emphasis to the modern reports we have of tunnels in the vicinity of Phoenix, Arizona, of which more in a while.

The Apaches called these people the *Numungkake* and said that they had originally come from another great island *before* settling in the subterranean tunnels. Was this island Atlantis and were these people Atlanteans, the same Atlanteans we have already read about who colonized a large part of South America? Harold Wilkins thinks they were, as he asserts in another of his books, *Secret Cities of Old South America* (1950):

> The Apache Indians say that their remote ancestors came from a great fire island in the eastern ocean, where there was a great port with an entrance of architectural masonry where ships had to be guided in by pilots. The Fire Dragon arose and made their ancestors flee from this island – which can be none other than the old Atlantean island of Pluto, mentioned by the lost and ancient Punic historian, Procles. The Apaches eventually reached the mountains of Tiahuanacu, where they were forced to take refuge in immense and ancient tunnels, through which they wandered for years carrying seeds and fruit plants.

Wilkins says that the Mandan tribe – a branch of the Sioux family who I mentioned earlier – claim that the first men to emerge from these old American tunnels were the Histoppa, or tattooed. They perished in the Deluge, having emerged too soon above ground to see how things were. The rest of the men stayed on below ground. And he adds: 'There are ancient

North American traditions which actually assert that these
mysterious tunnels were built or bored by an ancient race of
white men, long since dead and who caused an ancient
cataclysm!'

Such evidence of Atlanteans in North America is fascinating though not conclusive. As the Marquis de Nadaillac has
written in his study, *Pre-Historic America*:

> Similar myths are found among various Indian tribes; the
> legend of a deluge and of a saviour and benefactor of the
> human race extends to the Alaskan tribes and is in fact
> almost worldwide among all classes of men in some form
> or other. No dissemination of merely Christian ideas, since
> the conquest, is sufficient to account for these myths . . .
> That America was peopled at different times by scions of
> different races is highly probable from the physical differ-
> ences to be observed between the remains of pre-historic
> man and the complexion and features he bequeathed to
> his historic descendants.

What, in fact, the evidence does point to is that a race of
white-skinned people were abroad in America before the
Indians and were responsible for the construction of many of
the artifacts and, in particular, the great tunnel systems in
both North and South America.

The French scholar de Nadaillac again supports this argument with evidence from the Indians, telling how:

> The Shawnees are said to have claimed that the ancient
> inhabitants of Florida were white, and that when they
> arrived in the country they found there buildings and
> customs, with a civilisation very unlike their own. The
> Tuscaroras are said to possess a legendary chronology
> going back nearly three thousand years; according to
> them, their fathers were natives of the extreme north, of
> districts far beyond the Great Lakes, who came from
> tunnels in the ground to establish themselves upon the St
> Lawrence.

Still more emphatic are the words of W. S. Blacket in his
Lost Histories of America (1883), when he writes:

> It is part of the theory deducible from this work, that

America, in ancient times, has been the residence of a great race of men, frequently mentioned in the literature of Europe as Oceanides – that is to say, living in the Ocean. The inhabitants of this land were not isolated and alone, but in frequent intercourse with the rest of the world.

It was by a tunnel system which traversed the whole American continent and was then linked by way of Atlantis at one end, and via the Bering Strait at the other, I believe, that this 'intercourse with the rest of the world' – Europe, Africa and Asia, to be precise – was achieved. The conclusive evidence of this will become apparent later.

These, then, are the facts of an ancient tradition of subterranean tunnels in North America. What modern evidence is there to support their continued existence today? My researches have revealed that there is strong evidence to be found in each of the four localities mentioned in the foregoing Indian legends: California, the Dakota region, the area of the Bering Straits and perhaps most important of all, Arizona, where actual investigation is now taking place.

Let us start with California, though, for it is the land of 'startling antediluvian finds' according to Harold Wilkins, who cites several instances including 'a skull of a man of apparently Tertiary age found 130 feet deep in a mine with lava over it, an image of a man of a very archaic type with unknown letters on the sides of the carving, a mysterious causeway 18 feet under a desert, and granite tablets in a passageway with signs of some antediluvian mining'. Such, he suggests, are further signs of California's subterranean tunnels and underground dwellers which date back to at least the Atlantean era.

A remarkable story has also been told by Tom Wilson, an old Indian guide who was famous throughout Southern California for years until his death in 1968. Tom was a member of the Cahroc tribe, whose legends spoke of a man named Chareya, a venerable figure who had long, flowing white hair and wore a close-fitting tunic. He apparently appeared among the Cahrocs from time to time and disappeared once he had completed his mission into a deep passageway which ran 'no-one knew where' according to Tom Wilson.

Although most members of the Cahroc tribe believed that only the ghosts of the departed lived in the underworld, Tom was convinced there was an actual race of men and women living below the surface of California. His belief was founded on an extraordinary experience that his grandfather had undergone at the turn of the century. The elder Indian had apparently discovered a tunnel which ran for miles underground until it finally opened out into a cavern where dwelt a community of fair-skinned people. According to the old guide:

> My grandfather told me that these people made him welcome, and although he could not understand their language, he lived with them for some time. These people dressed in clothes that seemed to resemble leather, but which my grandfather said was not. Their cavern was illuminated by a pale, yellowish-green light from an unknown source.

Eventually the Indian returned to the surface world, where his story was greeted with predictable scepticism. When young Tom Wilson heard the story from his grandfather, however, he was so impressed by the old man's sincerity that he spent much of the rest of his life looking for the entry to the strange underground world. He remained convinced of its actuality until the day of his death, believing that the point of entry was somewhere in the regions where the Mojave Desert met the Sierra Nevada mountain range.

If we move up the west coast of America to the state of Oregon we come across the story of another subterranean dwelling place said to be linked to a number of secret passageways. Several experts, including Eric Norman, the author of *This Hollow Earth* (1972), believe this story to be related to the legends of the Sioux and Mandan Indians which speak of mysterious tunnels in the Dakota region also leading to an underground kingdom. It is a theory not easy to substantiate, but does, I think, confirm the likelihood of there being subterranean tunnels in this area of the United States which are part of the greater network spreading north to Canada, and south to Mexico and South America beyond.

The most recent discussion of the 'ancient subterranean metropolis' in Oregon appeared in a fascinating article,

'About Caves and Other Secret Hiding Places in the World',
by George Wagner Jr, published in the January 1967 issue of
Search. In discussing the various reports he had collected
about the mysterious place, Mr Wagner mentions some
specific details 'written to me recently by one of my correspondents, Mr. Azerland':

> He stated that about 75 miles northwest of Portland,
> Oregon, between Portland and the Seattle earth-faults, far
> down in the earth, where the earth was once flooded over,
> are the remains of a splendid city. My correspondent says
> that the city is about eight to ten miles underground, and
> is reached by a number of tunnels which radiate from it in
> different directions.

Mr Wagner's article gives the impression that he believes
the underground city to be of Atlantean origins (citing the
reference to flooding) and perhaps similar to other subter
ranean dwellings reported in South America and Asia. This
would certainly strengthen the argument for it being part of
the great world-network.

Continuing still further north, into Alaska and the region
of the Bering Strait, we can find more evidence of a subterranean tunnel. Among the people here, and in particular the
ethnic race of Indians, the Athapascans, there is a belief in a
subterranean race who have lived in harmony and secrecy
since before the arrival of the Indians themselves. In his fascinating book, *Arctic Adventure – My life in the Frozen
North* (1935), the intrepid adventurer Peter Freuchen makes
a number of references to stories he heard among the Indians
about the *Eqidleet*, or Inland People, who live below the
surface. In the heart of Alaska, not far from the town of
Tanana, he was shown crevices in the mountains where, he
was told by his guide Asayuk, men had disappeared over the
years to go and join the *Eqidleet*. Freuchen writes:

> The crevices were deep and broad, but Asayuk found a
> way in and out between them, seemed to know instinctively
> where they were, and took us safely to the land we sought.
> Asayuk told me of desperate men who had run away from
> home and gone into the mountains to get away from their
> fellow men. They had become ghosts or were taken in by
> the *Eqidleet*.

The Eskimos who dwell in the far north of the continent also have a number of legends concerning a race of people living beneath the earth's crust. These underground people have a system of tunnels through which they can travel to and from the surface world. According to William F. Warren in his book, *Paradise Found, or The Cradle of the Human Race* (1911), the Eskimos believe that their ancestors may well have come from this subterranean world which is lit by a perpetual light. They almost certainly knew of the whereabouts of the passageways, though these are now probably forgotten.

Fascinating though all these reports are, the most important evidence and conclusions have come from the south of the United States, in Arizona to be precise, where a dedicated researcher named Charles A. Marcoux has spent the last quarter of a century investigating the legends of a subterranean world. To formalize his work, Marcoux has established the Subsurface Research Center in Phoenix, Arizona, having picked this particular locality because he is convinced an entrance to the subterranean tunnels exists in a curiously named local mountain range known as the Superstitious Mountains.

Marcoux has made an intensive study of all the accounts of underground passageways throughout the world, and is already convinced that 'a network of tunnels exists from Canada to South America, especially under Brazil, all of which are connected by tunnels with other parts of the world'. However, the tunnel network which particularly interests him is 'the one that opens at various points in Central and South America, with an entrance in the Superstitious Mountains in Arizona'.

According to Dr Raymond Bernard, who knows the shy and rather self-effacing Marcoux well: 'He has been searching for twenty years for such an entrance; and while he has not yet found it, he claims to have achieved contact with subterranean people. He is continuing his search, since he believes that finding such an entrance is humanity's last hope of survival.'

We shall be examining Marcoux's claim of contact with subterranean people later in this book, but a word here about his plans *if* he finds the entranceway in the Superstitious Mountains. He believes that our atmosphere is being rapidly contaminated by radioactivity:

I know that mankind cannot survive on the earth's surface and must eventually go underground. Some believe that flying saucers will take them off the earth when the time comes, but my evidence on this matter proves to me that this is not possible. According to Heffling, the last time the earth was faced with the same problem which we face today, the Gods of Atlantis burrowed into Mother Earth and established underworld or subsurface kingdoms, and their remains can still be found there, along with their children. The same thing will have to be done today by present mankind in order to survive.

My purpose is to start a colony and gather a group who can give up the outside world and start a new life, one that will not be easy, but better than that which they left behind. That is the purpose of my entering the Subterranean World, where those who exist there will direct me what to do.

As I said, we shall return later to what Marcoux has to say on the Subterranean People and their lifestyle. But before leaving North America, there is one more extraordinary piece of information to be examined. This concerns the claim that a subterranean tunnel that is linked to the Agharti network actually exists beneath New York City!

The claim is made by Robert Ernst Dickhoff in his book, *Agharta* (1951) during a discussion on the various locations in America, Europe and Asia in which the underground tunnels have been reported.* 'Even New York,' he writes, 'can speak of elaborate tunnels which extend for miles under Central Park, of which most New Yorkers are blissfully unaware, except that it is admitted that these tunnels were dug by means unknown and are of great age.'

That is the sum total of Dickhoff's statement. While there are, of course, innumerable tunnels beneath New York through which the subway travels, and indeed other disused

---

* Another American writer on the theme of subterranean dwellers, Dr M. Doreal, believes that there are also passageways to the underground world under Mount Shasta in California, at Sulphur Springs, Oklahoma, and beneath the famous Mammoth Cave in Kentucky. Unfortunately, he cites no specific details as to where the entranceways might be, although there is a persistent belief that among the 226 passageways that branch out from the Mammoth Caves – spreading, it is said, for 160 miles – there might just be one that ultimately links up with a route to the underground world!

passageways, there is no evidence that I have been able to find to substantiate the claim they are in any way associated with the legend of Agharti. As the reader will see when I come to present my thesis later in the book on the actual location of the Agharti network, it leaves New York rather off the beaten track.

I do believe, however, that there *is* an explanation for suggestions of an underground passageway beneath New York, and that it lies in an extraordinary series of stories, presented ostensibly as based on truth, but in actual fact mostly fiction, which have become known as 'The Shaver Hoax'.

From the year 1945, there began to appear in an American 'pulp' magazine called *Amazing Stories* a series of related tales which put forward the theory that back at the dawn of time the Earth was the home of several races of people including the Titans and the Atlans. The author of the series, Richard S. Shaver (1907–1975), claimed that his information was based on a secret language, Mantong, he had discovered on pieces of rock covered with inscriptions which had been left by the Atlans and Titans before their departure from this planet.

The stories maintained that the Atlans and the Titans were godlike immortals who created mighty civilizations, but when the sun began to emit harmful radiation they built underground tunnels and caverns in which to escape the rays. These, however, failed to provide the necessary protection, and the immortals were forced to abandon the Earth, some 12,000 years ago, leaving behind the remnants of their peoples in the tunnels. The exiles fell into two groups: the 'Teros', a peaceful, highly intelligent species, and the 'Deros', small, malignant creatures bent on evil. It was these 'Deros', said Shaver that were responsible for all the evil in the world, the wars, disasters and accidents that have plagued mankind over the centuries. The writer also suggested that all the ancient ruin of the world, not forgetting the underground tunnels and caverns, which appeared to be well beyond the creative power of the people of the periods in which they were built, were actually the handiwork of the Atlans.

The series created a sensation when it appeared. The magazine's circulation was boosted enormously, and it attracted over 2,500 letters from readers whose reactions varied from passionate belief in Shaver's theories to outright ridicule. Som writers even claimed to have had actual encounters with the 'Teros' and 'Deros'. For the following five years, the controversy over the series raged backwards and forwards, Shaver all the while maintaining his facts were correct, while scientists and geographers denounced it as nonsense. Today, the extraordinary saga is regarded as a hoax pure and simple in most quarters, and by readers of Science Fiction as a fraud that did much harm to the embryo genre of SF which was then trying determinedly to be taken seriously as a literary form. Until the day of his death, Shaver never retracted a word of what he had written, and it has been accepted that he may well have genuinely believed what he wrote. From an objective standpoint, it is only possible to say that there are a few fragments of arguable truth amidst much highly imaginative fantasy.

As befitted a series which appeared in a Science Fiction magazine, most of the stories in Shaver's saga take place in space and feature the continuing activities of the Atlans and the Titans, who now move from place to place in the Flying Saucers which occasionally visit the Earth – to keep an eye on our planet, of course. But in one of the most crucial tales in the series, 'The Masked World' (*Amazing Stories*, May 1946), there is presented 'an incredible revelation of the world of horror hidden beneath modern New York – the caverns of the "Dero" '. In the course of this 50,000 word epic appears the following statement by Shaver:

Within the dense archean basalt that upholds our modern surface USA – deep within the solidity of dark rock where no water can ever penetrate – lies a city. It is not so well known as modern New York directly overhead, but it has its friends, its enemies, and its slums – its lords and plutocrats. It is part of the ancient, forgotten underworld, not entirely unknown to surface man, but unrecognized as a terrible truth, a harmful factor, of his life. Ontal is a part of the civilization under our feet that is called 'The Masked World' by those who know.

The underworld is an intricate maze of many levels of titanic caverns which reach everywhere under the surface of our modern surface world. But under New York the ancient highways that are in reality all part of one vast old planet-city that the Earth once was before it had a sun – here the ancient highways converge into a greater city of dwellings than anywhere else in the east . . . The underworld is so vast that little of it contains life, and not much has ever been fully explored. All of it is the handiwork of the ancient races who left earth those thousands of years ago.

Shaver also speaks intriguingly of a 'port of entry' in New York through which 'the favoured few' are allowed to enter 'The Masked World', but gives not the slightest indication as to where this might be. When readers of *Amazing* later urged him to prove his claim by 'leading a party into the caves', he responded sharply: 'I'm willing, but which entrance opens into a safe place where things are not waiting to engulf us? Naturally, I can't take people into a place where they would become beaten slaves!'

It is my belief that it is in the hugely publicized and controversial stories of Richard S. Shaver that we can find the origins of the rumours about mysterious tunnels under New York. I think, also, that there is little doubt that he found his inspiration for them in the books of Bulwer Lytton, Madame Blavatsky, Ferdinand Ossendowski, Nicholas Roerich and others that have been mentioned during the course of this book. Shaver made no secret of the fact that he was a voracious reader, and books on mysteries such as Subterranean Kingdoms and Secret Passageways filled his library shelves. He was actually only really following in the honourable footsteps of writers like Robert Paltock, who wrote *The Life and Adventures of Peter Wilkins* (1751), Ludvig Baron von Holberg, the author of *Niels Klim's Journey Underground* (1741), and Jules Verne, creator of the classic *Journey to the Centre of the Earth* (1864), as well as a host of lesser known twentieth-century writers, including Edgar Rice Burroughs with his novels about people living inside the globe, such as *At the Earth's Core* (1923) and its sequel, *Pellucidar* (1924). It was just Shaver's endless protestations that every word he wrote was true that ultimately diminished his work.

Perhaps the one element of the Shaver stories many readers found most difficult to accept was the 'Dero's' power to perpetrate all the evil that occurred on the surface of the earth. For to achieve this he said that they had at their command fearsome powers – powers that would certainly have got out of control in their destructive hands and resulted in the end of the world. It was a pity that Shaver could obviously not resist elaborating on the then developing fear of nuclear power – for if he had only looked closer at the works of Blavatsky, Ossendowski, Roerich, and in particular Bulwer Lytton's story *The Coming Race*, from which he clearly drew a number of the facets of his story, he would have found a force eminently more believable, and in most respects just as powerful. The force known as *Vril Power*.

Until this point in my study, we have only considered *Vril Power* in general terms. It is now time to look into its mysteries much more specifically . . .

Chapter 11

THE MYSTERY OF *VRIL POWER*

There is little doubt that the single most curious factor associated with the legend of Agharti is the strange force known as *Vril Power*. Ever since this mysterious element was first described in Bulwer Lytton's novel, *The Coming Race*, and the possibility of its existence cited in later reports about the secret underground kingdom, there has been mounting confusion as to just *what* it might be. And, more particularly, whether it really exists at all, or was just an invention of that ingenious Victorian novelist.

Perhaps before studying the facts that we have about *Vril Power*, it would be as well to remind ourselves of some of the things Bulwer Lytton told us about its capabilities. It is first mentioned almost immediately after the book's narrator arrives in the underground world and meets some of the inhabitants, known as the *Vril-ya*. They leave him in no doubt as to its importance in their lives.

Says our narrator:

There is no word in any language I know which is an exact synonym for *Vril*. I should call it electricity, except that it comprehends in its manifold branches other forces of nature, to which, in our scientific nomenclature, differing names are assigned, such as magnetism, galvanism, etc. These people consider that in *Vril* they have arrived at the unity in natural energic agencies, which has been conjectured by many philosophers above ground, and which Faraday thus intimates under the more cautious term of correlation:

'I have long held the opinion,' says that illustrious experimentalist, 'almost amounting to a conviction, in common, I believe, with many other lovers of natural knowledge, that the various forms under which the forces of matter are made manifest have one common origin; or, in other words, are so directly related, and mutually dependent, that they are convertible, as it were, into one another, and possess equivalents of power in their action.'

These subterranean philosophers assert that, by one operation of *Vril*, which Faraday would perhaps call 'atmospheric magnetism', they can influence the variations of temperature – in plain words, the weather; that by other operations, akin to those ascribed to mesmerism, electrobiology, odic force, etc., but applied scientifically through *Vril* conductors, they can exercise influence over minds, and bodies animal and vegetable, to an extent not surpassed in the romances of our mystics. To all such agencies they give the common name of *Vril*.

Through the medium of his narrator, Bulwer Lytton then explains more specifically the powers of *Vril*. He says that it can be used for expanding the consciousness of the mind, and allowing the transference of thoughts from one person to another by means of trance or vision. It was through the agency of *Vril*, he says 'while I had been placed in the state of trance, that I had been made acquainted with the rudiments of the *Vril-ya's* language'. (It should, of course, not be forgotten in this context that Bulwer Lytton was fascinated by mesmerism and had developed his own powers of telekinesis.)

Next, in discussing the rise of the *Vril-ya* civilization, he describes how this was achieved through harnessing all the latent powers of this 'all-permeating fluid'. It can, he says, 'be raised and disciplined into the mightiest agency over all forms of matter, animate or inanimate. It can destroy like a flash of lightning; yet, differently applied, it can replenish or invigorate life, heal and preserve.' The narrator explains that the underground people depend on it for the cure of disease, or rather – as he puts it – 'for enabling the physical organisation to re-establish the due equilibrium of its natural powers, and thereby to cure itself.'

Bulwer Lytton's young American is told that the force can also be harnessed to cut through solid rock as well as being directed as a destructive power against enemies. He is shown a *Vril Staff* and learns that 'the fire lodged in the hollow of the rod directed by the hand of a child could shatter the strongest fortress or cleave its burning way from the van to the rear of an

embattled host.' (Whether such a force can or cannot ultimately be attributed to *Vril Power*, is this not a remarkably
prophetic description of the modern laser-beam, almost a
century before it was fully developed?)

Further uses of the force include the motive power for
robots, the propulsion of land vehicles and flying contrivances,
and for supplying the light which illuminates the subterranean
world and nourishes all the life-forms therein, says the
narrator. Taken in total, *Vril* is seen as an enormous reservoir
of universal power, some parts of which can be concentrated
in the human body.

Is it any surprise, then, that people ever since have
wondered what truth there is in this amazing *Vril Power*?

Some of these attributes are, I am sure, clearly inventions of
Bulwer Lytton's fertile brain. But according to most commentators there seems to be an underlying truth, a feeling that a
force such as he describes *does* exist, and might not necessarily
be confined to the nether regions of the Earth.

I have, I believe, established earlier in this book in the
chapter devoted to Bulwer Lytton and *The Coming Race*, that
the author was a man of profound mystical knowledge who
drew on this secret information for his work. However, he
revealed little of his sources and was suitably enigmatic when
pressed to explain what *Vril Power* was. Writing to a close
friend shortly after the publication of the book, in his only
known comment on the subject, he said: 'I did not mean *Vril*
for mesmerism, which I hold to be a mere branch current of
this one great fluid pervading all nature.'

I find this explanation intriguing, though abstruse, as if
the usually precise Bulwer Lytton was regretful at already
having revealed too much. The Rosicrucian Brotherhood to
which he belonged took great pride in their oaths of secrecy,
and it seems likely to me that the author of *The Coming Race*,
in his straitened circumstances at the time, and urgent need of
money, employed information he had easily to hand in order
to complete his story quickly and also give to it the authenticity
that marked all his work. Although he would not discuss the
book further, he left a growing conviction that it concealed
certain basic truths – a conviction which, as I have shown,
gained its greatest support during the years that Adolf Hitler
was in power.

In an interesting article, 'UFO's and the Mystery of Agharti', which confirms my belief about Bulwer Lytton, Nadine Smyth has written:

> Certain highly-placed members of Hitler's Third Reich believed in Agharti and *Vril Power*, and it is their interest that has given the whole subject a sinister connotation which is largely undeserved. Occultism undoubtedly did play a part in the Nazi movement; but Hitler and his close followers twisted and perverted it to their own ends, and it may ultimately have rebounded upon them and destroyed them.

The Nazis were not, however, the first people to believe in *Vril Power* or to set out to learn its secrets. That credit goes to Madame Blavatsky, the Russian émigrée and Theosophist who had evidently read *The Coming Race* and been much influenced by it, for she mentions it in her first book, *Isis Unveiled*, published six years afterwards in 1877. In a section dealing with 'The Force that Moves Atoms' in which she expounds one of her persisting obsessions that 'every exertion of will results in a force', she writes:

> There is a force in existence whose secret powers were thoroughly familiar to the ancient theurgists but which is denied by modern sceptics. The antediluvian children – who perhaps played with it, using it as the boys in Bulwer Lytton's *The Coming Race* use the tremendous *Vril* – called it the 'Water of Phtha'; their descendants named it the *Anima Mundi*, the soul of the universe; and still later the mediaeval hermetists termed it 'sidereal light', or the 'Milk of the Celestial Virgin', the 'Magnes', and many other names. But our modern learned men will neither accept nor recognize it under such appellations; for it pertains to *magic*, and magic is, in their conception, a disgraceful superstition.

Having stated her conviction, Madame Blavatsky goes on to enlarge her argument:

> There has been an infinite confusion of names to express one and the same thing. The chaos of the ancients; the Zoroastrian sacred fire, or the *Antusbyrum* of the Parsees;

the Elmes-fire of the ancient Germans; the lightning of Cybelê; the burning torch of Apollo; the flame on the altar of Pan; the inextinguishable fire in the temple on the Acropolis, and in that of Vesta; the fire-flame of Pluto's helm; the brilliant sparks on the hats of the Dioscuri, on the Gorgon's head, the helm of Pallas, and the staff of Mercury; the Egyptian Phtha, or Ra; the Grecian *Zeus Cataibates* (the descending); the pentecostal fire-tongues; the burning bush of Moses; the pillar of fire of the *Exodus*, and the 'burning lamp' of Abram; the eternal fire of the 'bottomless pit', the Delphic oracular vapors; the Sidereal light of the Rosicrucians; the *Akasa* of the Hindu adepts; the Astral light of Eliphas Levi; the nerve-aura and the fluid of the magnetists; the *od* of Reichenbach; the fire-globe, or meteor-*cat* of Babinet; the *Psychod* and ectenic force of Thury; the atmospheric magnetism of some naturalists; galvanism; and finally, electricity, are but various names for many different manifestations, or effects of the same mysterious, all-pervading cause – the Greek *Archeus*. Sir E. Bulwer-Lytton, in his *Coming Race*, describes it as the *Vril*, used by the subterranean populations, and allowed his reader to take it for a fiction. 'These people,' he says, 'consider that in the *Vril* they had arrived at the unity in natural energic agencies'; and proceeds to show that Faraday intimated them 'under the more cautious term of correlation'.

Pausing briefly to give the quote from Faraday which I repeated at the start of this chapter, the authoress speculates that Bulwer Lytton 'coined his curious names by contracting words in classical language. *Gy* would come from *gune*; *Vril* from *virile*.' Then she continues:

Absurd and unscientific as may appear our comparison of a fictitious *Vril* invented by the great novelist, and the primal force of the equally great experimentalist, with the kabalistic astral light, it is nevertheless the true definition of this force. Discoveries are constantly being made to corroborate the statement thus boldly put forth.

Her conviction about the existence of *Vril Power* emerged again in her second book, *The Secret Doctrine* (1888). Here she wrote about its other powers, those of destruction, in a Chapter entitled, 'The Coming Force':

There is a terrible sidereal Force known to, and named by the Atlanteans *Mash-Mak*, and by the Aryan Rishis in their *Ashtar Vidya* by a name that we do not like to give. It is the *Vril* of Bulwer Lytton's 'Coming Race', and of the coming races of our mankind. The name *Vril* may be a fiction; the Force itself is a fact doubted as little in India as the existence itself of their Rishis, since it is mentioned in all the secret works.

It is this vibratory Force, which, when aimed at an army from an *Agni Rath* fixed on a flying vessel, a balloon, according to the instructions found in *Ashtar Vidya*, reduced to ashes 100,000 men and elephants, as easily as it would a dead rat. It is allegorised in the *Vishnu Purana*, in the *Ramayana* and other works, in the fable about the sage Kapilla whose *glance* made a mountain of ashes of King Sagara's 60,000 sons, and which is explained in the esoteric works, and referred to as the *Kapilaksha* – 'Kapila's Eye'.

And is it this Satanic Force that our generations were to be allowed to add to their stock of Anarchist's baby-toys, known as melenite, dynamite clockworks, explosive oranges, 'flower baskets', and such other innocent names? Is it this destructive agency, which, once in the hands of some modern Attila, e.g., a blood-thirsty anarchist, would reduce Europe in a few days to its primitive chaotic state with no man left alive to tell the tale – is this force to become the common property of all men alike?

As is the case in so much of Madame Blavatsky's work, she is all allusion and suggestion. She gives few *exact* details, but cites enough sources here to be considered reasonably factual, if over-sensational at times. However, there can be no denying how prophetic are those closing words from *The Secret Doctrine*. For what more fitting epithet could there be than 'a modern Attila' for the man who so soon after began earnestly seeking after the secrets of *Vril Power*, Adolf Hitler?

We have, of course, already gone into all the ramification of Hitler's fascination with the occult and mysticism, and his personal belief in a subterranean world where a race of 'supermen' dwelt. The subject is also dealt with in fascinating detail in J. H. Brennan's *Occult Reich* (1974), in which he discusses the German 'Luminous Lodge of the Vril Society' and how they interested the Fuehrer in their beliefs about *Vril Power*.

Mr Brennan tells us that Hitler was instructed in three important occult secrets, all of which deepened his belief in this mysterious force:

1) The control of a subtle energy, like Lytton's *Vril* or Mesmer's 'animal magnetism'. Once under conscious control, this force can be used as an aid to mystical enlightenment, as a healing agent or as a means to dominate others, depending on the temperament of the initiate.

2) The control of events and the creation of desirable situations on the physical plane. This is done by training the initiate's powers of concentration until he is able to focus his will like a laser. The preternaturally enhanced will-power is then directed by relevant and vivid visualization, usually of the situation that the magician wishes to bring about. The driving force behind the whole operation is heightened emotion. Once again, the *type* of events and situations created depends on the temperament of the initiate.

3) The establishment of lines of communication to super-human and sometimes alien entities held to operate on levels other than the physical (and now generally referred to by occultists as the 'inner planes'). But the neophyte soon discovers that techniques designed to put him in touch, as it were, with the heavens, can equally well be used to contrast the infernal regions.

'On the evidence before us,' says Mr Brennan:

it becomes increasingly likely that Hitler learned all three – and concentrated on the negative aspects of each. We have seen that his control of the subtle energy was of a very high order and survived even the breakdown of his health towards the end of his career. Proof of expertise in the second and most truly 'magical' aspect of occult training is obviously more difficult to obtain. But he certainly *thought* like a magician: his instincts and reactions were those of a man who had undergone the disciplines. His faith in will-power is very well known. Time and again he expressed the belief that all individuals and all situations would yield to a superior will. It should not require pointing out that this is a magical belief, but many historians have missed it.

There need be no doubt at all that Hitler mastered the third occult science. His lines of communication to the inner planes were well established – although psychologists are perfectly at liberty to conclude that the entities he reached were personifications of forces in his deep unconscious.

To support this third contention, Mr Brennan correctly cites the evidence we have already discussed from Hermann Rauschning, the *Gauleiter* of Danzig, who heard from Hitler's own lips of his experiences with the 'supermen'.

It has been suggested in certain quarters that Hitler was not only aware of *Vril Power*, but actually knew how to use it. It is said his ability to mesmerize huge crowds of people, to manipulate those who came into his presence, and draw 'mental nourishment' from the members of his staff like a kind of 'psychic vampire', is evidence of this force being operated. Though these qualities are certainly ones that Hitler possessed, that they stemmed from the utilization of *Vril Power* is not a theory I, personally, can accept. It was more likely the terrible aura of uncontrolled power and fear which surrounded him that bred, unchecked, these capabilities.

Francis King has perhaps best explained this phenomena in his *Satan and the Swastika* (1976):

> In psychological terms, Adolf Hitler was one of those rare individuals who have developed the capacity to fill themselves with energy derived from others, to expand emotional force in a physical experience – a public appearance in his case – and yet to end up with a greater charge of emotional energy than they possessed at the beginning of the experience.
>
> Such a psychological expression of the effects of an audience upon Hitler is more a description of that particular aspect of his character than an explanation of it. No psychological theory is, in fact, capable at the present time of providing such an explanation, and until it can one should at least consider the interpretation of Hitler's energization-by-audience put forward by some occultists.

It seems evident that Hitler, like many of those before him, was frustrated in his desire to unlock the secrets of *Vril Power*, although I have recently been able to examine copies of certain strange documents which once belonged to initiates of the German Vril Society. These purport to show that the members *had* pierced the mystery.

The documents claim that once a person has learned the control of *Vril Power*, he will have the ability to acquire all other powers. And this 'control' can apparently be done in either of two ways.

The first of these is described as 'The Scientific Way'. This requires the person seeking *Vril Power* to chemically isolate the particles of Proton Al which are contained in lead. Then, says the instructions, they must be 'captured in the photonic magnetism of Saturn or else in lava which has issued from an active volcano'. Next, under the effect of the radiations obtained from this process, 'the male sex glands activate all the *Korlos*, and confirm the ego in its physical centre of gravity.' *Vril Power* is now at the adept's fingertips, according to the documents.

The second method, described as 'The Mystic Way', is equally peculiar and baffling. It is apparently derived from a 'Higher Magic Ritual' performed before a *mandala* (or symbol) representing Shamballah, as the world-centre of Agharti. The adept should be bathed in a violet-coloured light made by an amethyst with 'the sound vibrations of the letter K endlessly repeated'. The documents indicate that the power can be more easily obtained if the sign of Saturn is present as well as the *Ankh*, the Egyptian ansate cross – a T-shaped cross with a loop above the horizontal bar – symbolizing life. During the ritual the initiate will 'effect a symbolic regression of life' before finding himself possessed of the miraculous powers of *Vril* the documents end.

If both these 'methods' tend to sound to the reader rather like the mumbo-jumbo associated with medieval witchcraft spells, then it is a feeling also shared by the author. However, as I am not a practising mystic – nor can I claim profound knowledge of the secrets of mysticism – I would not hastily denounce the documents or the 'secrets' they describe as complete nonsense. Rather, I think, they contain elements of truth presented in a disguised fashion to intrigue the casual reader while retaining the original secrets sacrosanct – if these were ever actually known. It is a very typical ploy found among similar allegedly secret occult and mystical documents which have somehow found their way into the public eye.

My belief is further substantiated by the fact that the explanation as to what *Vril Power* is, and how it may be obtained, is both easier to find and less elaborate to achieve, albeit without all the capabilities which Bulwer Lytton and other even more imaginative writers have suggested it possesses.

For my researches have shown that *Vril* is actually an ancient Indian name for the tremendous resources of energy which are made available as a result of mastering the Etheric Body (or Time Organization) and control of the life forces in the human body. It is, in essence, the control of what Bulwer Lytton called 'the one great fluid pervading all nature' and which the Hindu mystics call Kundalini. If I explain as concisely as I can the definition and complexities of Kundalini I think the reader will see how *Vril* is simply the attainment of this personal inner power force developed to its highest level. He will understand too, why Bulwer Lytton described it as the finest attribute of his superior subterranean race and why it has been much sought after by mankind.

As anyone who has made even the most cursory study of Indian mysticism – and its Tantric philosophies in particular – will know, trying to define any elements is extremely difficult because of the demand for great study and concentration under the teaching of a guru to attain the state of mind or body in question. Such is very much the case with Kundalini, which might, very simply, be described as a potential source of immense power lying dormant in man, represented by a tiny coiled serpent, which can be used for great good, but can be extremely dangerous if aroused without due care and attention. Perhaps as good a definition as any is to be found in Ajit Mookerjee and Madhu Khanna's *The Tantric Way* (1977), where they write:

> The Kundalini is the microcosmic form of universal energy or, more simply, the vast storehouse of static, potential psychic energy which exists in latent form in every being. It is the most powerful manifestation of creative force in the

human body. The concept of Kundalini is not peculiar to tantras but forms the basis of all yogic practices, and every genuine spiritual experience is considered to be an ascent of this power. The Kundalini is described as lying 'coiled', 'inactive' or in 'trance sleep' at the base of the spine, technically called the Muladhara Chakra or root centre, blocking the opening of the passage that leads to the cosmic consciousness in the brain centre. In most cases the Kundalini may lie dormant all through one's lifetime, and an individual may be unaware of its existence.

According to Mookerjee and Khanna, the closest parallel to this concept in modern terms is what behavioural scientists term the gap 'between our potential and actual self'. The findings of these scientists have shown that the average individual uses only 10% of his capacities, while the greater part of his potentialities, talents and abilities remain unrealized. However, the authors say that Kundalini should not be confused merely with a person's creative capacities, but should be conceived as a 'force which has the potency to awaken an undeniable psychic power inherent in all of us'. They add:

No tangible description of the Kundalini in symbolic or physiological terms will suffice, for it is a highly potential ultra-subtle vibration which eludes the 'surgeon's knife'. However elusive its nature, its efficacy can be judged only by experiencing it and the effect its arousal produces in the human body.

Many Western authorities have tried to describe the attainment of the power, but few better than Sir John Woodroffe in his various works on the Tantras, including *Shakti and Shakta* (1920), which devotes a whole section to the topic and from which I have drawn my broad outline, with due acknowledgement. Sir John begins by explaining that the Hindus believe that man is a microcosm – 'Whatever exists in the outer universe exists in him also.' He goes on:

The body may be divided into two main parts, namely the head and trunk on one hand, and the legs on the other. In man the centre of the body is between these two at the base of the spine where the legs begin. Supporting the trunk and throughout the whole body is the spinal cord. This is the axis of the body, just as Mount Meru is the axis of the earth. Hence man's spine is called Merudanda, the Meru or axis-staff.

Linked to this spinal cord are a number of invisible ganglia rather like veins, radiating out through the whole body. These strands come together at certain points, also connecting with the physical body, which are known as *Chakras* or 'wheels'. These *Chakras* are, quite simply, believed to be centres of super-physical energy, says Sir John, and may be thought of as 'psychic dynamos'. Although these 'wheels' have no tangible existence, they are said to be seven in number and situated as follows: one near the base of the spine, one close to the sex organs, another in the region of the solar plexus, the next close to the heart, the fifth by the throat, the sixth in the forehead above the bridge of the nose, and the final one on the crown of the head.

All of the *Chakras* are arranged along a shaft which can be imagined to run from the base of the spine to the top of the head. This shaft is referred to as the 'Rod of Brahma'. (Could this be the origin of Bulwer Lytton's '*Vril* Rod'?) At the base of the spine lies the Kundalini, the small, coiled serpent, as the Tantras describe it, which when made manifest releases great powers. What occurs in the wrong circumstances has been graphically described by Benjamin Walker in his recent work, *Hindu World* (1968):

In the astral body of the average person the Kundalini lies asleep, with its head blocking the central channel, the sus-humma of the 'Rod of Brahma', the 'gateway of ascent'; the man is left undisturbed by its presence and indeed unaware of its existence. This is all to the good. For the ordinary man it is important that the serpent should remain dormant, since it has a tremendous power when aroused. If disturbed, accidentally or by recourse to techniques ignorantly applied to awaken it, this force can prove very dangerous. Then the Kundalini raises its head and begins to move about in a dis-organised manner, raging unrestrained through the lower *Chakras* and causing an abnormal excitation of the baser instincts and passions.

However, when the awakening of Kundalini is achieved by

the discipline and practice which is necessary, a 'transformation and reorientation of the supreme power in the human body' occurs according to Mookerjee and Khanna:

> By activating its ascent it transcends our limitations. When the Kundalini sleeps man is aware of his immediate earthly circumstances only. When she awakes to a higher spiritual plane, the individual is not limited to his own perception but instead participates in the source of light. Thus in her ascent, the Kundalini absorbs within herself all the kinetic energy with which the different psychic centres are charged. By awakening the Kundalini's dormant force, otherwise absorbed in the unconscious and purely bodily functions, and directing it to the higher centres, the energy thus released is transformed and sublimated until its perfect unfolding and conscious realisation is achieved.

In the simplest terms, this unfolding opens up vast dormant areas of the brain – for it is a neurological fact that we only use a small percentage of the total capacity of our brains – and with it the attainment of supernatural powers, which the Hindus call *Siddhis*. There are said to be eight great *Siddhis*, and they seem to me to relate closely to those 'powers' or 'forces' credited to *Vril Power*. Mookerjee and Khanna have listed them as: mastery over the elements; the power of leaving and re-entering the body at will; supernormal hearing; weightlessness; the power to see things of the minutest size as well as enlarging the conceptions so that one can understand the functions of the solar system and the universe; the control of mind over matter; and, perhaps most significantly of all, the power to generate great motive forces.

It is no purpose of mine in a book such as this to even attempt to describe the complex technique required to awaken this 'coiled serpent', merely to indicate that it requires great learning, super-concentration, bodily control (including, especially, breathing and eye-focusing) and enormous discipline. For as Benjamin Walker has written:

> Those who wish to further their knowledge of Kundalini by practical experience, or who desire to achieve the powers that the aroused Kundalini engenders, have to submit to a long period of preparation, for the ability to control the

released force takes many years of arduous training to acquire.

To anyone who reads these pages and feels such a desire, I can only recommend the literature on the Tantric and Yoga doctrines as a starting point.

Yet it is surely not unreasonable to assume that the attributes I have listed would naturally be those of initiates of a high order, or the members of a super-race far advanced in their civilization? If such a race *does* exist beneath the surface of our world, is it not well within the realms of probability that they would have long ago achieved such a state of being, having never been distracted with the problems of numerous wars, conflicting political systems and social unrest which have beset all the nations of the surface world for centuries?

To conclude, then, I believe the practice of Kundalini may be the key to *Vril Power*. It certainly bears striking similarities to what we know of the strange force Bulwer Lytton brought so dramatically to our notice. If, as an initiate, he concealed and disguised some of its attributes, this is understandable and does not, I believe, detract from the validity of my assumptions. I therefore leave it to the reader to reach his own conclusions, for it is now time to return to trying to solve the remaining mysteries about the much more tangible world of Agharti and its subterranean tunnels. Once again, we shall be discovering some remarkable facts which lead to still more surprising conclusions . . .

Chapter 12

THE DISCOVERY OF SHANGRI-LA!

We are now nearing the end of our journey in search of the lost world of Agharti. In the foregoing pages I have, I trust, fully detailed the ancient traditions associated with the underground kingdom as well as recounting the modern developments in its story, and at the same time presented a wealth of material on the existence of the subterranean passageways which are believed to be linked to it. Much that I have recorded is based on facts that I consider beyond reproach, while the remainder is primarily the result of expert and carefully argued speculation. I think the case for both the reality of Agharti and the tunnel network is a convincing one. But there are still a number of important questions left to be answered.

Firstly, if the tunnels exist and, as the legends say, join the major continents of the world – how could they possibly provide a link between the American continent and those of Africa, Europe and Asia across the enormous fastness of the Atlantic Ocean? Secondly, can we pinpoint the actual locality of the heart of the subterranean world, the magical city of Shangri-La, known as Shamballah? And, thirdly, is there any evidence in our modern science that it is feasible for such an underground world to have been constructed at any age in the past and permit the existence of people in conditions so different to those in which we, the surface dwellers, live?

In the pages which follow, I shall endeavour to offer you positive answers to all of these questions.

To begin with, I should like to try to unravel the mystery of the tunnel network. As the reader will see from the map on the endpapers of this book, I have come to the conclusion from my researches that these passageways *did* exist and that the main artery followed the route I have marked. (I shall also mention the possibility of some diversions linking other countries in due course.) The reader will immediately appreciate from this that it is my belief, firstly, that the passageways provided communication between North America and Asia beneath the narrow strip of sea about fifty miles wide known as the Bering Strait. A perfectly feasible claim, I think, and one supported by the traditions of the Eskimos living there. In this context, Robert Ernest Dickhoff has written;

> Let no one underestimate the importance, the value, the existence, of these tunnels, especially those still open for use by such as know of their whereabouts . . . It is through them that the Eskimos travelled from Asia to Alaska and Canada. They claimed that they did not use a surface method of immigration as historians wish to put it, but these Eskimos insist that underground passageways connecting both Asia and the American continent running beneath the Bering Strait were used to accomplish the waves of migration.

However, while this may be a perfectly acceptable explanation as far as the Bering Strait is concerned, at the southern end it is a very different matter altogether, because here the distance between South America and the nearest landmass, Africa, is two thousand miles. Yet I believe the tunnel network *did* once link two mighty continents – *by way of the lost continent of Atlantis!*

It is my conviction that, in fact, these tunnels had no further to travel below sea than those in the Bering Straits, covering only a few dozen miles before reaching the landmass of Atlantis, where they continued in conditions no different to those anywhere else in the world. This is, of course, the hardest part of my hypothesis to prove, for the destruction of Atlantis obviously caused the obliteration of this part of the system. But without saying any more, let me tell you how I reached this no doubt surprising conclusion.

I came across the first clue on which I built my theory quite by chance come years ago when reading an ancient history book called the *Oera Linda Boch*. Written over a period of almost 500 years, but primarily by a Frisian named Ovira Linda in AD 803, the book is a compendium of historical records and facts collected from all over Europe assembled from both oral traditions and ancient manuscripts. In one of the later sections, evidently written by a descendant of the first author, a man called Hiddo Oera Linda, there is an appeal to the reader to 'keep these books with your body and soul'. And as I glanced over the pages, something else caught my eye which made me read on with growing interest:

> In these books are the histories of all our people, and of our forefathers. Last year I saved them in the flood . . . But they got wet and so began to perish. In order not to lose them I copied them on foreign paper. When you inherit them you must likewise copy them, and your children must do so, too. They may, therefore, never be lost.

Fascinating though these words were, it was the postscript beneath which really excited my interest: 'written in Liuwert (Ljuwert) in the 3,499th year after Atland (Atlantis) sank, or 1256, the year of the Christian reckoning.' Having long been intrigued by the legend of Atlantis, I continued to flip over the pages, reading about the exploits of the Frisian people and their contact with the rest of Europe.

A bit further on I came across another reference to Atlantis, but this time with an even more exciting reference. The writer of the *Oera Linda Boek* here said that Atland (or Atlantis) was destroyed when 'the Earth trembled, the heavens grew dark, and there were heavy explosions and reverberation of thunder.' At this, the King of Atlantis 'lead those of his people who were not destroyed through *tremendous and very ancient tunnels* to the land of Votan' (my italics).

In the edition of the *Oera Linda Boek* which I was reading (a translation made by William R. Sandbach in 1876) there was a footnote which explained that the 'land of Votan' was, in fact, Central America. So here was an early mention of a link between Atlantis and South America – a fact which I think further strengthens my earlier chapter on this topic – but more importantly a clear indication that the two continents had been linked by 'tremendous and very ancient tunnels'. It was a discovery never far from my mind when I came to research the legend of Agharti.

The second piece of evidence I found appeared in Harold Bayley's remarkable volume *Archaic England* (1919) and came to light when I was already at work on this book. Although I had not even begun to formulate my theory, there was something in one of his paragraphs which stopped me dead in my tracks. He wrote:

It is now well known that there was communication between the East and West long before America was discovered by Columbus, and there is nothing therefore improbable in the Chiapenese tradition that their Votan, after settling affairs in the West, visited Spain and Rome. The legend relates that Votan 'went by the road which his brethren, the Culebres, had bored.'

Here was a remarkable statement indeed. Clearly the road which the Culebres had 'bored' could only be a reference to a tunnel, and any tunnel which enabled a person in South America to visit Spain and Rome clearly must traverse the Atlantic Ocean. The reference in the *Oera Linda Boek* flashed into my mind with its talk of Atlantis linked by tunnels to the land of Votan. Had I stumbled upon the answer to an age-old mystery? The reason why there were uncanny similarities in the cultures of the peoples living on opposite sides of the Atlantic?

Harold Bayley went on to explain in his book that although it was difficult to establish who the Culebres of this Mexican tradition were, this should not detract from the probability of tunnels having once been built by people who lived either permanently or temporarily in Africa. He says:

The allusion to a road which the Culebres had bored might be dismissed as a fiction were it not for the curious fact mentioned by Livingstone that tribes lived underground in Rua: 'Some excavations are said to be thirty miles long and have running rills in them; a whole district can stand siege therein as long as required.'

Mr Bayley also tells us that he is totally convinced about the existence of Atlantis:

I incline to the opinion that Plato's story was well founded, and that the identities found in Peru and Mexico, Britain, the Iberian Peninsula, and North Africa, are due to these countries, like the Isles of the Mediterranean, being situated in the full sweep of Atlantian influence.

A third book in which I found further confirmation of my

now growing belief in the Atlantean tunnel system was Harold Wilkins's *Mysteries of Ancient South America* (1946), which I have already cited. He writes:

> A curious tradition of the old world of Asia, is that old Atlantis had a network of labyrinthine tunnels and passages running in all directions, in the day when the land-bridge between the drowned land and Africa, on one side, and old Brazil, on the other, still existed. In Atlantis, the tunnels were used for necromantic and black magic cults.

On what grounds Mr Wilkins makes his final deduction, I have not been able to ascertain, but he seems in no doubt about the existence of the intercontinental tunnel system.

Although it is not my intention to go into detail about the various similar artifacts and signs which have been found on opposite sides of the Atlantic pointing to a common source of inspiration – the works of Ignatius Donnelly, Colonel A. Braghine and H. S. Bellamy have already covered this in full – I should like to make a few comments about the continent of Atlantis itself to substantiate my belief that it provided a virtual land-bridge between America and Africa. The site of the island has, of course, been given in many different parts of the Atlantic by earlier writers, but I believe that Plato himself, the first great authority, is still the most reliable. Writing in *Critias*, he says:

> At that time, it was possible to cross the sea. There was an island beyond the gateway which, so you tell me, you call the Pillars of Hercules. This island was larger than Libya and Asia put together, and travellers could in those days pass from there to other islands, and thence on the far side of the sea, to a continent.

The Pillars of Hercules are of course, the Straits of Gibraltar, and the size of Atlantis as he gives it – 'larger than Libya and Asia' – would clearly occupy much of the ocean between the coasts of Africa and South America. The continent 'on the far side of the sea' is without question America: thus was the land-bridge formed.

My theory of contact with both America and Africa is shared by that redoubtable writer on ancient mysteries, Dr Lewis Spence, who has written several volumes on the lost continent including *The Problem of Atlantis* (1924), *The History of Atlantis* (1926) and *Will Europe Follow Atlantis?* (1942). One of his other books on the theme, *Atlantis in America* (1925), particularly addresses itself to the association between the lost continent and the Americas, and during the course of the book, he writes:

I hold that the occurrence on either side of the Atlantic of a civilisation having certain salient cultural characteristics proves that Europe and Africa on the one hand and America on the other must have received it from a common source – Atlantis. The chief components of this culture-complex are a common tradition of cataclysm, mummification, witchcraft, and certain art-forms and distinctive customs.

Dr Spence cites the evidence of another expert to support this theory:

Professor Edward Hull is of the opinion that 'the flora and fauna of the two hemispheres support the geological theory that there was a common centre in the Atlantic where life began and that during and prior to the glacial epoch great land bridges north and south spanned the Atlantic Ocean. I have made this deduction by a careful study of the soundings as recorded in the Admiralty charts.'

And by way of further proof Dr Spence adds:

An equal wealth of biological evidence regarding a former land connection between European and American soil also exists. The European carnivorous animals of the Tertiary times show a marked affinity with those of America. The burrowing *Amphisbaenidae*, or lizard snakes, are confined, sixty-four species of them, to America, Africa and the Mediterranean region. Kobelt shows conclusively that the land shells on the two opposite sides of the Atlantic imply an ancient connection having subsisted between the Old World and the New, which became ruptured only during the Miocene epoch of the Tertiary Period. Certain ants occur both in the Azores and America. Sixty per cent of the butterflies and moths found in the Canaries are of Mediterranean origin, and twenty per cent of these are to be found in America. Some crustaceans afford the best proof of an ancient connection between Europe and America.

On the similarities to be found in human characteristics, Robert Ernst Dickhoff has this to say:

Consider the enormous distance from ancient Babylon to Mexico, and begin to wonder just how it was possible for two such separated peoples living on separated continents, to have like beliefs and to portray these beliefs when they show pictures carved in stone, speaking of gods humanoid in their physical appearance, half man, half bird, or half man and the rest a serpent. That the spiritual, gifted pre-Mexican people understood the value of symbols is well expressed in their national emblem, which shows an eagle holding a serpent in his beak, and in one of his talons the serpent is rendered helpless. Babylonian – Mexico, the eagle-headed god Ashur holding the serpent god Quetzalcoatl in his beak and renders him helpless, in a land called Mexico [sic] . . . The logical solution to this riddle seems to point to the use of tunnels to explain the above unusual demonstration of a symbolic occurrence bordering on weird spiritual powers, called phenomen. [sic].

Having, I trust, established this land-bridge across the Atlantic, let us now look at the island of Atlantis itself, to which the passageways were linked. I think I need say little of the history of Atlantis, as the story of the destruction of this once mighty and advanced civilization by a holocaust about the year 9600 BC is familiar to every schoolboy. According to Plato's account, the continent must have covered an area of roughly 2,650,000 square miles, or slightly less than that of the continent of Australia.

In his *The History of Atlantis* (1926), Dr Spence gives us a splendid picture of the continent as he believes the evidence shows it to have been:

We must imagine Atlantis, an island nearly the size of Australia, as the seat of a great prehistoric civilisation of very considerable pretensions. A race of fine physique – such physique, indeed, as the world has not since beheld – inhabits it. It celebrates religious ceremonies in large caves decorated with elaborate paintings . . . Its public life circulates and flourishes around these cave temples, and it develops social classes, the protypes of these of the present day.

Dr Spence then presents two viewpoints on the precise location of the lost world – one, his own, and the other that of an earlier writer, both of which place it in the Atlantic between the coasts of South America and North Africa. The first writer, M. Pierre Termier, a French geologist, is quoted extensively, and this is the crucial sentence. 'There was,' he says, 'a South Atlantic, or African-Brazilian continent, extending northward to the southern border of the Atlas, eastward to the Persian Gulf and Mozambique Channel, westward to the eastern border of the Andes and to the sierras of Columbia and Venezuela.' By way of confirmation, M. Termier adds: 'Geologically speaking, Plato's theory of Atlantis is highly probable.'

Dr Spence then examines the evidence himself and concludes:

Supposing it to have lain, as Plato says, directly in front of, and at no great distance from, the Hispano-African coasts, then we must think of a landmass which extended westward at least to the 45th parallel of longitude, and from north to south, nearly from the 45th parallel of latitude to about the 22nd parallel of latitude. This area embraces not only the Azores and the Canary Islands, but much of the Sargasso Sea as well, though not its thickest part, and lies directly above the great banks surrounding the Azores and the Canaries. If we regard the Canaries as its south-eastern extremity (and it could not have come much farther in this direction without touching the African coast), and the Azores as the northern limit of the Atlantean landmass proper and prolong it westwards towards the 45th parallel of longitude, we have not only an area commensurate with that mentioned by Plato, but with those natural features which strikingly demonstrate its former presence.

In an interesting footnote to this argument, Dr Spence draws on even earlier authorities to support his claim and write:

Engel and the Comte de Corli learnedly insisted that the Atlantean boundaries had touched Europe and Africa on one side and America on the other. According to them, man had passed from the Old World to the New by way of an Atlantean land-bridge, the submergence of which had destroyed the ancient communication between the two continents.

So, now, we have the evidence of the landmass which would have made possible a tunnel system bridging that vast area of the Atlantic Ocean. But is there any evidence of such tunnels being built?

In his two works which refer to Atlantis, *Timaeus* and *Critias*, Plato informs us that utilizing their natural resources, 'the Atlanteans built temples, palaces, bridges and tunnels, also directing the waters, which flowed in a triple circle around their ancient metropolis, in a useful manner.' That they were capable of constructing huge underground passageways is surely made evident by the fact – which Plato also tells us – that they were able to build a canal well in excess of 1,000 miles long, parts of which were roofed over!

The claim that such tunnels were indeed created has been argued by an anonymous writer in the ancient history magazine *Papyrus*, in March 1921. He claimed that it was these passageways which enabled the Atlanteans to flee from the holocaust and thus populate much of the rest of the world. In his article, 'Some Notes on the Lost Atlantis', he writes:

> Atlantis sent her children over the entire world. Many of them are to this day living as Red Indians in Canada and the United States of America. They colonised Egypt, and built up one of the mighty Egyptian Empires. They spread over the North of Asia as the Turanians and Mongols – a tremendous and prolific race, still constituting a majority of the population of the earth.

Perhaps, though, the most convincing evidence of the tunnel network emerges when we study the evidence about underground passageways running through the major continents of the world which all unerringly lead to the site of Atlantis – just as they do to the lost world of Agharti. The map makes this evident, I think, but I should like to augment the route with some specific details.

We have, of course, already traced the route through North

and South America, with the tunnel, at its northernmost point, crossing beneath the Bering Strait into Russia. We shall pick it up from there in a moment. At the southern end it is lost in Brazil and from here traverses – as I have shown – what was formerly Atlantis to emerge in Africa. Let us continue the route from this point. Naturally, there is not evidence for every mile of this journey – or else the mystery would not have persisted for so many ages! – yet what we have does enable us to draw an authentic route.

The strongest tradition of subterranean passages in Africa is to be found in the north, as Harold Bayley has written:

> That the Atlanteans colonised the North of Africa is gener-ally supposed, whence it becomes likely that the marvellous excavations at Rua were related to the worship of the serpentine Rhea: these are mentioned by Livingstone who wrote, 'Tribes live in underground houses in Rua. Some excavations are said to be 30 miles long, and have running rills in them: a whole district can stand a siege in them.'

There are also stories of ancient underground tunnels which were once used as hiding places by the natives, to be found in Nigeria, in the district of Wama – an appropriate name which several authorities believe to have derived from the word 'womb'. According to an old legend, there is a tunnel here which stretches for hundreds of miles 'unto the sea'. As the nearest sea is the Atlantic Ocean, this in all probability indi-cates that the point at which the African tunnel made its crossing to Atlantis was somewhere along the west coast of the continent in the vicinity of Guinea.

This is not all the evidence of tunnels in Africa, for as Harold Bayley also tells us:

> The existence of underground ways seems to be not infre-quent in Africa, for Captain Grant, who accompanied Captain Speke in his exploration for the source of the Nile, tells of a colossal tunnel or subway bored under the river Kaoma. Grant asked his native guide whether he had ever seen anything like it elsewhere and the guide replied, 'This country reminds me of what I saw in the country to the south of lake Tanganyika': he then described a tunnel or subway under another river named also Kaoma, a tunnel so

lengthy that it took the caravan from sunrise to noon to pass through. This was said to be so lofty that if mounted upon camels the top could not be touched: 'Tall reeds the thickness of a walking-stick grew inside; the road was strewed with white pebbles, and so wide – 440 yards – that they could see their way tolerably well while passing through it. The rocks looked as if they had been planed by artificial means.'

Such evidence leaves me in no doubt of a unique and extremely lengthy passageway traversing Africa which was certainly not the handiwork of the indigenous population.

The trail next leads us to Egypt, and that collection of wonders of the ancient world, the pyramids around Cairo. For here at El Giza, there is said to be a tunnel which actually has an entranceway concealed in the basement of one of the pyramids. Once found, this doorway provides 'a tunnel running clear to Tibet' according to an old account. The belief in a subterranean world is firmly entrenched in Egyptian lore, and one of the main panoply of gods was Osiris, Lord of the Underworld. The tunnel system in question is also claimed to be referred to in this reference in the ancient *Book of the Dead*: 'I am the offspring of yesterday; the tunnels of the Earth have given me birth and I am revealed at my appointed time.'

Dr Raymond Bernard, that expert on Agharti we met earlier, has made a special study of the tunnels in Egypt and firmly believes in their link with both the subterranean kingdom and lost Atlantis. He has written:

A tunnel that opens at the base of the pyramids in Egypt is claimed to go on in the direction of South Africa for a distance of 900 kilometres. Another tunnel that opened on the west coast of Africa was claimed to go underwater to the site of the vanished Atlantis. This same tunnel also goes in the opposite direction to another city, claimed to be the capital of the network of subterranean passages.

It is probable that the gigantic statues believed to be early Egyptian kings were really Atlantean gods or supermen dwelling in the Subterranean World, with whom the early Egyptian kings were in contact. A tunnel connected with the subterranean chamber of the Pyramid of Gizeh [Giza] connected Atlantis with its Egyptian colony, and it was through this tunnel that the god-kings of Atlantis appeared among the Egyptians in their immense temples.

Still in the context of Egypt, a curious story is related by Harold Wilkins about a French explorer named Monsieur Frot, who in 1938 claimed that there was evidence to be found in Bolivia of ancient Egyptian excursions into South America. M. Frot said he had discovered an inscribed stone on an old Carthaginian trail that 'proved that the ancestors of the Egyptians, long before they passed to Africa and the Nile, had established an ancient South American empire, ranging from what is now Bolivia to Bahia'. The Frenchman apparently disappeared somewhere on the Mato Grosso shortly afterwards without adding further to this theory – which, if we are prepared to accept it, does seem to add further evidence of concourse between Africa and South America by people who must surely have been Atlanteans!

We next pick up details about the tunnel system in India where, as I related much earlier in the book, the French Orientalist Louis Jacolliot first secured information on the kingdom of Agharti and presented it to Western readers. Not wishing to repeat what has gone before, just let me quote from Eric Norman's book *The Hollow Earth*, which summarizes the Indian tradition:

> There is an ancient legend among the Hindus of India that tells of a civilisation of immense beauty beneath central Asia. Several underground cities are said to be located north of the Himalayan mountains, possibly in Afghanistan, or under the Hindu Kush. This subterranean Shangri-la is inhabited by a race of golden people who seldom communicate with the surface world. From time to time, they travel into our land through tunnels that stretch in many directions. Entrances to the tunnels are believed to be hidden in several of the ancient cities of the Orient. Tunnel entrances are said to be in Ellora and the Ajanta caverns in the Chandore Mountain range of India.

We have now almost homed in on the heart of the subterranean passageways, the city of Shamballah, but before doing so we must also trace the remaining part of the tunnel system – that which runs from the Bering Strait across Russia, Siberia, Mongolia and China.

Ferdinand Ossendowski and Nicholas Roerich have already given us a clear picture of the knowledge existing in the USSR concerning Agharti, and so we can go immediately to one of the two most important sites in the country, at Kilyma near the Cherskiy Range of mountains. Here, several hundred miles from the Bering Strait, a network of tunnels exists that have scarcely been explored since they were first discovered during the last century. The passageways have been known about for hundreds of years, but had always been regarded simply as large caves until explorers found that they stretched away endlessly beneath the mountains in a generally southwesterly direction.

Inspection of the tunnels along a considerable distance made it evident that while some stretches had clearly been formed naturally, there were other parts that had received the attention of human hands. Where this had occurred the surface of the wall was almost smooth, as if it had been bored by some kind of machinery.

These tunnels, which I believe run on to Mongolia and beyond, are very similar to another system discovered less than a quarter of a century ago in Azerbaijan. There, strange noises and lights which seemed to emanate from a bottomless well caused Soviet scientists to investigate and stumble upon 'a whole network of tunnels, which turned out to be linked with others in Georgia and throughout the Caucasus' according to Peter Kolosimo in his book *Timeless Earth* (1968). He writes of this discovery:

These were at first thought to be prehistoric caves: near their mouths were found graffiti and human remains, but on inspection it turned out that the bones were of much later date than the drawings. It was also discovered that most of the caves led to tunnels carved in the mountainside . . . One large tunnel, which it was possible to follow for a considerable distance, led to a spacious underground hall or piazza more than 65 feet high. Clearly this was the work of intelligent beings, but for what purpose? No clue has yet been found; the answer to the mystery may lie further on, in the blocked portion of the tunnels.

Mr Kolosimo is, I believe, right in his assumption, and even more right – though he may not realize it – in what he writes next in his book. 'The main entrances to these tunnels are regular in form,' he says, 'with handsome straight walls and narrow arches. The most curious fact about them is that they are almost identical with similar tunnels in Central America.'

And so they should be, as they form part of the same global network!

Mr Kolosimo tells us that some Soviet archaeologists believe that the tunnels are part of a huge network stretching out towards Iran and perhaps linked with those discovered near the Amu Darya in Turkmenistan and on the Russo-Afghan border. 'Or even', he adds, 'the underground labyrinths of central and Western China, Siberia and Mongolia.'

In Siberia there are stories of subterranean passages in the area of the Altai Mountains with their snowbound and dangerous passes. Somewhere close, a place called Ergor is said to be an entrance to what the local people call *Belovodye* – The Blessed Land, their interpretation of Agharti.

According to an article by T. Beloshinov, 'The History of Belovodye', in *The Journal of the Western Siberian Geographical Society* in 1916, people in the area believe implicitly in the legend and say that the underground kingdom is an 'earthly paradise where there are no persecutions'. Apparently an old man told the author: 'If despite all the dangers your spirit is ready to reach this spot, the people of *Belovodye* will greet you, and, should they find that you are worthy, they may even permit you to remain with them. This rarely happens, however, and many people have tried to reach *Belovodye*.'

Commenting on these remarks Beloshinov says: 'These old believers made great efforts to find this fairy land; for some time Altai came to be looked upon as *Belovodye*, but gradually the legendary realm began to move in the direction of the Himalayas.'

Moving south into Mongolia we find that the tradition of an 'earthly paradise' is even stronger. Robert Dickhoff reports:

Tribes of Inner Mongolia believe that Agharti is a creation of an antediluvian civilisation, incredibly old and located in a recess of Afghanistan, and that this mysterious city is linked by means of tunnels coming from different regions of the world.

Nicholas Roerich was convinced that not only the local people and learned lamas knew about this mysterious kingdom, but also members of the government, although they in particular were reluctant to speak about the matter to outsiders. Roerich also collected a folk tale at Ulan Bator about some strange stone circles which were supposed to mark one of the openings to Agharti. Pointing to the stones, an old man told him:

Here the Chud went under the earth. When the White Tsar came to our Altai and when in our region the white birchwood began to bloom, the Chud did not wish to remain under the White Tsar. They went underground and closed the passage with mighty stones – there, can you see it? But the Chud did not go forever. When a new era will come, when the people from *Belovodye* will return and will give to the people a new knowledge then the Chud will come back with all acquired treasures.

Roerich tells us that the Gobi Desert has long been associated with the legend of Agharti, and there are those who think the capital city, Shamballah, lies beneath its sands. He adds: 'In Mongolia we were not astonished to find many signs about Shamballah. In these countries psychic powers are rather developed.'

However, on the southeastern edge of the Gobi, in Chinese territory, there is positive evidence of subterranean passageways. The place in question is called Tunhwang, and it sits on the very borders of Tibet.

Located in rocky terrain about sixteen kilometres to the north of the city is an artificial series of grottoes known as 'The Caves of the One Thousand Buddhas'. They were constructed at some time between AD 357 and 384, when Buddhism came to China, and were to serve as a monument to the religion. What makes the caves fascinating from our point of view is that a concealed stairway leads from one of the grottoes into a labyrinth of tunnels which disappear in Stygian gloom in a due south direction. This fact clearly fascinated Peter Kolosimo, whom I quoted earlier, for in another of his books, *Not of The World* (1969), he writes:

> It is said that the first caverns were not actually built by Buddhist monks but by someone who had preceded them by thousands of years; and such structures must have hidden the entrance to the labyrinths stretching under vast areas of Central Asia. They are the tunnels of the legendary kingdoms of Shamballah and Agharti. It is also said that the first section of the galleries would have been blocked up by the priests to stop bandits getting inside and stealing their hidden treasures.
>
> But there is one certain thing about Tunhwang: in the grotto numbered 58 by the archaeologists there is an altar showing a sleeping Buddha, behind whom are crowds of the faithful, together with good and bad genii. We can ignore the latter as being unknown or simply due to the artists' whims – but there are some which clearly show by their clothes and facial features that they are just like the American Indians!

Is this yet another extraordinary piece of evidence of contact between the American continent and the remote heartland of Asia? It is difficult to find any other explanation.

With these details from China, our circumnavigation of the Earth by way of the subterreanean system is all but complete. We have traced it through the length of America, via Atlantis, to the south and on across Africa, Egypt and India to the Himalayas; and to the north by way of the Bering Straits across Russia, Mongolia, Siberia and China. One country now lies between a junction of these two arteries: the mysterious land of Tibet. And it is below this remote country perched on a barren plateau that I believe the tunnels converge on the subterranean kingdom of Agharti, actually meeting at the place called Shamballah, its fabled and much sought after capital city, the legendary Shangri-la.

Tibet is surely one of the most mysterious places on Earth, and has been shut off from the rest of the world for generations. Although under only nominal Chinese suzerainty from about 1700 to the present century, this claim was made effective in 1951, when the historic ruler, the Dalai Lama, was driven out of the country, and the large percentage of the population who were monks, forced out of their monasteries. In 1965 the Chinese control was made absolute when Tibet was declared an autononous region of China. The veil of secrecy which hangs over the 471,000 square miles of country is now, if anything, more impenetrable than ever.

Already, of course, a number of the experts quoted in this book have made their suggestions as to where Shamballah might be. Some have said it lies in the fastness of the Hindu Kush, others below the hostile sands of the enormous Gobi Desert. A case has been made for poor Afghanistan, recently overrun by Russian forces, and no less than two sites are proposed in China. Robert Dickhoff is in no doubt that it is 'located in the Sangpo Valley, China' though he gives no facts to support his claim, while Eric Norman quotes an American explorer named 'Doc' Anderson who says the entrance lies beneath 'seven pyramids (?) near Sian-fu, the capital of Shensi province'. Apparently an old Chinese lama told Anderson that the secrets of Agharti were concealed in these mysterious structures. 'He said there were tunnel entrances beneath the pyramids. The tunnels are said to connect up with the pyramids in Egypt, the highest monasteries, and they run under the oceans to connect every land.'

Reasonable though most of these suggestions are, I am convinced from my own research that Shamballah undoubtedly lies beneath Tibet. More specifically it is below an area at the head of the valley of the River Brahmaputra, one of the few places in the country from which air and water, prime requirements of any underground settlement, may be drawn easily and unobtrusively.

My conviction is based on a detailed study of the classic Tibetan work, *The Way to Shamballah*, written by the Tashi Lama III about three hundred years ago. Only one translation from the Tibetan has ever been made, by the great German Oriental scholar Albert Grunwendel, in 1915. Grunwendel, an expert on both China and Tibet, and the author of two classic works on the mystical beliefs of the countries, *Mythologie du Buddhisme au Tibet et en Mongolie* (1900) and *Altbuddhist: Kultstatten in Chinesisch-Turkestan* (1912), was an ideal person to tackle a translation of the Tashi Lama's book. For its mixture of geographical hints and symbolic allusions make it a difficult work to read and even harder to interpret, and it is

Grunwendel's helpful notes that actually make it possible to draw positive conclusions. Nicholas Roerich, who also studied the book, has written as follows of the complexities facing the seeker after Shamballah:

> In the east, they know that there exist two Shamballahs – an earthly and an invisible one. Many speculations have been made about the location of the earthly Shamballah. Certain indications put this place in the extreme north, explaining that the rays of Aurora Borealis are the rays of the invisible Shamballah. This attribution to the north is easily under-stood – the ancient name of Shamballah is Chang-Sham-bhala, and this means the Northern Shamballah. The epithet of this name is explained as follows: The teaching originally was manifested in India where everything coming from beyond the Himalayas is naturally called the North.
>
> Several indications, blended in symbols, have put the position of Shamballah on the Pamir, in Turkestan or Central Gobi . . . This relativity and the many misconcep-tions of these geographical locations of Shamballah have quite natural reasons. In all books on Shamballah, in all verbal legends, speaking of the same place, the location is described in a most symbological language, almost unde-cipherable to the uninitiated. Only great knowledge of old Buddhist places and of local names can help you to disen-tangle somehow this complicated web.

Undeterred by these pitfalls, however, I worked methodic-ally through the German translation and finally discovered what I believe are the important clues to the location of Shamballah.

Firstly, the Tashi Lama is quite specific in his book that the underground kingdom lies 'in a valley to the west of Lhasa' and makes a number of enigmatic references in this context to a large community called 'Mount Sumeru' somewhere in the vicinity. By looking at a map of Tibet, it is not difficult to spot the valley running to the west of the capital city, that of the River Brahmaputra. On the banks of this picturesque river, about 150 miles from Lhasa, stands Shigatze, the second largest town in Tibet, with its immense fort spread out across the valley and the magnificent monastery of Tashi Lhunpo. A little research establishes that the name of Shigatze means 'a glorious mass' or 'Mount Sumeru' – the explanation, surely, of the Tashi Lama's reference? 'Mount Sumeru', apparently, was a legendary mountain in Buddhist Scriptures.

Secondly, the Tashi Lama declares that Shamballah is 'bounded on its further side by a sacred lake'. By tracing up the valley of the Brahmaputra beyond Shigatze we can again find the 'sacred lake' he clearly describes: Lake Manasarowar. This stretch of water, octagonal in shape and covering an area of about 100 square miles, is said to be the highest body of fresh water in the world, its elevation being about 15,500 feet above sea-level. It is called simply *Tso Rinpoche* (Sacred Lake) by the Tibetans, and it has a special place in Hindu mythology because within a radius of a few miles rise four of the greatest rivers of India, the Indus, the Sutlej, the Ganges, and, of course, the Brahmaputra. If I had any doubts that this *was* the lake, these were dispelled by the Tashi Lama's further reference to a 'holy mountain in whose shadow it stood'. For on the northwestern corner of Manasarowar stands Kailas Parbat, or Peak, esteemed by the lamas and towering above the other mountains lying to the north of the lake. It rises about 7,000 feet above the surrounding plain, is snowcapped, and is said to have a number of caves and ravines about its base.

Thirdly, and perhaps most importantly of all, the Tashi Lama says that it was through openings in a holy mountain that 'certain lamas have met with the holy men of Shamballah in days gone by'. Once again by diligent research I found confirmation that I had not been mistaken in my calculations. In Captain C. G. Rawling's classic study of the locality, *The Great Plateau* (1905), was a description of Kailas Perbat which said: 'This spot is believed by Hindus and Mahomedans alike to be the home of all the gods, that of the waters of its lake they drink, and that *in its unexplored caverns they dwell;* to them it is *the* Holy Mountain.'

All the clues I had unearthed seemed to tie in perfectly with the holy lama's words, and I was sure I had found the locality of Shamballah – lying beneath the Brahmaputra Valley, bounded by Shigatze to the east and Lake Manasarowar to the west. There seemed every indication, also, that there was an entranceway to the underground city in Kailas Parbat. In a second book I consulted as a result of my careful examination of Grunwendel's translation, I found another reference which further strengthened my belief, The work was *Three Years in Tibet*, by the Japanese Theosophist Ekai Kawaguchi, published in 1909. In describing Manasarowar and its environs he wrote:

> It is the only real paradise on earth, with a living Buddha and five hundred saints inhabiting Mount Kailasa on its north-west, and five hundred immortals making their home on Man-ri, that rises on its southern shore, all enjoying eternal beatitude . . . I believe that anybody would desire to see the spot; but the things mentioned in the Scriptures cannot be seen with our mortal eyes. The real thing is the region in its wonderfully inspiring character and an unutterably holy elevation is to be felt there.

Knowing what we do of the Theosophists and their belief in Agharti, Shamballah and the King of the World, does this not seem like another clear indication that someone else also shares my conviction?

Such facts, I believe the reader will agree, present a very strong possibility that the heart of the subterranean world of Agharti lies directly beneath this area of Tibet. It is only to be regretted that until the country is once more open to visitors from the West, neither I nor anyone else will be able to put this theory to the test.

However, whether this solution answers the mystery or not, we still have some unresolved issues concerning the underground world to consider. In particular the tunnels which converge on Agharti. Is it possible that human beings *could* have used the passageways to cover the enormous distances we know are involved, and if so, by what means of transport? And, more importantly, who could such people have been, and what modern evidence might there be of their continued existence? And, finally, who is the mysterious ruler of the kingdom known only as 'The King of the World'?

These are the points which I propose to examine in the final chapter of our strange story.

Chapter 13

THE REALM OF 'THE KING OF THE WORLD'

During the years in which I was researching this book, I occasionally came across references to subterranean passageways in connection with Agharti which, at the time, seemed to be far away from the global route I traced in the previous chapter. It would, of course, have been convenient to ignore these stories, to assume that they were not in any way associated with the subject I was investigating. Yet there was something about a group of them which told me I would be being less than honest if I took this course of action. So I filed away those various pieces of information, deciding to return to them at the conclusion of my inquiries.

Now that I have had a chance to look back over the references concerning these out-of-the-way underground tunnels, a startling conclusion seems likely to me. That the tunnel system to Agharti might just have a number of subdivisions which give it access to an even wider area of the Earth's surface! It seems probable that these diversions may have been constructed to lead off from the main network and thereby link more countries on the major continents to the 'golden road', as a South American legend describes the main tunnel system to Agharti. And this fact stated, I can see no reason why Great Britain, as well as its European neighbours France and Germany, are not among those places also linked to the underground kingdom by a secret route. Certainly there is evidence to be found — as well as that extraordinary experience of my own which I recounted right at the start of this book! Let us look, then, at some of these references.

One of the first to catch my eye occurred in a book called *The Mysterious Unknown* by the French archaeologist and journalist Robert Charroux, published in 1969. This proved to be a fascinating collection of strange and secret facts said to be known only to Initiates, and in it the author claimed that man had actually lived on this planet for a very much longer period than was generally supposed: indeed, he was just the latest of many races to inhabit Earth.

In the book, Charroux devotes a chapter to 'The Mystery of Agartha and of Shamballah', in which he writes:

> Agartha is a mysterious subterranean kingdom that is said to lie under the Himalayas and where all the Great Initiators and the Masters of the World in the present cycle are still living. Agartha is an initiatory centre, and is understood to function on a principle similar to that of the pyramids, the Himalayas forming the external monument, and the crypt being the kingdom far removed from earthly and cosmic contamination. But how could the higher powers of the spirit, intensity of thought and contemplation, be developed in a neutralised cavity? All in all, it seems probable that the vast potentialities of the human and super-human ego can manifest more successfully in a secluded retreat than in the open, exposed to the contagion of its surroundings. On the other hand, one might think that, theoretically, perfection had no need to evolve further.

Charroux then follows up this interesting observation with the information:

> Traditionally, there are four entrances to Agartha: one between the paws of the sphinx at Giza, another on the Mont-Saint-Michel, a third through a crevice in the Forest of Broceliande, and the main gate at Shamballah in Tibet.

What struck me immediately about this statement was that while I knew all about two of the entrances – those thousands of miles apart in Egypt and Tibet – it was curious that the remaining two were both in the author's native France! As he did not seek to substantiate the claim with any facts, I decided to make my own inquiries.

In both cases I was disappointed. I could find nothing other than oral traditions to support Charroux's claim of extensive subterranean tunnels beneath the beautiful Mont-Saint-Michel and in the mystery-haunted Forest of Broceliande which might link them with the legend. But, because of the very nature of the puzzle of Agharti, I should stress that this does not mean they do not exist.

However, I did find some more concrete evidence of

enormous tunnels in France in Sabine Baring-Gould's classic work, *Cliff Castles and Cave Dwellings of Europe* (1911). In it he describes how a church at Gapennes in Picardy, 'perhaps one of the most ancient provinces of France', collapsed during the night of 13 February, 1834:

> At first, it was supposed that this was the result of an earthquake, but after a while the true cause was discovered. The church had been erected over a vast network of subterranean passages and tunnels, and the roofs of some of these had given way. This led to an exploration, and the plan of this subterranean world was traced as far as possible.
>
> But Gapennes is not the only place where such passages exist throughout the province. Something like a hundred have been found, and more are every now and then coming to light. Indeed, it may safely be said that there is scarcely a village between Arras and Amiens and between Roye and the sea, between the courses of the Somme and Authie, that does not have these underground tunnels. The character of all is very much the same. To what date, or period, do they belong? Some doubtless are of extreme antiquity.

Earlier commentators than myself have suggested that these subterranean ways might just have some relationship to the ancient legend of Agharti.*

A second book then led me to the possibility that there might be similar tunnels in Germany. It was *The Inner Earth* by Dr M. Doreal, published privately in America in 1946 in the wake of the 'Shaver Mystery' which I referred to earlier. Dr Doreal claimed that there were a number of entrances to the subterranean world, including Tibet, the Gobi Desert, South America (Yucatan), North America (California), Canada, and the Harz Mountains of Germany.

In this underground kingdom, he says, live the remnants of 'a god-race who existed on the earth before the Adamites were

---

* There is also a curious French tradition that from time to time strange noises have been heard in some deep caverns near Marseilles. The historian E. Lucan has written: 'It is reported that the ground is shaken and strangely moved, and that dreadful sounds are heard from the caverns.' It has been suggested that this may have some significance to the Agharti legend because the noises resemble 'throbbing machines' and sometimes flashing green lights are seen in the vicinity: two factors which we shall be examining later in the book.

gases like the British 'Will-o'-the-Wisp', he preferred to believe that they were caused by 'some kind of subterranean metal'. Dr Raymond Bernard and Robert Dickhoff, for their part, have already gone on record in the earlier chapter dealing with Brazil that they believe the green glow to be the means of illumination in Agharti.

I also came across a personal experience of this light which seemed to confirm all the stories. It was reported by Peter Kolosimo in his *Timeless Earth*. He writes:

An explorer in the Amazon jungle is said to have found his way into an underground labyrinth illuminated 'as though by an emerald sun'. He retreated hastily to avoid the clutches of a monstrous spider, but before doing so saw 'shadows like men' moving at the end of a passage.

An experience with a certain similarity to this also happened to an English woman in the completely contrasting locality of an underground cellar, according to W. T. Stead in his *Real Ghost Stories* (1897). The events occurred at the end of the last century, and I quote them here without comment because they have been described by the magazine *Man, Myth and Magic* as a typical example of 'the belief that a low type of subterranean being sometimes appears in astral form on the Earth's surface'. The woman told Stead:

To my great surprise I suddenly saw a peculiar light about six feet from me. In less time than it takes me to write it, I saw this light develop into a head and face of yellowish greenish light, with a mass of matted hair above it. The face was very wide and broad, larger than ours in all respects, very large eyes of green, which, not being distinctly out-lined, appeared to merge into the yellow of the cheeks; no hair whatever on the lower part of the face, and nothing to be seen below. The expression of the face was diabolically malignant, and as it gazed straight at me my horror was as intense as my wonder. I felt that such an awful thing could only be Satanic, so keeping my gaze fixed on the thing, I said to it, 'In the name of Christ, be gone,' and the fiendish thing faded from my sight.

My research also established that the strange rumbling noises which I had been conscious of while in the Yorkshire cave had similarly been reported in other stories about the subterranean world. In Canada, for instance, I discovered accounts by the Eskimos that they had quite often heard 'mysterious drumming sounds' which seemed to emanate from deep, unexplored caves. There are several such tales from Mexico, too, and William Hickling Prescott, who wrote the definitive study, *History and Conquest of Mexico* (1843), says that the natives told him of 'great noises that shake the earth' which they had experienced in the vicinity of the old tunnel networks in Palenque and elsewhere.

Harold Wilkins also came across similar sounds in Mexico, in the ruined cities on the borders of the states of Tehuantepec. He records:

> Here, this *Oohah*, or mysterious drumming, is heard coming from afar over the environing jungle and ranges. One such dead city stands on a *mesa* girdled by cliffs. The region is covered with shrouded pyramids to which lead ancient roadways of massive paved blocks. In vaults of this dead city the Indians of Chiapas say there are hidden, and guarded by the ghosts of Mayan priest-rulers, 'books' written on gold leaves recording the history of ancient things and races of Ante-diluvian, or later Mayan times. Competent exploration is, of course, necessary, before these riddles can be solved.

Wilkins also cites another interesting case about a stone city further south in the mountain wilderness of South-Western Darien:

> Old legend says this stone city (called Dahyba) had a secret *subterranean* temple at the bottom of a cavern, where strange rites of the underworld were performed. No smoke without fire in these legends of mysterious America! A native whisper in Darien says these rites are by no means extinct, nor the subterraneans, today!

Disturbances heard in the vicinity of ancient stoneworks in Peru are also believed to signify 'ancient rituals of subterranean dwellers' according to what Dr John James Von Tschudi, the German geographer, learned during his explorations of the country, and recorded in his book, *Peruvian Antiquities* (1854). Another German explorer, Von Humboldt, who actually heard the noises when in the vicinity of the 'dead city' near Trujillo in Northern Peru in 1820, later theorized that the sound – rather like that of galloping horses – might be caused by changes in temperature or underground waters. This idea has not been supported by subsequent research, however, and the mystery sounds remain unsolved.

In Asia, as Ossendowski reported, mysterious noises carried on the winds and accompanied by the ground trembling are believed to herald some activity of 'The King of the World', and bring both the human and animal worlds to a standstill.

There are other examples of sounds emanating from the vicinity of the subterranean network in Africa, India and certain parts of Russia, but I have no wish to labour the point further. I think the case for the appearance of green lights and mysterious sounds in these passages is now clearly established. But this still does not prove that the kind of enormously long tunnels we are talking about *could* exist. When we consider the extreme difficulties in creating such underground ways even today, with all the modern equipment at our disposal, it seems almost inconceivable that people from a much earlier time than our own could have possessed the necessary skills and equipment. Yet there are experts who are quite convinced they *did*.

There seems little doubt that such a system would need to take advantage of cavities in the rocks below the Earth's surface, and scientific evidence proves that such cavities do exist.* As I noted earlier, the Earth consists of a molten core, and outside it, two main layers. Of these, the one nearer the core is subject to heat and pressure which put the rock in a state of 'flowage', while in the upper, cooler zone 'fracture' can occur.

The possibility of such subterranean cavities has been the subject of some study by Professor Frank D. Adams of

*In support of this statement, I would simply quote from Dr George Hartwig's classic study, *The Subterranean World* (1871), in which he writes of underground tunnels: Many are mere rents or crevices in the disrupted rocks; others wide vaults, not seldom of hall or dome-like dimensions, or long and narrow passages branching out in numerous ramifications. Not seldom the same cave alternately expands into spacious chambers, and then again contracts into narrow tunnels or galleries. The walls of many are smooth and nearly parallel; the sides of others are irregular and rugged. Many have narrow entrances and swell at greater depths into majestic proportions; while others open with wide portals, and gradually diminish in size as they penetrate the rock.'

Montreal, who has shown by actual experiment that the might well exist in granite to a depth of at least eleven miles His findings have been supported by a mathematician, Loui V. King, who has calculated that, at normal temperature, cavity could exist at depths down to between 17·2 and 20· miles.

With the availability of these cavities, and the Earth fault to follow from one to the next, the ancient tunnellers had thei first requirements. But what about the technology of thei mining?

I think Robert Charroux has found an important clue wher he tells us about Eupalinos, who constructed a tunnel i ancient times on the island of Samos:

> The works were begun simultaneously from both ends. Th tunnel is 1,000 yards long, it is absolutely straight and th two teams met each other exactly according to plan. Th French and Italian engineers who tunnelled under Mon Blanc had at their disposal electronic measuring devices radar, magnetic detectors and ultrasonic equipment Eupalinos, as far as we know, did not even have the use of compass.

Should we doubt such a feat of technical engineering, Char roux reminds us:

> Equally astounding from the technical point of view are th basalt sculptures of unknown age discovered in 1939 in th heart of the Mexican jungle – five enormous heads, recall ing the well-known monuments of Easter Island – and othe prodigious works of statuary found in the Andes, Asia an Oceania.

The indefatigable Erich Von Daniken, who, as I reporte earlier, investigated the tunnel system in Ecuador, has n doubt as to how the passageways were built. Describing h experience in *The Gold of the Gods* (1972), which continue his theory that extraterrestrial beings once lived on Earth, h says they were constructed by a kind of *thermal drill*. This the centrepiece of his argument:

> The newly landed astronauts went underground. They du themselves in, created subterranean communication rout

over great distances and built strongpoints deep under the earth that afforded them safety, although they could emerge from them to cultivate areas of their new homeland and include them in the plans for a carefully thought out infrastructure. I can refute the objection that the tunnel-builders must have 'betrayed' themselves by enormous quantities of debris excavated while making the tunnels. As I credit them with an advanced technology, they were presumably equipped with a *thermal drill* of the kind described in *Der Spiegel* for 3 April 1972, which reported it as the latest discovery.

Von Daniken describes how the drill was developed at the US Laboratory for Atomic Research at Los Alamos. It is made of wolfram and heated by a graphite heating element. There is no waste material from the drill, as it melts the rock through which it drills and presses this waste against the walls, where it cools down. He also believes that the ancient tunnellers had an electron ray machine at their disposal. Von Daniken then adds:

> I was stimulated to make these speculations by the tunnel system in Ecuador. Juan Moricz (my guide) thinks that the long straight galleries in particular have glazed walls and that the large rooms were made by blasting. Neatly blasted layers of rock are clearly recognisable at the tunnel entrance, as is the right-angled door blown out of the rock face. The technical care with which the tunnel system was planned is proved by the ventilation shafts that recur at regular intervals. These shafts are all accurately worked and on average are between 5ft 10 ins and 10ft long and 2ft 7 ins wide . . . It was here, in the impenetrable depths, that the 'gods' decided to create men 'in their image', many years later, when they were no longer afraid of being discovered.

Whether or not we can accept that the tunnel system was made by men from space, there can be no disputing the skill of its original builders. Peter Kolosimo, who is also fascinated by the origins of the tunnels, says that one old Tibetan lama who was questioned about them replied: 'Yes, they exist; they were made by giants who gave us the benefit of their knowledge when the world was young.'

There are, indeed, several theories as to who were the original creators of the tunnels, and by association the kingdom of Agharti, and these are worth looking at individually.

The earliest of our speculators, Louis Jacolliot, the Marquis Saint-Yves d'Alveydre, and Madame Blavatsky, were, as we have seen, convinced that the people of the lost world were the remnants of one of the original 'root' races of the world. They had remained in their secret kingdom hidden from the eyes of later men, content with just the occasional contact with surface humanity. With the destruction of Atlantis, their tunnel network was broken and then evidently much less used than in previous ages.

Ferdinand Ossendowski and Nicholas Roerich both incline to the Oriental view of Agharti, that it was founded some 60,000 years ago by a holy man and a tribe of his people who disappeared under the surface of the earth, creating the tunnel system to allow them access to other points of the Earth. As Ossendowski wrote in *Beasts, Men and Gods*:

All the people there are protected against Evil and crimes do not exist within its bournes. Science has there developed calmly and nothing is threatened with destruction. The subterranean people have reached the highest knowledge. Now it is a large kingdom, millions of men, with 'The King of the World' as their ruler. He knows all the forces of the world and reads all the souls of humankind and the great book of their destiny.

Dr Lewis Spence, Harold Wilkins and their contemporaries, who have devoted so much time to the legend of Atlantis, are convinced that the tunnels were built by the Atlanteans and used by them to escape the holocaust that overwhelmed their continent. The survivors then re-established themselves in various parts of the world, although a group of them chose to remain below ground and create a secret kingdom where they felt they would be safe from any future catastrophe.*

*An American writer on prehistory, Brad Steiger, recently commented that this explanation has apparently become widely accepted amongst Occultists. Writing in an article entitled, 'The Smoky God, Deros and Other Dwellers of Inner Earth' (*Strange Magazine*, Vol. 1. No. 3, 1971) he said; 'Occultists interpret Agharti to be a continuation of the civilisation of Atlantis, whose inhabitants are content to remain in their peaceful network of subterranean cities with only occasional excursions to the outer world.'

The theories of the modern writers are even more grandiose. The Buddhist, Robert Dickhoff, says categorically:

The early builders of these tunnels were not of earth, but visitors, colonisers from a world now called Mars. These alien settlers here envisioned competition, and in anticipation of a battle for the possession of the earth the defensive tunnel systems and underground gathering centres or cities were set up, which included Agharti.

In his book, *Agharta*, he also explains how the tunnels were built:

I envision that the straight line is indeed the shortest distance between two given points and also believe the ancient builders were aware of this universal rule, thus incorporating this fundamental idea when boring their tunnels in straight lines from one continent to another in order to accomplish swift communication, transportation, and at the same time enjoy mining this earth for precious metals and for matter which could be converted into fuel for their hungry space crafts, space ships, or whatever you may call these fire-spitting dragons, remembered by all the ancient races of earth, as having descended from the heavens with a cargo of alien creatures from another world.

Dickhoff believes that the actual builders of the tunnels were men of huge stature, and that they are referred to in the Biblical quotation found in Genesis: 'There were giants in the earth in those days.'

Since Genesis mentions these giants or Titans were *in* the earth and not *on* the earth, this must account for their being the actual tunnel diggers, living by necessity in the bowels of the earth, groundhog fashion. Fossils of such giants have been found in Java as being the most primitive man who lived some 500,000 years ago.

He also claims that the Martians themselves went underground permanently after the sinking of Atlantis, and there began the creation of the human race:

The synthetic ones created by their scientific father from Mars soon mingled and interbred with the product of natural evolution on the earth, and the human race was well on its way . . . The human and subhuman race of earth is old, much older than most of us are led to believe.

The Frenchman, Robert Charroux, on the other hand, has written about a claim that the tunnel builders were Venusians! It is not his own theory, he says, but one deduced from the Indian *Vedas* and Tibetan *Bardo Thodol*. Apparently the Venusians came to this planet in the year 701,969 of the era of Lucifer – the name is here used in its literal sense of 'Light Bringer' – and it was they who created the great initiatory centre of Shamballah. Charroux then quotes Paul Gregor, whom he describes as an expert on the subterranean people. Gregor says:

For obscure reasons, they are said to have built tremendous altars, and to have excavated shafts by which to go down into the bowels of the earth, to the core where all the fire and all the water of the earth have their origin, from whence all the streams of lava of all the volcanoes erupt. Down below, among the sombre foundations of the whole universe, the bulk of a people called the Mysterious Builders are believed to have settled.

Charroux says the Theosophists also believe in the Venus theory:

Theosophical Teachers say that the Lords of Venus founded the Grand Lodge of Initiation as soon as they reached the earth; their present dwelling is symbolically called by the ancient name, Shamballah . . . The legend of the subterranean realm where the Masters and the secret archives of the world are kept in security is a glorious reality.

Dr Raymond Bernard shares the more Earthbound ideas of Ossendowski and Roerich that a kind of 'Atlantean Noah' founded the underground kingdom. 'Most of the human population of Agharti,' he says, 'as distinct from the superhuman inhabitants of Hyperborean, Lemurian and Atlantean origin, consist of Hindu Yogis and Tibetan lamas who gained admission as a result of lifelong persevering effort.'

In his book, *The Subterranean World*, Dr Bernard quotes what he calls 'a number of rumours circulating in Brazil'. He says several Brazilians have told him that the kingdom is a kind of Garden of Eden, illuminated by a strange glow, where the men, women and children live almost exclusively on a diet of different kinds of fruits. These people enjoy excellent health, live free from worry, and crime is unheard of. 'They live in a state of perfect continence,' says Dr Bernard, 'with no marriage. The women not only live apart from the men but produce children without need of male fertilization. These people compose a super race whose members never grow old and never die, but live for centuries in a state of youth, in fact for thousands of years.'

By way of example, he paraphrases two accounts that were given to him:

A man came to us and said he entered a subterranean city some distance from Paranagua in South Brazil. It was illuminated and had much fruit – including huge clusters of grapes, a strange fruit not known on the surface, apples and other fruits, which compose the sole diet of the people. He said he entered a subterranean vehicle operated by a strange motive power, which spiralled down until it brought him to the hollow interior of the world, where he beheld the central sun and tall godlike beings (Atlanteans). After visiting this 'New World' he returned to the city. Later he travelled through a tunnel to another subterranean city over a hundred miles away. The entrance of the tunnel had a waterfall of warm water falling in front of it. This was near Iguassu Falls, on the Paraguay border.

In the second account, another Brazilian describes how he travelled through a 'smooth-cut, illuminated tunnel' for three days, twenty hours a day, until he came to an immense illuminated space filled with buildings and a fruit orchard. 'The people who lived there were all an exact copy of each other, with no individual variation,' the narrator told Dr Bernard. 'The sexes lived apart and the women all looked as if in their teens, even though they were centuries old. These women produced children by parthenogenesis, and were all virgin mothers.' The man later returned to the surface world by an exit tunnel, apparently none the worse for his remarkable encounter!

Dr Bernard is quick to point out that he has no proof that

such stories are true, 'since the persons who made them were, in most cases, impelled by monetary motives'. 'But,' he adds, 'in the main they agree with each other regarding (1) these subterraneans cities being illuminated (2) being inhabited by a super race, and (3) connected with each other by a network of tunnels.'

Charles A. Marcoux, the director of the Subsurface Research Center in Phoenix, Arizona, who has been researching the legend of Agharti for twenty years, also believes the inhabitants are of Atlantean stock: fair-skinned, with blue eyes and blonde hair. Despite dwelling underground, they enjoy a subtropical climate, and ventilation is provided by means of the tunnel system and disguised air shafts. He says they also have air purifying machines resembling rotating radar detectors which clear the atmosphere of all impurities:

> This is a 'sweep ray' which literally 'sweeps' the atmosphere of all radio-active elements. Most of them are mobile and have a fan-like antenna, and are designed like a spider web, which draws in the radioactive particles from the air and processes them through filters, which remove all substances harmful to life.

Marcoux claims that these machines not only remove poisons from the air but add to it health-giving substances that have a beneficial effect on both vegetable and human life. The people live mostly on fruit, having a number of varieties unknown on the surface world. 'A white and red grape is common there and is purer than the blue,' he says. 'Melon meats are made into a juice which helps stimulate the mind and makes it more receptive to beneficial thought currents. Bathing is done in natural stream waters which exist there.'

The claims of this remarkable American researcher, which he says are mainly based on 'mind messages' he has received, seem to coincide very much with our idea of a utopian, vegetarian society much concerned with radioactivity and atmospheric pollution.

Perhaps, though, Marcoux's most remarkable claim concerns the method by which the people of the underground kingdom travel along their tunnels. *For according to his report, they are the creators of what we commonly call Unidentified Flying Objects or 'Flying Saucers'. And not only do* these mysterious craft utilize the tunnel system, but occasionally they appear in our skies, too! If this theory is true – and there are other supporters of the idea – then it offers one of the most fascinating solutions to the riddle of the Flying Saucers that has baffled mankind for many years now. And it also explains the strange enigmas of Ossendowski's 'cars of a type unknown to Western races' which rush through the subterranean world and Roerich's 'spheroid form with shiny surface' in the sky over Mongolia; and adds weight to the conviction of writers like Erich von Daniken that the creators of Agharti might originally have been space people.

Flying Saucers are certainly one of the strangest and most persistent mysteries of the twentieth century – although researchers have shown that reports of strange 'lights' and 'shapes' in the skies corresponding to their description have been reported since the days of the Ancient Greeks. Until this century, however, it has always been assumed that they were of extraterrestrial origin, appearing above the Earth on scouting missions from some civilization elsewhere in the galaxy.* The man who actually first proposed the idea that they might come from much nearer home – from planet Earth itself – was a Brazilian Professor, Dr Henrique Jose de Souza.

Professor de Souza, who lived in Sao Lourenço, and was President of the Brazilian Theosophical Society, developed the theory with a close friend, Commander Paulo Strauss, a member of the Brazilian navy. Their conclusions were first published in a series of articles which appeared in the Brazil-

---

*Recently, in a fascinating article, 'UFOs and the Mystery of Agharti', in *Prediction*, January 1979, Nadine Smyth addressed herself to this problem and wrote: 'The extraterrestrial explanation of the UFOs is today being widely questioned among students of this subject: especially as the space-probes directed at our nearest neighbours in the solar system have disclosed no life or possibility of life as we know it. More and more, experts on UFOs are considering the possibility of a psychic rather than a physical explanation. They suggest that UFOs come, not from other planets but from other dimensions; "an invisible world coincident with the space of our physical Earth". As Air Marshal Sir Victor Goddard expressed it in a lecture he gave at Caxton Hall in 1969. The Inner Earth! Is *this* the real truth about Agharti and Shamballah? That the legends about the inner earth, the hidden world, and so on, are really attempts to express a paraphysical reality? This would tie up with one account of Shamballah, that it is located in the Gobi Desert, but can be seen only by initiates and is invisible to everyone else. Are the two mysteries of Agharti and of the UFOs, really one mystery? Is there both a physical and a non-physical Agharti? And are its inhabitants benign, malignant, or some of both? These questions may well be dismissed as fantastic; but on the other hand, they may be more important than we think.'

ian magazine, *O Cruzeiro* in February 1955. In three issues, Professor de Souza and Commander Strauss argued that while it was evident that no nation on Earth had created the flying machines – certainly not the Russians or the Americans for they would have taken great propaganda advantages from the fact, the two men suggested – it was also equally clear from space research that it was inconceivable such craft could have travelled from the very far distant planets where it was just possible, though not proven, that life of some kind might exist. This only left the possibility that the UFOs had originated from Earth – and from the interior of the Earth, according to de Souza and Strauss.

Professor de Souza, in his capacity as leader of the Brazilian Theosophists, had for years been interested in the Agharti legend, and the more he pondered over the underground kingdom and its network of tunnels, and how it was conceivable that anyone might utilize them without a very special form of transport, the more he came to the conclusion that the Flying Saucers were the answer. That the subterranean dwellers were an advanced people seemed beyond doubt, so if they were capable of living and thriving beneath the Earth's surface there was surely no reason why they should not have developed a form of transport far more sophisticated than anything known on Earth. And the very shape, manoeuvrability and speed with which these craft were credited seemed to make them ideally suited for traversing the network of tunnels that lead to and from the underground kingdom.

In 1957, the ideas of de Souza and Strauss were carefully examined by a writer named O. C. Huguenin in a book called *From The Subterranean World To The Sky: Flying Saucers*. After declaring that 'the hypothesis of the extra-terrestrial origin of the flying saucers does not seem acceptable', Huguenin wrote:

We must consider the most recent and interesting theory that has been offered to account for the origin of flying saucers: the existence of a great Subterranean World with innumerable cities in which live millions of inhabitants. This other humanity must have reached a very high degree of civilization, economic organization and social, cultural and spiritual development, together with an extraordinary scientific progress, in comparison with whom the humanity that lives in the Earth's surface may be considered as a race of barbarians. According to the information supplied by Commander Paulo Strauss, the Subterranean World is not restricted to caverns, but is more or less extensive and located in a hollow inside the Earth large enough to contain cities and fields, where live human beings and animals, whose physical structure resembles those on the surface.

Huguenin then describes how these people, far in advance of the rest of humanity in terms of scientific development, devised machines called *Vimanas* that 'flew in the skies and the tunnels like aircraft, utilising a form of energy obtained directly from the atmosphere'. They were, he says, 'identical with what we know as Flying Saucers'.

He continues:

Prior to the catastrophe that destroyed Atlantis, the Atlanteans found refuge in the Subterranean World, to which they travelled in their *Vimanas*, or Flying Saucers . . . ever since then, their Flying Saucers have remained in the Earth's interior, and were used for purposes of transportation from one point to another.

In the intervening years since 1957, this theory has been argued again on several occasions, more than once by the American, Ray Palmer, who declared in 1959 that: 'there is a tremendous mass of evidence to show that there is an unknown location of vast dimensions below the earth's surface where the Flying Saucers can, and most probably do, originate.' Dr Raymond Bernard believes the UFOs from Agharti may actually be driven by *Vril Power*:

The tragic death and disappearance of Captain Mandell, who pursued a fleeing flying saucer until the latter lost patience and caused him to vanish by being disintegrated into atoms, would indicate that the race have at their command a superior form of energy referred to by Bulwer Lytton by the name of '*Vril*', which is the power that operates their craft and which they only use for destructive purposes when driven to do so in self defence.

And John A. Keel has made the intriguing observation that as strange people of Oriental appearance have been associated with a number of Flying Saucer sightings this may be another clue to tie them in with Agharti and its centre beneath Tibet. Interestingly, all these writers believe that the UFOs have a 'mission' to prevent the world destroying itself through a radio-active catastrophe.

As I said earlier, this theory does provide us with an explanation for two unusual remarks in the works of Ferdinand Ossendowski and Nicholas Roerich. In his *Beasts, Men and Gods*, published back in 1923 long before the terms UFO or Flying Saucer were coined, Ossendowski describes how the people of Agharti 'in cars strange and unknown to us rush through the narrow cleavages inside our planet'. What else could they be but Flying Saucers, several experts have asked? And these same people also quote Roerich, from his book *Heart of Asia* (1928):

> We notice something shiny, flying very high from the north-east to the south. We bring three powerful field glasses from the tents and watch the huge spheroid body shining against the sun, clearly visible against the blue sky and moving very fast. Afterwards we see that it sharply changes its direction from south to south-west and disappears behind the snow-peaked Humboldt Chain. The whole camp follows the unusual apparition and the lamas whisper, 'The Sign of Shamballah'.

The reader should remember that no aircraft of that size, shape, speed or manoeuvrability had been invented in 1928.

Such a mountain of evidence, then – the strange green lights, the persistent rumbling sounds, the geological possibility of habitable cavities below the Earth's surface, the wherewithal for a massive tunnelling project, and the scientific capability to run a subterranean world – all these plus the legends and histories I have recounted, convince me that Agharti *is* a reality. That somewhere below the plateau of Tibet lies the heart of this nation, a super-race of remarkable people who still exist and live out their lives: as much a mystery as any of the other mysteries which still flourish in our world and which likewise only our lack of knowledge prevents us from understanding.

Quite *who* these people are still puzzles me. The reader is invited to judge for himself whether they are remnants of the lost Atlantean civilization, people of an antediluvian culture, or even beings from another world across the galaxy. Of less doubt, I think, is the massive network of passageways that girdles the Earth; a tribute to their remarkable skills as constructors. That much of this labyrinth is lost beyond discovery may well be true: but I think enough remains to substantiate the hypothesis I have argued in these pages.

One final element in the story of Agharti still remains to be considered: the claim that this subterranean world is ruled by an all-powerful overlord, 'The King of the World'. Ossendowski, Roerich and others have written about this mysterious figure, each independently describing him as the 'guiding light of the Earth', a man attuned to both god and humanity, able to direct life and inspire the religions of the world. Such claims are somewhat difficult to accept, *ipso facto*, and while I would not dismiss the idea of a supreme ruler of the underground kingdom, I think his powers may be somewhat overstated. If he does exist, I believe he is probably an initiate of a very high order, preserving the traditions of his people from the earliest times. I am drawn to this conclusion because most descriptions of him tend to be obscure and overblown: perhaps the most convincing and acceptable being that of Ferdinand Ossendowski in *Beasts, Men and Gods*. In the book, Ossendowski relates how an old Tibetan lama told him of a visit of 'The King of the World' to a lamasery in Lhasa:

One night in winter several horsemen rode into the monastery and demanded that all the lamas should congregate into the throne room. Then one of the strangers mounted the throne, where he took off his *bashlyk* or cap-like head covering. All of the lamas fell to their knees as they recognised the man who had been long ago described in the sacred bulls of Dalai Lama, Tashi Lama and Bogdo Khan. He was the man to whom the whole world belongs and who has penetrated all the mysteries of Nature. He pronounced a short Tibetan prayer, blessed all his hearers and afterwards made predictions for the coming half century. This was thirty years ago, and in the interim all his prophecies are being fulfilled.

During his prayers before that small shrine, a huge red door opened of its own accord, the candles and lights before the altar lighted themselves and the sacred braziers without coal gave forth great streams of incense that filled the room. And then, without warning, The King of the World and his companions disappeared from among us. Behind him remained no trace save the folds in the silken coverings which smoothed themselves out and left the throne as though no one had sat upon it.

Two facts about this statement particularly intrigued me. Firstly, the talk about prophecies that had come true, and, secondly, mention of a door through which 'The King of the World' had disappeared. Could this, I wondered, be one of the gateways to Agharti?

My subsequent research has led me to believe that it was: and that the gateway still exists, in the heart of the palace of the exiled Dalai Lama, the Potala, which sits on top of a small mountain, surrounded by monasteries and temples, in Lhasa. My conviction was first strengthened by a rather enigmatic statement from a lama quoted by Roerich: 'The capital of Agharti is surrounded with towns of high priests and scientists. It reminds one of Lhasa where the palace of the Dalai Lama is the top of a mountain covered with monasteries and temples. They are joined spiritually and physically.' The inference of this I found inescapable, and then I secured an illustration of the huge red door in the throne room in the Potala – which is reproduced in this book – and found that it matched Ossendowski's description so closely I was left in no doubt that here lies one of the authentic tunnels to Agharti. Perhaps the day will come when I, or some other intrepid soul from outside the closed borders of Tibet, will have the chance of putting this theory to the test and at last opening the way to the mysterious world underground.

The intriguing possibility that 'The King of the World' had also made a number of predictions which had subsequently come true also set me off on one last search for his original statement. When I found it, I saw that the claim of the old lama that Ossendowski had quoted had not been far short of the mark. According to the Tibetan, 'The King of the World' made his pronouncements 'thirty years ago', which we can assume to be about thirty years prior to the publication of Ossendowski's book in 1922.

This, then, is what he foresaw for the future of the world way back in 1890, and I leave it to the reader to interpret for himself the King's vision of world war, the fall of monarchs, the rise (and ultimate decline!) of Communism, and the inexorable degeneration of mankind. Perhaps his closing remarks on the need for the people of Agharti to serve as the agents of salvation for our doomed world are the most poignant on which I could end a book such as this. Indeed, there are those believers in the Kingdom who say this is *precisely* what they have been waiting to do in their subterranean fastness for untold ages . . .

More and more the people will forget their souls and care about their bodies. The greatest sin and corruption will reign on the earth. People will become as ferocious animals, thirsting for the blood and death of their brothers. The 'Crescent' will grow dim and its followers will descend into beggary and ceaseless war. The conquerors will be stricken by the sun but will not progress upward and twice they will be visited with the heaviest misfortune, which will end in insult before the eye of the other peoples. The crowns of kings, great and small, will fall . . . one, two, three, four, five, six, serve, eight . . . There will be a terrible battle among all the peoples. The seas will become red . . . the earth and the bottom of the seas will be strewn with bones . . . kingdoms will be scattered . . . whole peoples will die . . . hunger, disease, crimes unknown to the law, never before seen in the world.

The enemies of God and of the Divine Spirit in man will come. Those who take the hand of another shall also perish. The forgotten and pursued shall rise and hold the attention of the whole world. There will be fogs and storms. Bare mountains shall suddenly be covered with forests. Earthquakes will come . . . Millions will change the fetters of slavery and humiliation for hunger, disease and death. The ancient roads will be covered with crowds wandering from one place to another. The greatest and most beautiful cities shall perish in fire . . . one, two, three . . . Father shall rise against son, brother against brother and mother against daughter . . . Vice, crime and the destruction of body and soul shall follow . . . Families shall be scattered . . . Truth and love shall disappear . . .

Then I shall send a people, now unknown, which shall tear out the weeds of madness and vice with a strong hand and will lead those who still remain faithful to the spirit of man in the fight against Evil. They will found a new life on the earth purified by the death of nations. In the fiftieth year only three great kingdoms will appear, which will exist happily seventy-one years. Afterwards there will be eighteen years of war and destruction. Then the peoples of Agharti will come up from their subterranean caverns to the surface of the earth.

BIBLIOGRAPHY

HAROLD BAYLEY, *Archaic England*, Chapman & Hall 1919.

DR RAYMOND BERNARD, *The Subterranean World*, University Books, 1960.

J. H. BRENNAN, *Occult Reich*, Futura Publications, 1974.

W. S. BLACKET, *Lost Histories of America*, New York, 1883.

HELENA BLAVATSKY, *Isis Unveiled*, Theosophical Publishing House, 1877.

— —, *The Secret Doctrine*, Theosophical Publishing House, 1888.

ANDRE CHALEIL, *Les Grandes Inities de Notre Temps*, Pierre Blefond 1978.

ROBERT CHARROUX, *The Mysterious Unknown*, Neville Spearman, 1969.

ROBERT ERNST DICKHOFF, *Agharti*, Health Research Co, 1951.

ERICH VON DANIKEN, *The Gold of the Gods*, Souvenir Press, 1972.

SABINE BARING-GOULD, *Curious Myths of the Middle Ages*, Rivingtons, 1894.

— —, *Cliff Castles and Cave Dwellings of Europe*, Seeley 1911.

DR ANTONIN HORAK 'A remarkable Underground Grotto', *National Speleological Society News*, 1965.

O. C. HUGUENIN, *The Subterranean World To The Sky: Flying Saucers*, Rio de Janero, 1957.

LOUIS JACOLLIOT, *La Bible Dans L'Indie*, Paris, 1868.

— —, *Le Spiritisme dans le Monde*, Paris, 1875.

— —, *Histoire des Vierges*, Paris, 1879.

— —, *Occult Science in India*, Ryder, 1884.

FRANCIS KING, *Satan and the Swastika*, Mayflower Books, 1976.

PETER KOLOSIMO, *Timeless Earth*, Sugar Editore, 1968.

— —, *Not of the World*, Souvenir Press, 1969.

230   BIBLIOGRAPHY

LUDVIG, BARON VON HOLBERG, *Niels Klim's Journey Underground*, 1741.

EDWARD GEORGE BULWER LYTTON, *Zanoni*, George Routledge, 1842.

— —, *A Strange Story*, George Routledge, 1861

— —, *The Coming Race*, George Routledge, 1871.

WALTER MAPES, *De Nugis Curialium*, c.12th Century.

AJIT MOOKERJEE & MADHU KHANNA, *The Tantric Way*, Weidenfeld & Nicolson, 1977.

PROFESSOR FRIEDRICH MAX MULLER, *Sacred Books of the East*, London, 1875.

MARQUIS DE NADAILLAC, *Pre-Historic America*, New York, 1885.

ERIC NORMAN, *This Hollow Earth*, Lancer Books, 1972.

JOSEPH O'NEILL, *Land Under England*, Victor Gollancz, 1935.

FERDINAND OSSENDOWSKI, *Beasts, Men and Gods*, Edward Arnold, 1923.

— —, *Man and Mystery in Asia*, Edward Arnold, 1924.

LOUIS PAUWELS & JACQUES BERGIER, *The Morning of the Magicians*, Anthony Gibbs & Phillips, 1960.

TREVOR RAVENSCROFT, *The Spear of Destiny*, Neville Spearman, 1972.

HERMANN RAUSCHNING, *Hitler Speaks*, Thornton Butterworth, 1939.

CONSTANTINE NICHOLAS ROERICH, *Altai-Himalaya: A Travel Diary*, Jarrolds, 1930.

— —, *Shamballah*, Jarrolds ,1930.

— —, *Abode of Light*, David Marlow, 1947.

J. A. SAINT-YVES D'ALVEYDRE, *The Mission of India in Europe*, Paris, 1886.

PROFESSOR HENRIQUE JOSE DE SOUZA, 'Does Shangri-La Exist?' *Brazilian Theosophical Society Journal*, 1960.

LEWIS SPENCE, *Myths of the North American Indians*, Rider, 1914.

— —, *The Problem of Atlantis*, Rider, 1924.

— —, *Atlantis in America*, Rider 1925.

— —, *The History of Atlantis*, Rider, 1926.

JOHN LLOYD STEPHENS, *Incidents of Travel in Central America*, Harper's, 1838.

TASHI LAMA III, *The Way to Shamballah* (Trans) Munich, 1915.

HAROLD T. WILKINS, *Mysteries of Ancient South America*, Rider, 1946.

— —, *Secret Cities of Old South America*, Rider, 1950.

SIR JOHN WOODROFFE, *Shakti and Shakta*, Calcutta, 1920.